Key Terms in Language and Culture

Key Terms
in
Language and Culture

Edited by
Alessandro Duranti

First published 2001

The material included in this book first appeared as a special issue of the *Journal of Linguistic Anthropology* (Volume 9, Numbers 1–2, 1999) published by the American Anthropological Association for the Society of Linguistic Anthropology.

2 4 6 8 10 9 7 5 3 1

Blackwell Publishers Inc.
350 Main Street
Malden, Massachusetts 02148
USA

Blackwell Publishers Ltd
108 Cowley Road
Oxford OX4 1JF
UK

Library of Congress Cataloging-in-Publication Data is available for this book.

ISBN 0-631-22665-6 (hardback); 0-631-22666-4 (paperback)

British Library Cataloguing in Publication Data

A CIP catalogue record for this book is available from the British Library.

Typeset in 10 on 11 pt Palatino
by Ace Filmsetting Ltd, Frome, Somerset
Printed in Great Britain by T.J. International, Padstow, Cornwall

This book is printed on acid-free paper.

CONTENTS

v

CONTRIBUTORS

Asif Agha Department of Anthropology, University of Pennsylvania, 33rd and Spruce Street, Philadelphia, PA 19104-6398.
asifagha@sas.upenn. edu

Laura M. Ahearn Department of Anthropology, University of South Carolina, Columbia, SC 29208.
ahearn@sc.edu

Celso Alvarez-Cáccamo Linguística Geral, Faculdade de Filologia, Universidade da Corunha, 15071 A Corunha, Galiza, Spain.
lxalvarz@udc.es

Benjamin Bailey Department of Anthropology, Box 6000, Binghamton University, Binghamton, NY 13902-6000.
bbailey@binghamton.edu

Giorgio Banti Istituto Universitario Orientale di Napoli, Italy. Mailing address: via le del Vignola 73, I-00196 Roma, Italy.
g.banti@agora.stm.it

Patricia Baquedano-López Graduate School of Education, University of California, Berkeley, Berkeley, CA 94720-1670.
pbl@uclink4.berkeley.edu

John Baugh School of Education, Stanford University, Stanford, CA 94305.
jbaugh@leland.stanford.edu

Richard Bauman Folklore Institute, Indiana University, 504 North Fess, Bloomington, IN 47405.
bauman@indiana.edu

William O. Beeman Department of Anthropology, Brown University, Providence, RI 02912.
william_beeman@brown.edu

Dan Ben-Amos Department of Asian and Middle Eastern Studies, University of Pensylvania, Philadelphia, PA 19104-6305.
dbamos@sas.upenn.edu

Niko Besnier   Department of Anthropology, Victoria University of Wellington, P.O. Box 600, Wellington 6000, New Zealand.
niko.besnier@vuw.ac.nz

Susan D. Blum   Department of Anthropology, 314 O'Shaughnessy Hall, University of Notre Dame, Notre Dame, IN 46656.
Susan.Blum.24@nd.edu

Charles L. Briggs   Department of Ethnic Studies, University of California, San Diego, La Jolla, CA 92093-0522.
clbriggs@weber.ucsd.edu

Penelope Brown   Max Planck Institute for Psycholinguistics, PB 310, NL 6500 AH Nijmegen, Netherlands.
penelope.brown@mpi.nl

Mary Bucholtz   Department of English, Texas A&M University, College Station, TX 77843-4227.
bucholtz@tamu.edu

Aaron V. Cicourel   Department of Cognitive Science, 9500 Gilman Drive, Dept. 0515, University of California, San Diego, La Jolla, CA 92093-0515.
cicourel@cogsci.ucsd.edu

Haruko M. Cook   Department of East Asian Languages and Literatures, University of Hawaii at Manoa, 1890 East West Road, Honolulu, HI 96822.
hkcook@hawaii.edu

Regna Darnell   Department of Anthropology, University of Western Ontario, London, Ontario N6A 5C2, Canada.
rdarnell@julian.uwo.ca

John W. Du Bois   Department of Linguistics, University of California, Santa Barbara, Santa Barbara, CA 93106.
dubois@humanitas.ucsb.edu

Alessandro Duranti   Department of Anthropology, University of California, Los Angeles, Los Angeles, CA 90095-1553.
aduranti@ucla.edu

Joseph Errington   Department of Anthropology, 51 Hillhouse Avenue, Yale University, New Haven, CT 06520-8277.
j.errington@yale.edu

Susan Ervin-Tripp   Department of Psychology, University of California, Berkeley, Berkeley, CA 94720-0001.
ervin-tr@cogsci.berkeley.edu

Steven Feld   Department of Anthropology, New York University, 25 Waverly Place, New York, NY 10003.

Aaron Fox   Department of Music, MC 1822, Dodge Hall, Columbia University, New York, NY, 10027.

Kathleen R. Gibson   Department of Basic Sciences, University of Texas Houston, Dental Branch, P.O. Box 20068, Houston, TX 77225.
kgibson@mail.db.uth.tmc.edu

Victor Golla   Department of Native American Studies, Humboldt State University, Arcata, CA 95521.
vkg1@humboldt.edu

Ward H. Goodenough   Department of Anthropology, University of Pennsylvania, 33rd and Spruce Streets, Philadelphia, PA 19104-6398.
whgooden@sas.upenn.edu

Charles Goodwin   Department of Applied Linguistics, University of California, Los Angeles, 3300 Rolfe Hall, Los Angeles, CA 90095-1531.
cgoodwin@humnet.ucla.edu

Marjorie H. Goodwin   Department of Anthropology, University of California, Los Angeles, Los Angeles, CA 90095-1553.
mgoodwin@anthro.ucla.edu

Laura R. Graham   Department of Anthropology, 114 MH, University of Iowa, Iowa City, IA 52242.
laura-graham@uiowa.edu

Allen D. Grimshaw   2211 Woodstock Place, Bloomington, IN 47401.
grimsha@indiana.edu

John J. Gumperz   Department of Anthropology, University of California, Berkeley, Berkeley, CA 94720.
gumperz@education.ucsb.edu

Kira Hall   Department of Anthropology, 51 Hillhouse Avenue, Yale University, New Haven, CT 06520-8277.
kira.hall@yale.edu

William F. Hanks   Department of Anthropology, University of California, Berkeley, CA 94720-3710.
wfhanks@nwu.edu

John B. Haviland   Department of Anthropology, Reed College, Portland, OR 97202.
Johnh@reed.edu

Jane H. Hill   Department of Anthropology, University of Arizona, Tucson, AZ 85721.
jhill@u.arizona.edu

Ingjerd Hoëm   University of Oslo, Department of Linguistics, P.O. Box 1102, Blindern, N-0317 Oslo, Norway.
ingjerd.hoem@ilf.uio.no

Dell Hymes   Department of Anthropology, University of Virginia, Charlottesville, VA 22903.

Vyacheslav Ivanov   Department of Slavic Languages and Literatures, University of California, Los Angeles, Los Angeles, CA 90095-150205.
ivanov@ucla.edu

Sally Jacoby   Department of Communication, University of New Hampshire, Horton Social Science Center, 20 College Road, Durham, NH 03824-3586.
swj@hopper.unh.edu

Marco Jacquemet   Department of Anthropology, Barnard College, 3009 Broadway, New York, NY 10027.
mjacquem@barnard. columbia.edu

Barbara Johnstone   Department of English, Carnegie Mellon University, Pittsburgh, PA 15213-3890.
bj4@andrew.cmu.edu

Christine Jourdan   Department of Sociology and Anthropology, Concordia University, 1455 de Maisonneuve W., Montreal H3G 1M8, Canada.
jourdan@vax2.concordia.ca

Paul Kay   Department of Linguistics, University of California, Berkeley, Berkeley, CA 94720.
kay@cogsci.berkeley.edu

Webb Keane   Department of Anthropology, University of Michigan, Ann Arbor, MI 48109.
wkeane@umich.edu

Elizabeth Keating   Department of Anthropology, University of Texas, Austin, TX 78712-1086.
ekeating@mail.utexas.edu

Harriet E. Manelis Klein   Department of Linguistics, State University of New York at Stony Brook, Stony Brook, NY 11794.
hklein@notes.cc.sunysb.edu

Paul V. Kroskrity   Department of Anthropology and Interdepartmental Program in American Indian Studies, University of California, Los Angeles, Los Angeles, CA 90095-1553.
paulvk@ucla.edu

Joel Kuipers   Department of Anthropology, 2112 G Street NW, X201, George Washington University, Washington, DC 20052.
kuipers@gwu.edu

John Leavitt   Département d'Anthropologie, Université de Montréal, C.P. 6128, Succursale Centre-Ville, Montréal, Quebec, H3C 3J7, Canada.

Stephen C. Levinson   Max Planck Institute for Psycholinguistics, P.O. Box 310, NL-6500 AH Nijmegen, The Netherlands.
levinson@mpi.nl

John A. Lucy   Committee on Human Development, University of Chicago, 5730 S. Woodlawn Ave., Chicago, IL 60637.
johnlucy@midway.uchicago.edu

Bruce Mannheim   Department of Anthropology, University of Michigan, Ann Arbor, MI 48109.
brucem@quriurqu.anthro.lsa.umich.edu

Norma Mendoza-Denton   Department of Anthropology, University of Arizona, Tucson, AZ 85721-0030.
nmd@u.arizona.edu

Leila Monaghan Department of Anthropology, Temple University, Philadelphia, PA 19122.

Robert E. Moore Department of Anthropology, New York University, 25 Waverly Place, New York, NY 10003.
rem10@is5.nyu.edu

Marcyliena M. Morgan Department of Anthropology, University of California, Los Angeles, Los Angeles, CA 90095-1553.
mhmorgan@ucla.edu

Elinor Ochs Department of Anthropology, University of California, Los Angeles, Los Angeles, CA 90095-1552.
ochs@humnet.ucla.edu

Carol Padden Department of Communication, University of California, San Diego, La Jolla, CA 92093.
cpadden@ucsd.edu

Mariella Pandolfi Départment d'Anthropologie, Université de Montréal, C.P. 6128, Succursale Centre-Ville, Montréal, Quebec, H3C 3J7, Canada.
pandolfm@anthro. umontreal.ca

Antonio Perri Via Baldo degli Ubaldi 96, 00167 Rome, Italy.
a.perri@pronet.it

Susan U. Philips Department of Anthropology, University of Arizona, Tucson, AZ 85721.
sphilips@u.arizona.edu

Ben Rampton King's College London, School of Education, Waterloo Road, London, SE1 8WA, United Kingdom.
ben.rampton@kcl.ac.uk

Alan Rumsey Australian National University, Canberra, ACT 0200, Australia.
alan.rumsey@anu.edu.au

Betsy Rymes Department of Language Education, The University of Georgia, Athens, GA 30602-7123.
brymes@coe.uga.edu

R. Keith Sawyer Department of Education, Washington University, Campus Box 1183, St. Louis, MO 63130.
ksawyer@artsci.wustl.edu

Marina Sbisà Dipartimento di Filosofia, Università di Trieste, via dell' Università 7, 34123 Trieste, Italy.
sbisama@univ.trieste.it

John H. Schumann Applied Linguistics, 3300 Rolfe Hall, UCLA, Los Angeles, CA 90095-1531.
schumann@humnet.ucla.edu

Ron Scollon Department of Linguistics, Georgetown University, Washington, DC 20057.
scollonr@gusun.georgetown.edu

Jack Sidnell Department of Anthropology, Northwestern University, 1810 Hinman Avenue, Evanston, IL 60201.
jsidnell@nwu.edu

Michael Silverstein Department of Anthropology, University of Chicago, 1126 East 59th Street, Chicago, IL 60637-1539.
m-silverstein@uchicago.edu

Debra Spitulnik Department of Anthropology, Emory University, 1557 Pierce Drive, Atlanta, GA 30322.

Dennis Tedlock Department of English, SUNY at Buffalo, Buffalo, NY 14260.
dtedlock@acsu.buffalo.edu

James Wilce Department of Anthropology, Northern Arizona University, Flagstaff, AZ 86011-5200.
jim.wilce@nau.edu

Kwesi Yankah Linguistics department, University of Ghana, Legon, Ghana.
kwyankah@libr.ug.edu.gh

PREFACE

In the winter of 1998, I volunteered to organize an "educational" session on the state of the art in linguistic anthropology for the Annual Meetings of the American Anthropological Association, to be held in December in Philadelphia. The session, one of a series for each of the major subfields in anthropology, was meant to inform the AAA members about contemporary research in linguistic anthropology.

I thought that the best way to accomplish this goal was to invite as many people as possible to talk about what they knew best about language matters in anthropology. As the number of contributors and topics grew, I realized that despite the three hours and forty five minutes alloted for the session, there was not going to be sufficient time for a series of fifteen-minute papers. One solution was to limit the time of each presentation to seven minutes. That is how the idea of papers structured as entries of a lexicon emerged. I asked each author to write about one thousand words on one key concept in the study of language. The result was a very original and thought-provoking series of statements that kept the audience at the AAA meetings engaged for almost four hours (the room was filled beyond capacity and many people could not get in). After the session, I decided that the papers should be collected and published. Free from the temporal constraints of the meetings, I also realized that I could include other topics and authors. As I approached more colleagues or wrote again to those who had not been able to participate in the session because of previous commitments, the list grew to include about ninety potential contributors. Of those to whom I wrote, the great majority responded with enthusiasm, despite the short notice and the close deadline I had set. The question then arose as to where to publish the papers. I thought that the *Journal of Linguistic Anthropology* would be the ideal place to publish the entries. Under editors Ben Blount and Judith Irvine, the journal has acquired a reputation for high quality contributions in a wide range of research topics and paradigms within our field. This book reproduces the special issue (*JLA* vol. 9) I edited under the title *Language Matters in Anthropology: A Lexicon for the Millennium*, an ambitious collective attempt to push the boundaries of our discipline even further into realms that just a generation ago would not have been thought of as linguistic anthropology. The contributors to this collection give voice to research programs and intellectual agendas that, each in their own unique way, celebrate the complexity and the richness of language as the ever present instrument and living record of the human experience on Earth.

Most of the contributors to this volume are linguistic anthropologists, but there are also colleagues from other fields, including folklore, linguistics, philosophy of language, psychology, sociology, ethnomusicology, conversation analysis, biological anthropology, and medical anthropology. Although not everything you always wanted to know about linguistic anthropology – or language – is represented here, the entries and authors in this issue cover a vast territory of knowledge about linguistic matters. They are written to inform, suggest, provoke, and open up new horizons while looking back at our relatively short, no more than a century-long, history. If they succeed in engaging the readers with new ideas and making them reconsider or deepen their views of language matters, they will have accomplished their goal.

This project required a considerable amount of work by many people. I want to thank all the contributors for their willingness to adapt to the format of the entries and the strict deadlines without losing their creativity. The original session was made possible by the encouragement of the 1998 Annual Meetings Program Chair, Susan Greenhalgh, and the hard work of Lucille Horn at the AAA office in Arlington. In editing the volume, corresponding with the contributors, and making sure that I would not forget anything or anyone, I was fortunate to have the support of three skillful and energetic editorial assistants, Adrienne Lo, Sarah Meacham, and Vincent Barletta. Finally, this was my first collaboration with the publication staff at the AAA headquarters. Many thanks to John Neikirk, Neada Ross-Fleming, and the rest of the staff who made this at first improbable enterprise something that you can hold in your hands and read. The publication of the *JLA* special issue as *Key Terms in Language and Culture* would not have been possible without the skillful negotiation and support of Susi Skomal at AAA headquarters and Jane Huber at Blackwell, and without the expert editorial assistance of Margaret Aherne. I am also grateful to Tracy Rone for compiling the index.

In making the original collection available to a wider audience, I hope that this book will invite reflections and reactions that will widen and deepen our understanding of and commitment to the study of language as both a human capacity and a human activity.

Alessandro Duranti

■ *Susan Ervin-Tripp*

Acquisition

Acquisition of a language refers to learning enough about it to understand what speakers mean. A language used in late childhood for inner speech and abstraction can survive in memory the rest of life, as we see in the last speakers of dying languages. What's acquired is knowledge of the sound system of an oral language, syntax, vocabulary or lexical system, semantics underlying both, and the pragmatic or sociolinguistic system that relates language to conditions of use.

Three conditions are necessary for acquisition: capacity, access, and motive. Language requires the capacity to form classes of classes, an ability only humans have. There must also be a peripheral system – touch, vision, or sound. Both cognitive and social development in children affect the order of acquisition. The increase in capacity, as well as transfer from first language, explains why second languages are acquired so fast in late childhood. On the other hand, after puberty, a first language has never been learned successfully, and attaining the skill of a native speaker of a second language is variable.

Second, there must be access to exchanges with others in which language forms co-occur with information about meanings. This is necessary for semantic mapping to forms. What is learned about forms from access includes what forms occur together, what is happening physically and socially at the time, who is speaking, and so on. Where there is a regular, distinctive co-occurrence of any of these events with linguistic form, the information may be stored. Language is acquired readily from siblings and older play partners because they are likely to provide frequent and easy conditions for mapping.

Third, there has to be a motive to attend to or to speak a language. While not an issue for dependent infants, if speakers of a variety aren't valued, listeners may not get enough access to come to understand new vocabulary, styles, dialects, or languages, and they may be even more unwilling to be heard speaking in other varieties. This is a place where social ideology has an impact on acquisition. In relaxed informal speech, phonetic choices, vocabulary, and other aspects of style reflect the speech of valued others, usually of childhood peers. However, we know that children have heard and stored a great variety of detailed information about who talks, and how, because we see it if four-year-olds do role-playing, as demonstrated by Elaine Andersen.

All the components of language are being developed simultaneously, but those aspects that reach their relatively mature state first are the phonological system, core syntax, and probably some basic aspects of the semantic system for the first language. Vocabulary growth is very sensitive to the physical and social environment, since it is a form of mapping of objects and concepts, as well as changes throughout life. It has three facets: the representation of the form of the word, its grammatical properties, and its denotation, connotations, and social implications. Taboo words and insults provide a clear case where the child often acquires these features separately.

Vocabulary development is both affected by and affects the semantic and cognitive organization of the child, so it can be a focus for socialization. The semantic system reflects those features that the syntax and vocabulary single out for marking, so it varies for different languages – for instance, differentiating tight and loose fit for some Korean prepositions, identifying shapes of objects for Navajo verbs, identifying sources of information for Turkish (which has evidential markers), and identifying age and status in Korean.

The structure of first sentences is sensitive to the context of language used for and by children. Two-year-olds' speech is usually brief – telegraphic – and often includes only the core information. In one language there may at first be much more naming of things, in another more naming of actions, or of changes of location or state. As children's capacity increases, they complicate syntax by including several types of information at once, such as place and action. They start to add formal features demanded by their particular language. If they speak a language that requires coding the gender of a speaker or the relative time an event occurred in every utterance, they begin adding that, though they may still have omissions at the age of three or four. Both complexity and ease of marking affect order; markers that are at the ends of turns are acquired earlier than those in the middle, just because of salience.

Traditionally, studies of acquisition focused most on the development of reference and ideational communication, but speech is also organized as to turn participation, speech actions, social relations marking, register or variety, speech genres like joking or narration, and speech events like weddings or trials. Children mark turn organization very early; by three they have replies with linguistic features showing dialog skill. In English we find "I can too" or "Because he does," and some topical coherence across turns. Infants first learn the speech acts, such as greeting rituals, that have similar turns to mimic. They use an increasing variety of kinds of acts during childhood – requesting, challenging, justifying, apologies, and so on. Linguistic forms that mark important or salient social acts are candidates for early acquisition, so they vary culturally. Complex genres and their situating in larger speech events can continue acquisition throughout life.

Social indices in speech range from address terms, to mitigating or aggravating of speech acts by tone of voice or explicit formal choices, to selection of registers or styles in which multiple choices must be made. Register variation appears before two – in whispering, for instance – but by four includes variation in subtle features like the discourse markers "well" or "uh." By four there is very clear mitigating when a child is imposing, as in requests. Children with access to more than one variety learn from the beginning some of the constraints on use, varying language with addressee or place, for instance. Such rules of use may be explicitly taught or – as with the rest of language – acquired from adequate access to observation.

(See also *body, brain, endangered, genre, particles, register, socialization, style, turn*)

Bibliography

Andersen, Elaine
  1992[1977] Speaking with Style: The Sociolinguistic Skills of Children. London, New York: Routledge.
Barrett, M.
  1999 The Development of Language. Sussex, UK: Psychology Press.
Berman, Ruth A., Dan Isaac Slobin, Ayhan A. Aksu-Koç, Michael Bamberg, et al.
  1994 Relating Events in Narrative: A Cross-linguistic Developmental Study. Hillsdale, NJ: Lawrence Erlbaum Associates.
Ervin-Tripp, S., J. Guo, and M. Lampert
  1990 Politeness and Persuasion in Children's Control Acts. Journal of Pragmatics 14(2):307–332.
Ervin-Tripp, S. M., and C. Mitchell-Kernan
  1977 Child Discourse. New York: Academic Press.
Goodwin, Marjorie H.
  1990 He-Said-She-Said: Talk as Social Organization among Black Children. Bloomington: Indiana University Press.
Ninio, A., and C. E. Snow
  1996 Pragmatic Development. Boulder, CO: Westview Press.
Ochs, Elinor, and Bambi B. Schieffelin, eds.
  1979 Developmental Pragmatics. New York: Academic Press.
Ochs, Elinor, and Bambi B. Schieffelin
  1983 Acquiring Conversational Competence. London, Boston: Routledge and Kegan Paul.
Shatz, M.
  1994 A Toddler's Life: Becoming a Person. New York: Oxford University Press.
Slobin, Dan Isaac, Julie Gerhardt, Amy Kyratzis, and Jiansheng Guo
  1996 Social Interaction, Social Context, and Language. Mahwah, NJ: Lawrence Erlbaum Associates.

■ *Marina Sbisà*

Act

In everyday talk, we sometimes oppose "only saying" something to "doing" something. But if we reflect on how we use language, it is undeniable that language is often (if not always) a tool for doing: it enables us to achieve various kinds of effects on our interlocutors, playing an important role in collaborative action, and contributes to the establishment and management of social relationships. Thus it is sensible to wonder whether and how the idea of "doing something" should be applied to language.

The trend in the philosophy of language and in pragmatic research known as speech act theory has contended that (1) utterances of *every* kind can be considered as acts, and has tried to distinguish different senses in which the issuing of an utterance constitutes or involves the performing of an act, claiming that (2) a distinction should be drawn between what an utterance says and what is done in using it (its "force").

The first contention was already present in the later work of Ludwig Wittgenstein, particularly in his proposal to view language as consisting of rule-governed activities, or "language games." J. L. Austin emphasized the operative character of language, introducing the term "performative" with reference to those declarative sentences that, issued in appropriate circumstances, are not reports or descriptions, but performances of such acts as baptisms ("I name this ship 'Queen Elizabeth' ") or promises ("I promise that I'll come tomorrow"). Austin also claimed that all of our utterances can be reformulated as performatives, and that such reformulations make it explicit what act is performed in issuing the utterance. It is remarkable that for speech act theory, not only ritual utterances such as baptisms or appointments or apologies, and not only non-declarative utterances that cannot be deemed true or false such as orders, advice, and promises, but also assertions or statements are acts.

The second claim has been inspired by Gottlob Frege's distinction between the proposition (the thought expressed by a declarative or interrogative sentence) and the judgment that the proposition is true (which turns the proposition into an assertion), i.e., the assertive force. Austin extended the notion of

4

force to all kinds of utterances, distinguishing the "locutionary meaning" of an utterance (what it says) from the way in which the utterance is used, namely, its illocutionary force, indicated by linguistic devices including performative verbs, mood, modals, adverbs and connectives, intonation, or punctuation. John Searle reformulated this distinction as a distinction between the illocutionary force of an utterance and its propositional content. It should be noted that the term "illocutionary" was constructed by Austin from "in" + "locutionary": the illocutionary force of an utterance corresponds to the act that is performed *in* issuing it. The identification of force as a specific level of the speech act's overall meaning has made possible a principled analysis of what we do in speaking.

Speakers perform illocutionary acts in issuing utterances insofar as there are socially accepted conventional procedures for achieving certain conventional effects, which involve the use of utterances of certain kinds in appropriate circumstances. Thus a first kind of analysis made possible is the exploration of the requirements for the performance of illocutionary acts, namely, of their "felicity" or "successfulness" conditions, as well as of what happens when the requirements are not met ("infelicities"). A second kind of analysis that has been practiced even more extensively regards the classification or typology of illocutionary acts. Among the classes that have been proposed, within classificatory frameworks sometimes in competition with each other, there are verdictives (judgments), assertives (committing the speaker to the truth of a proposition), exercitives (involving the exercise of authority), directives (attempts to get the addressee to do something), commissives (committing the speaker to a course of action), and expressives (expressing inner states). It should be noted that classifying illocutionary acts presupposes distinguishing them both from linguistic activities belonging to the locutionary, or propositional, level, and from acts performed "by" speaking (as opposed to "in" speaking), namely, perlocutionary acts (such as persuading or getting someone to do something, alerting, deterring, etc.), which are the achievement of material as opposed to conventional effects. A third area of interest is the linguistic strategies used for performing illocutionary acts of a given kind in different situational or cultural contexts.

The evolution of speech act theory has reduced the import of conventions in the analysis of speech acts, boosting the role of the speaker's intentions. It has become common to think of most speech acts as having as their effect the recognition of the speaker's communicative intention on the part of the hearer. The speaker's intentions are often held to determine which speech act is performed, and the role of the hearer is reduced to getting these intentions right. I believe this is a limitation of the theory, since it leaves no room for collaborative achievements or negotiations about what is done. In contrast, if we grant an active role to the hearer we can see what it means to claim that illocutionary acts have "conventional" effects: speaker and hearer implicitly agree on what the speaker counts as having done.

Another serious limitation of the theory is its primary concern with utterances of the size of a complete sentence and the consequential difficulty in dealing with conversational turns, conversational sequences, and texts. Are speakers really "doing," and intending to do, something definite in each of the sentences they utter, and only if they utter a complete sentence? This does not seem to be true. But it is still true that as discourse proceeds, the participants' statuses are partly confirmed and partly modified.

There is a range of human activities connected with the management and fine-tuning of interpersonal relationships, which involve the creation of commitments, the assignment and elimination of rights and entitlements or obligations, the legitimation of expectations, and the like. I believe that this area could still be fruitfully explored by taking inspiration from speech act theory in the framework of a conception of language closely connecting language and action, but avoiding philosophical oversimplifications.

(See also *agency, intentionality, participation, performativity, power, relativity, truth, turn*)

Bibliography

Austin, John L.
 1962   How to Do Things with Words. Oxford: Oxford University Press.
Bach, Kent, and Robert M. Harnish
 1979   Linguistic Communication and Speech Acts. Cambridge, MA: MIT Press.
Blum-Kulka, Shoshana, Juliane House, and Gabriele Kasper, eds.
 1989   Cross-cultural Pragmatics: Requests and Apologies. Norwood, NJ: Ablex.
Caffi, Claudia
 1999   On Mitigation. Journal of Pragmatics 31:881–909.
Mey, Jacob
 1993   Pragmatics. Oxford: Blackwell.
Sbisà, Marina
 1984   On Illocutionary Types. Journal of Pragmatics 8:93–112.
Searle, John
 1969   Speech Acts: An Essay in the Philosophy of Language. Cambridge: Cambridge University Press.
 1979   Expression and Meaning. Cambridge: Cambridge University Press.
Streeck, Jürgen
 1980   Speech Acts in Interaction: A Critique of Searle. Discourse Processes 3:133–154.
Tsohatzidis, Savas L., ed.
 1994   Foundations of Speech Act Theory. London: Routledge.

■ *Laura M. Ahearn*

Agency

T he term *agency* appears often in academic writing these days, but what scholars mean by it can differ considerably from common usages of the word. When I did a keyword search in our university library cata- logue for *agency*, for example, the system returned with 24,728 matches. (And that's just books, not articles.) Among these were books about travel agen- cies, the Central Intelligence Agency, social service agencies, collection agencies, the International Atomic Energy Agency, and the European Space Agency. Few, if any, of these books use agency in the way scholars do: as a way to talk about *the human capacity to act*. In fact, ironically enough, the commonsense notion of the term in English often connotes a lack of what scholars would call agency because the everyday definition of agent involves acting on behalf of someone else, not oneself.

The concept of agency gained currency in the late 1970s as scholars across many disciplines reacted against structuralism's failure to take into account the actions of individuals. Inspired by activists who challenged existing power structures in order to achieve racial and gender equality, some academics sought to develop new theories that would do justice to the potential effects of human action. Feminist theorists in particular analyzed the ways in which "the personal" is always political – in other words, how people's actions in- fluence, and are influenced by, larger social and political structures. In the late 1970s and early 1980s, sociologist Anthony Giddens first popularized the term *agency* and, along with anthropologists such as Pierre Bourdieu and Marshall Sahlins, focused on the ways in which human actions are dialect- ically related to social structure in a mutually constitutive manner. These scholars, in addition to cultural Marxists such as Raymond Williams, noted that human beings make society even as society makes them. This loosely defined school of thought has been called "practice theory" by Sherry Ortner, a theorist who has herself carried forward this program of study. The riddle that practice theorists seek to solve is how social reproduction becomes so- cial transformation – and they believe agency is the key.

Note that agency in these formulations is not synonymous with free will.

7

Rather, practice theorists recognize that actions are always already socially, culturally, and linguistically constrained. Agency is emergent in sociocultural and linguistic practices. Furthermore, although some scholars use *agency* as a synonym for resistance, most practice theorists maintain that agentive acts may also involve complicity with, accommodation to, or reinforcement of the status quo – sometimes all at the same time.

Scholars who use the term *agency* must consider several important issues. Can agency only be the property of an individual? What types of supra-individual agency might exist? The field is wide open for theorists to explore and distinguish among various types of institutional and collective agency exercised by entities such as states, corporations, anthropology faculties, unions, lineages, families, or couples. Similarly, we might also be able to talk about agency at the sub-individual level (or the "dividual," as McKim Marriott, E. Valentine Daniel, Bonnie McElhinny, and others call it), thereby shedding light on things like internal dialogues and fragmented subjectivities. The level of analysis appropriate for scholars interested in agency should not automatically be considered to be the individual, since such a tight focus on individual agency is likely to render invisible larger social structures such as gender, race, and class that shape possibilities for, and types of, agency. Scholars analyzing agency must also decide whether agency can act below the level of awareness. What sorts of actions are truly "agentive" (or "agentic" or "agential")? Must an act be fully, consciously intentional in order to be agentive? How could a scholar ever know?

Another avenue for potential research involves investigating theories of agency that people in other cultures or speech communities might espouse. In my own work I have analyzed Nepali marriage narratives and love letters in order to ascertain how people in other societies interpret actions and assign responsibility for events – by blaming or crediting others, by attributing the events to fate, or by naming a supernatural force. Instead of attempting to locate, label, and measure agency, I try to discover how people in other societies conceptualize it. Who do they believe can exercise agency? Do they view it as differentially or hierarchically distributed somehow?

Linguistic anthropologists are well situated to contribute to the scholarship on agency. Recognizing that language shapes individuals' thought categories even as it enables them at times to transcend those categories, linguistic anthropologists interested in agency examine specific speech events in order to illuminate how people think about their own and others' actions. Because language is social action, studies of language use (such as can be found, for example, in Dennis Tedlock and Bruce Mannheim's recent edited volume) reveal how culture in all its forms emerges dialogically from everyday linguistic interactions that are themselves shaped by sociocultural formations.

The work of Alessandro Duranti exemplifies how attention to language can shed light on human agency. Duranti looks at the attribution of agency in Western Samoa by examining what is known as an ergative marker – a grammatical form found in some languages in which the subjects of transitive verbs and intransitive verbs are encoded differently. Duranti maintains that the Samoans' use of ergative markers reveals how they attribute agency, especially in cases of praise or blame. Powerful individuals are more likely to use the ergative marker when they want to accuse someone of a malicious act, whereas less-powerful individuals try to resist such accusations by suggesting alternative linguistic definitions of events. Thus Duranti's "grammar of praising and blaming" demonstrates how agency is embedded in and shaped by the linguistic forms that a speaker uses.

Researchers need not look only at ergative markers and transitive or intransitive verbs for evidence of how agency is exercised through language. Analyzing other linguistic features such as pronoun use, turn-taking, overlapping discourse, or the narrative structure of stories can be extremely instructive. Linguistic anthropologists working in the field of language and gender have made especially important contributions to the study of human agency by investigating the multifunctionality of specific linguistic features and by demonstrating how human actions and words shape and are shaped by gendered social structures.

Whichever aspects of agency researchers pursue, it is crucial that scholars interested in agency consider the assumptions about personhood, desire, and intentionality that are built into their analyses. Some studies of agency reinforce received notions about Western atomic individualism, while others deny agency to individuals, attributing it instead only to discourses or social forces. No matter how agency is defined, implications for social theory abound. Scholars using the term must define it clearly, both for themselves and for their readers. This is where linguistic anthropology, with its focus on concrete interactions, can provide guidance as scholars attempt to understand the micro- and macro-processes of social life.

(See also *body, gender, intentionality, narrative, participation, performativity, relativity, turn*)

Bibliography

Duranti, Alessandro
  1994   From Grammar to Politics: Linguistic Anthropology in a Western Samoan Village. Berkeley: University of California Press.
Duranti, Alessandro, and Charles Goodwin, eds.
  1992   Rethinking Context: Language as an Interactive Phenomenon. Cambridge: Cambridge University Press.
Giddens, Anthony
  1979   Central Problems in Social Theory: Action, Structure and Contradiction in Social Analysis. Berkeley: University of California Press.
Hall, Kira, and Mary Bucholtz, eds.
  1995   Gender Articulated: Language and the Socially Constructed Self. New York: Routledge.
Hill, Jane H., and Judith T. Irvine, eds.
  1992   Responsibility and Evidence in Oral Discourse. Cambridge: Cambridge University Press.

McElhinny, Bonnie

1998   Genealogies of Gender Theory: Practice Theory and Feminism in Sociocultural and Linguistic Anthropology. Social Analysis 42(3):164–189.

Ochs, Elinor, Emanuel A. Schlegloff, and Sandra A. Thompson, eds.

1996   Interaction and Grammar. Cambridge: Cambridge University Press.

Ortner, Sherry B.

1996   Making Gender: Toward a Feminist, Minority, Postcolonial, Subaltern, etc.,
   Theory of Practice. *In* Making Gender: The Politics and Erotics of Culture.
   Sherry B. Ortner, ed. Pp. 1–20. Boston: Beacon Press.

Taylor, Charles

1985   Introduction and What Is Human Agency? *In* Human Agency and Language: Philosophical Papers 1. Charles Taylor, ed. Pp. 1–44. Cambridge: Cambridge University Press.

Tedlock, Dennis, and Bruce Mannheim, eds.

1995   The Dialogic Emergence of Culture. Urbana: University of Illinois Press.

■ *Mariella Pandolfi*

Body

Over the centuries the history of the human body – especially in Western cultures – has been characterized by an ever-increasing separation between matter and spirit, between flesh and soul. In cultures where the relation between human beings, deities, and nature is interpreted as a harmonic and constantly interpenetrating rapport of the human with the sacred, the experience of the body has been different. Such is the case in the scholarly traditions of Ayurvedic and Chinese medicine, as well as the bodily practices that derive from them: Yoga, Shiatzu, Tai Ji Quan, Qigong, or acupuncture. Such practices imply complex cosmologies that view the human body as intimately interconnected with cosmic forces and tensions. For these traditions the body is not merely a mechanism entirely controlled by biology, but a site where signs of harmony or disharmony can be read. From Asia to Africa different religions and philosophies have developed ritual practices whereby the social body and the individual body are placed in a common vision of human reality. Symptoms and illnesses at the level of the individual are thus interpreted as expressions of tensions within society, while all suffering is contextualized in a wider field of forces more complex than the purely biomedical etiology. Diagnoses and therapies entail, then, the reorganization of individuals' roles in the social order. In these cultures the social identity of each human being is strengthened or modified through specific ritual practices that underscore the individual's growth and the ensuing transformation of his or her social role. Initiation rituals, therapeutic rituals, and rites of passage are all symbolic practices that transform the human body into an altar that mediates the metamorphosis of the personal identity and the equilibrium of the social body. The body as altar is a means to re-establish social order after an illness or a witch attack; it creates the symbolic space that allows human beings, ancestors, and gods to communicate with each other. Becoming a shaman or a healer, being possessed or sick, the transition from puberty to adulthood – are all processes whereby the body is endowed with symbols and discourses marking the transition from one state to another. In all processes of transmission or metamorphosis of identity the body is the main vector of symbolic communication. Thus the body surface can be viewed as a social skin – the boundary between society and the psycho-biological individual, a sort of stage on which human beings interpret the drama of their socialization. Through complex social, cultural, and linguistic processes the body surface may also be seen as a constructed entity, capable of transforming both its biological character and its own rhetorical and symbolic potential, capable of inducing ritual possession despite a modern rejection of ancient practices, and still capable of blocking memories of traumatic events in a body whose rituality could become merely narrative. Anthropology has shown us how we can read bodies as topographies that relate memory and community. These bodily traces create belonging and exclusion.

It is extremely difficult to define the body of Western cultures as homogeneous. The medicine of both Hippocrates and Galen shows that the theories of humors, the relationship between melancholy and bile, between psychological and physical suffering, are themselves the roots of modern biomedicine. Yet we can still attempt to simplify the complex trajectory of the different Western theories if we remember that since the eighteenth century the body has been the object of a long history of control and repressive interventions. Through ethics and science, such disciplinary practices have aimed at separating the body from emotions and at punishing the body – especially the female body – at first through the accusation of witchcraft and of possession and later through the diagnoses of hysteria and other pathologies. The body as machine subject to the social imperative of reproduction and the body of passions are today conceived of as objects to be monitored, manipulated, and rendered passive. The female body has been the locus of many images of madness: from Plato's itinerant uterus to today's eating disorders, anorexia and bulimia. The woman's body seems incapable of escaping the paradox of being a porous body continuously absorbing violence. At the same time its complex somatic, expressing its communicative power, implicitly reveals an autonomous discourse of resistance.

Drawing from psychoanalysis and phenomenology, recent critics have radically criticized the reduction of the body to its purely biological features and rejected its subjugation to any formal logic. Jacques Lacan, Gilles Deleuze, Michel Foucault, and Jacques Derrida have all argued for a new dimension of the body, namely, the body as a political arena or major battleground where identities are wrought. To have or to be a body is a phenomenological paradox today, an outmoded expression that does not capture the tragedy of a ruptured dialogue between the individual body and the social body.

In addition to the techniques of the body, whereby Marcel Mauss argued that each culture is able to transmit its traditions, today there are technologies of the contemporary body that determine the reproduction of the same blueprint. An agile, muscular, and lean body strives to forget the violence of genocide and the holocaust of wars by projecting all over the world the model of a young, and thus innocent, body. The body has increasingly become a flexible and docile space on which one can read the contradictions of contemporary societies: emancipation and repression at one and the same time. A number of such body techniques may seem to be transgressive and antisocial in character, free from external constraints thus capable of fostering an agenda of individual freedom and the utopia whereby a subject can decide how and what his or her identity may be. In reality, each technique unveils the contradiction existing in the quest for hedonism. According to Arjun Appadurai, to be effective, body techniques imply painful and exacting social disciplines that gradually become a specific *habitus*, a form of repetitive behavior that actually limits rather than enhances invention and creativity. What in contemporary culture appears to be the search for originality and novelty is in reality only a symptom of a deeper discipline through which desire is shaped according to an aesthetic of the ephemeral, which by way of consumption practices truly becomes an engagement requiring continuous dedication and attention. Ornaments and clothes have always determined the rules of the power of beauty and have made possible societal, group, and class identification of each individual and, consequently, his or her negotiating power. In Western societies, for example, it is impossible to identify the body without thinking of all those accessories that have been the markers of epochs and values: crinoline, garters, bra, stockings, tie. Today, though, especially among the younger generations, the body seems to be in the process of losing all ornament and becoming both the object and the subject of a new aesthetics. With the help of computer technology that is capable of simulating how body parts may physically be changed, the "biological body" becomes a virtual reality. The naked body tends to acquire a power stronger than that of any garment. Through photography, magazines, cinema, and television, new universal aesthetic norms emerge together with bodily practices that tend to homogenize age and genders. The young body tends to wear the same clothes, to adopt similar postures and to build an undifferentiated ideal image on which to inscribe, through direct interventions like tattooing or piercing, its subjective specificity. These are ways of bodily discourse that tend to set aside or efface all forms of discourse.

(See also *healing, identity, indexicality, individual, intentionality, metaphor, power, prophecy, space, theater, writing*)

Bibliography

Appadurai, Arjun
  1996 Modernity at Large. Cultural Dimensions of Globalization. Minneapolis: Minnesota University Press.
Crapanzano, Vincent
  1996 Riflessioni frammentarie sul corpo, il dolore, la memoria. *In* Perché il corpo. Utopia, sofferenza, desiderio. Mariella Pandolfi, ed. Rome: Meltemi.
Gil, José
  1998[1985] Metamorphoses of the Body. Minneapolis: University of Minnesota Press.
Grosz, Elisabeth
  1994 Volatile Bodies: Toward a Corporeal Feminism. Bloomington: Indiana

University Press.

Lock, Margaret

    1993 Cultivating the Body. Anthropology and Epistemologies of Bodily Practices and Knowledge. Annual Review Of Anthropology 22:133–155.

Mauss, Marcel

    Techniques du corps. In Sociologie et anthropologie. Pp. 363–386. Paris: PUF.

Pandolfi, Mariella, ed.

    1996 Perché il corpo. Utopia, sofferenza, desiderio. Rome: Meltemi.

Starobinski, Jean

    1980 Le passé de la passion. Nouvelle Revue de Psychanalyse 21:51–76.

Strathern, Andrew

    1996 Body Thoughts. Ann Arbor: University of Michigan Press.

Turner, Terence

    1979 The Social Skin. *In* Not Work Alone. I. Cherfas and R. Lewin, eds. Pp. 111–140. London: Temple Smith.

■ *John H. Schumann*

Brain

I n the most basic terms, the brain can be seen as consisting of a posterior sensory system, an anterior motor system, and a more or less anterior and ventral appraisal system. The appraisal system assesses the motivational relevance and emotional significance of agents, actions, and objects perceived by the sensory mechanism in order to determine the appropriate mental or motor action to take with respect to stimulus.

We think and act on the basis of relevance or value. Value is of three kinds: homeostatic, sociostatic, and somatic. Homeostatic value relates to biological stasis and the basic functions of the body. We behave in order to maintain appropriate respiration, body temperature, satiety, and physical safety, and we appraise environmental stimuli in terms of their relevance to these functions. Sociostatic value relates to our innate tendencies to interact with conspecifics, to form attachments and achieve social affiliation. We pay attention to faces, voices, and bodily movements of others in order to determine their intentions and dispositions, and we act according to value determined by such social cognition. Finally, somatic value relates to value accrued in the lifetime of the individual and consists of preferences and aversions acquired through socialization, enculturation and education. Much of homeostatic value is evolutionarily inherited and innate. Sociostatic value may also be under genetic control to the extent it entrains us to be sensitive to the facial expression, voice, and musculoskeletal activity of others. Somatic value involves dispositions to form preferences and aversions, likes and dislikes based on experience during one's lifetime.

The major brain mechanisms involved in stimulus appraisal are the amygdala in the temporal lobes on the sides of the brain, the orbitofrontal cortex in the frontal lobes above the orbits of the eyes, and the body proper via the autonomic nervous system, the endocrine system, and the musculoskeletal system. The amygdala appears to make appraisals about stimuli in terms of what threats they pose to the organism. People with amygdala damage appear to have reduced sensitivity to stimuli that normal individuals find fearful or threatening. However, some researchers believe that the amygdala is also responsive to rewarding stimuli. The orbitofrontal cortex seems to be involved in the appraisal of both positive and negative stimuli and seems to function particularly in determining changes in reward contingencies. In other words, the orbitofrontal cortex seems to subserve the recognition of positive stimuli that cease to be rewarding and negative stimulus situations that cease to be aversive.

Psychologists have been interested in defining the categories that we use to appraise stimuli. Several highly congruent models have been proposed, and that developed by Klaus Scherer appears to capture the dimensions identified in most of them. He identifies five stimulus evaluation checks: novelty, intrinsic pleasantness, goal/need significance, coping potential, and norm/self compatibility. The novelty check determines whether the stimulus is familiar or whether it is new. The pleasantness check determines whether the stimulus is intrinsically pleasant. The goal/need significance check assesses whether the stimulus situation will facilitate or interfere with the individual's meeting his or her needs or achieving his or her goals. The coping potential check evaluates whether the individual is capable of meeting the physical, mental, and emotional demands of the situation. The norm/self compatibility check assesses whether the stimulus situation is compatible with societal expectations and personal standards.

In sum, then, the brain inherits some preferences and aversions (homeostatic and sociostatic value) and acquires others (somatic value). One of the functions of society appears to be to capture or entrain an individual's appraisal system so that the individual will ultimately share the preferences and aversions of the culture of which he or she is a member. A society socializes individuals to preferences in foods, religious beliefs, social behaviors, and moral standards, as well as particular knowledge and skill domains.

An interesting way to observe the entrainment of stimulus appraisal systems is to observe how different societies socialize individuals to learn a second language. In Holland it is extremely rare to find a Dutch person with a university degree who is monolingual; educated people in Holland are likely to have a substantial command of English, French, or German. The acquisition and possession of this knowledge and skill is part of being Dutch. All academics in Holland know English. In general, this is not a product of identification with English speakers. In other words, in Holland one does not necessarily acquire English to become British-like or American-like. One acquires it to be a particular kind of Dutch person – a university teacher or researcher.

Dutch society expends considerable effort and resources to entrain its members' value systems to get them to make the effort to acquire these second languages. English, for example, is required and taught at the elementary, secondary, and university levels, and a significant number of university courses are taught in English. English, French, and German movies on Dutch television are not dubbed; they are in the native language with Dutch subtitles. Dutch students who eventually receive university degrees are encouraged by families and educational institutions to spend various periods during their education abroad.

In North America, particularly in the United States, there is very little expectation that people will acquire a language other than English. To be considered an educated American, it is not necessary to speak another language. A major reason for this is that there is no obvious language for the society as a whole to choose. The Dutch stress English because there are very few Dutch speakers in the world, and English is the language of commerce and science. France and Germany are neighbors with whom Holland has extensive relations. Therefore, when an American born to monolingual English-speaking parents does acquire a second language, it is because of a particular idiosyncrasy of his or her stimulus appraisal system. The system appraises some aspect of the language-learning situation positively – its speakers, the culture or the language itself. This appraisal creates an incentive motive, and then the learner makes efforts to learn the language to achieve that goal. His or her neural appraisal mechanism assesses stimuli in the environment (teacher, method, materials, the target language itself) and, if the appraisal is positive enough (in terms of pleasantness, goal/need significance, coping potential, and self and social image) such that the intellectual effort is made over a long enough period of time (generally several years), the language may eventually be acquired. But unlike the case in Holland, what language is learned and to what degree is very variable. English-speaking North American society does not organize to entrain its members' neural appraisal systems to acquire any particular second languages to any particular degree.

In sum, what society values has an impact on how the brain appraises certain stimuli, and that appraisal determines how the brain acquires and processes certain information. The brain, in turn, allows societal institutions to work. In societies where the acquisition of certain second languages is both necessary and expected, sufficient instruction will be provided and that instruction will be effective. This does not mean that second languages are taught better in Holland. It simply means that because the society needs its citizens to know English, German, or French, the society will provide the requisite instructional opportunities, and the citizens will make the effort to learn from those opportunities.

The simple view of the brain (sensory system, value system, motor system) provided here shows the brain's enormous power. The value system generates motor and mental activity vis-à-vis the stimulus situation. This simple neural system determines such large-scale societal phenomena as who learns what foreign language and how well. In general, the brain is not designed to like some things and to dislike others. Rather, it is designed to acquire such preferences and aversions, sometimes idiosyncratically as individuals (e.g., North Americans' acquiring a second language) or socially as groups (e.g., Dutch speakers' acquiring English). The preferences and aversions control what is learned and to what degree.

(See also *acquisition, category, contact, evolution, identity*)

Bibliography

Brothers, Leslie
   1997   Friday's Footprint: How Society Shapes the Human Mind. New York: Oxford University Press.
Damasio, Antonio
   1994   Descartes' Error: Emotion, Reason and the Human Brain. New York: G. P. Putnam's Sons.
Edelman, Gerald
   1992   Bright Air Brilliant Fire: On the Matter of the Mind. New York: Basic Books.
LeDoux, Joseph
   1996   The Emotional Brain. New York: Simon and Schuster.
Rolls, Edmund
   1999   The Brain and Emotion. New York: Oxford University Press.
Scherer, Klaus
   1984   Emotion as a Multi-component Process: A Model and Some Cross-cultural Data. *In* Review of Personality and Social Psychology. Vol. 5: Emotions, Relationships and Health. P. Shaver, ed. Pp. 37–63. Beverly Hills, CA: Sage.
Schumann, John
   1997   The Neurobiology of Affect in Language. Malden, MA: Blackwell Publishers.

■ *Ward H. Goodenough*

Category

F undamental to all learning and hence to culture is the categorization of experience. Sensory input, other than that evoking a reflex response, must be equatable with past sensory input if it is to have stimulus value. Learned responses are to stimulus categories, not to unique sensory inputs. Purposeful behavior, whether in humans or animals, is based on learning to relate categories of means to categories of ends. For a sensory input to have value as a stimulus with an associated learned response, it must be perceived as an instance or member of a categorical set.

Categories are fundamentally subjective. People objectivize them through language and other forms of symbolic representation. We tend to think of categories, therefore, as things that words designate. Words are, indeed, the means by which we are able to be aware of categories and their role in human cognition. But the categories that vocabularies designate are only the objectified visible tip of the much larger domain of categories in subjective cognitive processes.

Like other animals, humans are genetically programmed to find certain sensory inputs to be highly salient by contrast with others. Certain places on the range of color hues, for example, are invariant foci of reference for designating colors verbally, regardless of cross-linguistic differences in the number of basic color terms and the range of hues they are said to encompass. (Basic terms do not refer to natural objects, such as "grass color," and their referents are not perceived as subsets of what other terms designate.) Differences in color terminologies reflect differences in how people have clustered for verbal objectification the wider range of subjective color categories they distinguish perceptually.

Color categories illustrate the many kinds of categories, especially those based on direct sensory inputs, that are to be understood as "defined" by prototypic referents. These prototypes may be based on genetic proclivities (as with color), on primacy of experience, on intensity or frequency of experience, or on some combination of these. Such categories have imprecise or fuzzy boundaries, as implied by describing something as "yellow-brown."

19

Named land areas (spatial categories) in some societies are defined as the regions around focal landmarks, rather than the spaces between boundaries, with resulting zones of indeterminacy between them.

Basic categories are not perceived as composed of combinations of other categories. They can be defined only by pointing to illustrative examples, and many of them have no verbal representation as such in language. Most of the categories in terms of which people apprehend their world and events within it are complex, consisting of combinations of other categories. Complex categories that belong to non-overlapping complementary sets can be defined in terms of the constituent subcategories by which they can be distinguished from one another (their distinctive features). Thus the sound categories that distinguish between the different words of a language – the language's phonemes – can be defined in terms of the combinations of phonetic categories that distinguish among them, such as voicing/non-voicing, mode of articulation, position of articulation, etc. The latter categories are basic and defined by focal points of reference, but the phonemes defined in terms of them are conceptually discrete even if their concrete articulation is occasionally fuzzily ambiguous. The purely conceptual categories of relationship variously designated by kinship terms in different languages can be defined only in terms of other conceptual categories. They are thus definable, through componential analysis, in terms of categories that serve as distinctive features discriminating among them. Some subcategories of relationship within the set of subcategories designated by a kinship term may appear as more focal within the set, serving as a stereotype for the set as a whole. Thus where "mother" can refer to aunts as well as one's female parent, the latter may be described as "principal mother," revealing it to be the focal subcategory. The set of subcategories may also be defined in terms of extension rules applied to the focal one, the latter being distinguished from the focal subcategories of other sets by combinations of distinctive features.

Analysis shows that more than one set of distinctive features can reliably discriminate among verbally designated categories. Thus people may use a word denotatively in the same way while having different cognitive bases for doing so. Most drivers may stop at a red traffic light because they see it to be red, whereas some color-blind persons may stop because they perceive it to be at the top of the bank of lights. For people to have a sense that they share understanding about what percepts or concepts belong to a given category, redundancy in how it can be reliably defined is very helpful.

Categories tend to be organized in hierarchies. Basic categories, already mentioned, are those whose combinations produce and discriminate among other categories. Combinations of the latter in turn give rise to higher-level categories, and so on. Taxonomies exemplify elaborate, objectified categorical hierarchies, consisting of varieties, grouped into sub-species, then species, genera, families, orders, classes, and phyla. Research shows that verbal designation of categories tends to be (1) at a practical utilitarian level (akin to that of genus): oak, elm, robin, canary, horse, elephant, tuna, whiting, bee, ant, chair, table, etc.; and (2) at a much higher, broadly encompassing level:

tree, shrub, bird, animal, fish, insect, furniture, etc. Lower levels, when there is need to talk about them, are designated by descriptive expressions, often binomial ones such as white oak, weeping willow, striped bass, mountain goat, red ant, armchair, etc. This tendency is found cross-linguistically.

Experimental evidence shows that children tend to perceive words as designating categories that are mutually exclusive. They do not expect words to designate the same or overlapping categories. They learn later that words can refer to broader categories in a taxonomic hierarchy, "toy" encompassing both "doll" and "blocks." That people perceive some categories as more alike than others, even though they lack words for these hierarchical clusters, has also been established experimentally.

Since human learning is in terms of associations of categories of things, acts, persons, animals, and feeling states in various categories of relationship – such as means-ends, hierarchical, supportive – people attach differential value to them. Categories thus are not simply discriminated entities, they are good, bad, desirable, undesirable, etc., depending on how people have experienced them. Experiments show that people have richer associations with words designating nominal categories (things, persons, etc.) than with words designating adjectival ones.

Contextual association of categories of things and acts leads people to infer causal relations, which, formulated in words, become propositions. These associations lead to recipes for purposeful behavior. People order the conduct of activities, moreover, in terms of categories of situation, social identity, and context. How members of a family interact, for example, shifts with the arrival of a guest in their home, the category "guest" being a culturally significant contextualizer for how things are done, how language is used, and what things may be taboo. Since all perception is categorical, moreover, shifts in how one categorizes the same sensory or information inputs changes what one perceives, something that religious teachers, politicians, and trial lawyers, among others, seek to exploit to their various ends.

People organize their categories in many complicated ways, allowing some to co-occur and others not (as with foods) and some categories of person to enter into particular social relationships while prohibiting others from doing so (as with priestly celibacy). There are, as it were, grammatical and ungrammatical ways to associate categories, and some categories serve as contextualizing signals or markers that govern these associations.

Categories, moreover, are designated not only by words but by various other signs, including body language. Anything that makes a difference in how people perceive or respond to things marks a significant categorical difference. Human knowledge and beliefs and the organization of human activities and social relationships – indeed all of culture – is based on the categories humans construct out of experience and the ways in which they interrelate them.

(See also *brain, color, evolution, identity, maxim*)

Bibliography

Berlin, Brent O., and Paul D. Kay
  1966   Basic Color Terms. Berkeley: University of California Press.
Brown, Cecil H.
  1984   Language and Living Things: Uniformities in Folk Classification and Naming. New Brunswick, NJ: Rutgers University Press.
D'Andrade, Roy
  1995   The Development of Cognitive Anthropology. Cambridge: Cambridge University Press.
Goffman, Erving
  1974   Frame Analysis. New York: Harper and Row.
Goodenough, Ward H.
  1955   Componential Analysis and the Study of Meaning. Language 32:185–216.
  1990   Evolution of the Human Capacity for Beliefs. American Anthropologist 92:597–612.
Goodwin, Charles
  1995   Professional Vision. American Anthropologist 96:606–633.
Lakoff, George
  1987   Women, Fire, and Dangerous Things: What Categories Reveal about the Human Mind. Chicago and London: University of Chicago Press.
Lounsbury, Floyd G.
  1964   A Formal Analysis of the Crow and Omaha-type Kinship Terminologies. *In* Explorations in Cultural Anthropology: Essays in Honor of George Peter Murock. Ward H. Goodenough, ed. Pp. 351–393. New York: McGraw-Hill.
Markman, Ellen M.
  1989   Categorization and Naming in Children: Problems of Induction. Cambridge, MA: MIT Press.

■ *Celso Alvarez-Cáccamo*

Codes

C ommunicative codes are general procedures that both senders (speakers or signers) and receivers have to signal the communication of intentions (and to somehow interpret these intentions) by means of multimodal resources such as linguistic and paralinguistic signals, prosody, gaze, gestures, kinesics, and posturing. For the concerted production of meanings, senders' signaling alone is not enough; receivers then inferentially map perceived signals against communicative expectations and previous communicative experiences. In this sense, both senders and receivers are active and productive. Strictly speaking, receivers cannot replicate intentions, since these are abstract properties of the senders' minds; rather, receivers apply their own communicative codes to generate interpretations. These interpretations then affect the receivers' own cognitive states, and a certain sense of "understanding" ensues. Thus communicative codes, applied both to signal intentions and to construct interpretations from signals, are forms of an individual's competence that are alternately (or simultaneously) activated in interaction.

The notion of "code" in linguistics derives from information theory. In information theory, a code is a mechanism to pair two sets of signals in non-ambiguous, reversible, and context-free ways. For instance, in morse code the letter "s" is always rendered as three dots, regardless of particular circumstances (context independence); "s" can only be rendered as three dots (non-ambiguity); and three dots are always to be understood as "s" (reversibility). Morse code is not the inventory of dot-and-line combinations equivalent to letters, but the abstract rule or cypher that relates letters to those combinations.

This "code" notion was systematically applied to speech first by information theorists (Fano) and, then, fundamentally, by Roman Jakobson. Jakobson reframed Saussure's *langue/parole* dichotomy in terms of code/message. In this model, the speech signals would match "meanings" in the linguistic "code," equivalent here to "grammar." However, Jakobson's model is not exempt from ambiguities, loose ends, and perhaps contradictions. For instance, many pragmatic meanings, such as most conversational implicatures, cannot be accounted for by linguistic structures per se. Second, the interplay between linguistic and other systems in interaction (e.g., between grammar, prosody, and gestures to convey irony) produces apparent incongruences between literal and unstated contents that the linguistic-code model cannot account for either. Third, in much of face-to-face interaction, the various signaling values of oral or visual languages cannot be detached from non-linguistic body signals, as language use and other practices are mutually intertwined (see, e.g., Charles Goodwin's work on conversational organization).

These problems in the strict application of the "code" notion to human interaction have been widely pointed out. Philosophers, anthropologists, and linguists such as Paul Grice, John Searle, John Gumperz, Charles Goodwin, Alessandro Duranti, and Dan Sperber and Deirdre Wilson highlight the context-bound nature of most interpretation, the ambiguity of unstated meanings, and the variable interplay of understanding and misunderstanding. Inferential views of communication propose that most understanding depends on the particulars of the relationship between literal contents and contexts. Notions such as "background/mutual/shared/common knowledge," "common/shared assumptions," "mutual cognitive environment," or, simply, "cultural values" are thus construed as crucial variable contexts for interpretation.

This has led to a disabling of the applicability of the "code model" to human communication. However, a loose notion of codes still can and should be applied to communicative processes. Some reasons for this perspective are the following:

First, even for proponents of an inferential view of communication, it is beyond contention that at least some contents (e.g. literal or "sentence" meanings) that also enter interaction can safely be said to be "coded" (an explicit point in, for example, Sperber and Wilson's work). If I say "It's hot in here," I am in principle also predicating about the room temperature regardless of any possible additional interpretations (e.g., "Let's go to the park" or "Bad day to attend a lecture").

Second, and most important, the work on inference and contextualization also emphasizes the *regularities* in peoples' interpretations of signals or "contextualization cues," as interaction is by definition a social and cultural fact, not a purely individual one in which each person reinvents meaning anew in each encounter. In this sense, ethnomethodologists maintain that human sense-making is based on the inherently "overwhelming order" of conversational "normative practices." Likewise, interactional sociolinguists and anthropologists emphasize the build-up of assumptions through common "interactional histories," which helps explain highly regulated interpretations of others' utterances and acts. Unstated, inferred meanings also derive from systematic associations between signals (utterances, gaze, etc.), their literal interpretations, and contexts (social, interactional, discursive, cognitive).

In sum, although important properties of codes in information theory (non-ambiguity, reversibility, and context-independence) are problematic for human interaction, understanding is still governed by strongly patterned associations between material signals of various types and cognitive contents. A code model of interaction is applicable, then, if we conceive of coding procedures as inherently loose, intentional, and interpretive, and not as closed formal operations that preclude any meaning negotiation.

Communicative codes are therefore those general principles that first link intentions with sets of signals – regardless of their form – and then link these sets of signals with interpretations. The physical signaling resources that codes organize are multiple. Evidence that human interaction is inherently multimodal calls for a model that accounts for the integrated ways in which signals are deployed. In signaling intentions, codes mobilize whatever communicative resources humans have at their disposal. Just as morse code is not the inventory of dot-line combinations, communicative codes are not the signals (verbal or otherwise) themselves, but abstract associative procedures that relate them to contents.

Contents that are signaled through codes include referential-propositional contents, propositional dispositions, assumptions, beliefs, values, affect, knowledge, and, crucially, intentions about the signaling of these contents as well. For instance, a given participant in an interaction may intend to simultaneously signal beliefs about the world, the "definition of the situation," representations of locally relevant identities, overall interactional goals, the activity at hand, the turn-construction value of a given action (verbal or otherwise), the illocutionary force of an utterance, and the intentions to signal all those contents. However, communicative codes do not manifest meanings in non-ambiguous ways. In the dynamic feedback process of interaction, signals both point to contents in senders' minds and are the raw materials for others (or for the senders themselves) to produce meanings. This dual location of signals can help explain both the understandings and the misunderstandings that make up the fabric of daily interaction.

An implication of this view of communicative codes as essentially loose, intentional/interpretive procedures is that, by definition, intention-signaling and signal-interpretation differ substantially. Senders creatively apply intention-encoding principles, while receivers creatively apply signal-encoding principles that select meaning values and operate changes in their own mental states. We may thus speak separately of two one-way-only codes: "intentional communicative codes" and "interpretive communicative codes," which both senders and receivers possess as competence. Intentional and interpretive codes thus have different properties and roles, although their common basis must be broad enough to guarantee that the process of semantic mimesis deceive each interlocutor into a sense of sufficient understanding.

Another implication is that the "switching of codes" consists, precisely, of a recontextualization of interaction by which participants "indicate otherness," as sociolinguist Peter Auer asserts, to call attention to previously non-relevant contents by means of multimodal clusters of contextualization cues. Since the respective indexical values of linguistic varieties alone cannot be preassumed, switching of codes has thus less to do with the so-called code-switching, which merely juxtaposes speech varieties, than with the various, contrasting ways (including, but not exclusively, language alternations) by which humans selectively expose intentions.

(See also *functions, genre, identity, ideology, intentionality, literacy, power, switching, syncretism, translation, variation*)

Bibliography

Auer, Peter, and Aldo Di Luzio, eds.
   1992   The Contextualisation of Language. Amsterdam: John Benjamins.
Duranti, Alessandro, and Charles Goodwin, eds.
   1992   Rethinking Context: Language as an Interactive Phenomenon. Cambridge: Cambridge University Press.
Eco, Umberto
   1976   A Theory of Semiotics. Bloomington: Indiana University Press.
Givón, Talmy
   1989   Mind, Code and Context: Essays in Pragmatics. Hillsdale, NJ, and London: Lawrence Erlbaum.
Goodwin, Charles 1981
   Conversational Organization: Interaction between Speakers and Hearers. New York: Academic Press.
Gumperz, John J.
   1982   Discourse Strategies. Cambridge: Cambridge University Press.
Jakobson, Roman
   1990   On Language. Linda R. Waugh and Monique Monville-Burston, eds. Cambridge, MA: Harvard University Press.
Sacks, Harvey
   1995   Lectures on Conversation. Vols. 1 and 2. Gail Jefferson, ed. Oxford and Cambridge, MA: Blackwell.
Sperber, Dan, and Deirdre Wilson
   1986   Relevance: Communication and Cognition. Cambridge, MA: Harvard University Press.
Thibault, Paul J.
   1997   Re-reading Saussure: The Dynamics of Signs in Social Life. London and New York: Routledge.

■ *Paul Kay*

Color

C olor has been of interest to anthropologists of the twentieth century as the empirical domain par excellence in which to argue for (and against) the linguistic relativity thesis. Nineteenth-century scholars were aware that all languages do not reflect identical lexical classifications of color. The classicist (and politician) William Gladstone concluded that differences in color lexicons reflect differences in perceptual abilities: "the organ of color and its impressions were but partially developed among the Greeks of the heroic age." But the ophthalmologist Hugo Magnus recognized that failure to distinguish colors lexically need not indicate inability to distinguish them perceptually, insisting that a naming distinction and a perceptual distinction must be tested for independently. These and other late-nineteenth-century scholars tended strongly to view differences in color lexicons in evolutionary terms.

By the mid-twentieth century cultural evolutionism had largely run its course in the United States. Beginning with Boas and Sapir in the twenties and thirties, the tide of cultural and linguistic relativity was on the rise. In 1940, Whorf wrote that the world presents itself to us "in a kaleidoscopic flux of impressions which have to be organized in our minds." The categories in which this organization takes place, Whorf said, are largely supplied by our language. Thus language dictates perceptual organization.

The idea of semantic universals induced by perceptual universals runs directly counter to the rhetorical thrust of Whorfian relativism, although there is no necessary contradiction between language sometimes influencing perception and perception sometimes influencing language. Phenomena of both types probably exist. Indeed, it is ironic that the early Whorfians chose color as their parade example. Color represents one of the few lexical domains for which humans possess dedicated peripheral receptors. In the retina, the rods and (at least) three different families of cones are devoted to detecting variations in wavelength and luminance information. That the mid-century relativists chose color as their empirical battleground stands as a tribute to their self-confidence and a rebuke to their common sense.

There have been two major traditions of empirical research on color language stemming from the relativity thesis: a within-language, correlational line of research and a cross-language, descriptive one.

In the 1950s and 1960s, a series of studies was initiated by Eric Lenneberg, Roger Brown, and John M. Roberts that attempted to establish a correlation between a linguistic variable distinguishing colors (codability or communication accuracy) and a non-linguistic cognitive variable over colors: memorability. Since it was *assumed* at the time that any linguistic variable would vary across languages, correlation between a linguistic and the non-linguistic variable within a single language (almost always English) was taken to validate the doctrine that the coding systems of different languages induce differences in the non-linguistic cognition of their speakers.

In 1972, Eleanor Rosch challenged this assumption on the basis of the apparent universal lexical salience of certain "focal" colors. Rosch showed that among the Dani of New Guinea, universal perceptual salience determines both the non-linguistic and the linguistic variables of the correlational approach, thus undercutting the logic of this line of research. Rosch's view, and her procedures, were criticized by Lucy and Shweder in 1979. Lucy and Shweder's procedures were in turn challenged in 1984 by Kay and Kempton. Also, in a rigorous restudy, Linda Garro was unable to replicate the Lucy and Shweder result. However, Kay and Kempton also showed that differences in lexical classification of color can influence certain non-linguistic color similarity judgments.

In the tradition of cross-language description, the studies of the 1950s and 1960s sought to discover and celebrate the differences among color lexicons. In 1969, using the original stimulus set of Lenneberg and Roberts, Brent Berlin and Paul Kay compared the denotations of basic color terms in twenty languages and, based on these findings, examined descriptions of seventy-eight additional languages from the literature. They reported that there are universals in the semantics of color: the major color terms of all languages being focused on one of eleven landmark colors. Further, they postulated an evolutionary sequence for the development of basic color lexicons according to which black and white precede red, red precedes green and yellow, green and yellow precede blue, blue precedes brown, and brown precedes purple, pink, orange, and gray.

These results were challenged on methodological grounds, primarily by anthropologists, and largely embraced by psychologists and linguists. Subsequent field studies have confirmed the main lines of the universal and evolutionary theory but challenged details of Berlin and Kay's specific formulation. Taking into account both the new data on cross-language color naming and what was known about color perception from the vision literature, Kay and Chad K. McDaniel formulated in 1978 a reconceptualization of the model of color lexicon evolution, based in part on earlier, unpublished work of McDaniel that had established the identity of some of the universal semantic foci of Berlin and Kay with the psychophysically determined unique hues. Kay and McDaniel introduced the notion of fuzzy set into a formal model of the typology and evolution of color lexicons and shifted the emphasis away from the eleven universal color foci of Berlin and Kay to (1) the six primary colors of the Hering opponent process model (black, white, red, yellow, green, and blue), (2) certain categories present in early color terminology systems that consist in fuzzy *unions* of two or more primaries (e.g., [green OR blue]), and (3) categories occurring mostly in later color terminology systems based on fuzzy *intersections* of Hering primaries (e.g., = [red AND yellow], i.e. orange).

Kay and McDaniel also related the universal semantics of color to the neurophysiological results of Russell De Valois and his associates. The De Valois findings of the 1960s, based on recordings from LGN (optic nerve) cells of the macaque, were widely considered to provide the neurological locus of the opponent system. It was subsequently recognized that (1) the cells studied by the De Valois group provided no account of the long wavelength red response observed in humans psychophysically, and (2) the specific crossover points between excitation and inhibition for these cells did not correspond well to the psychophysically determined unique hue points. Current vision science continues to maintain the opponent process model on psychophysical grounds while rejecting the specific neurological substrate proposed by De Valois.

Since 1978, two important surveys of color lexicons have been conducted, both supporting Berlin and Kay's two broad hypotheses of semantic universals and evolutionary sequence in the lexical encoding of colors: the World Color Survey of Berlin, Kay, and William Merrifield, and the Middle American Color Survey of Robert MacLaury. Kay and Luisa Maffi, in recent work, have proposed, on the basis of the World Color Survey data, a model of the evolution of color terminology systems that attempts to derive the typology and evolutionary trajectories of basic color term systems from facts of color appearance. This model also takes account of the Emergence Hypothesis, according to which not all languages necessarily have a small set of words (or word senses) of pure color meaning whose denotations jointly partition the perceptual color space.

The universalist/evolutionary tradition of research on color categorization has continued to receive methodological criticism from relativists, such as John Lucy and the team of B. Saunders and J. van Brakel, and universalists with competing paradigms, notably Anna Wierzbicka and her associates. The emphasis in these methodological critiques has shifted away from challenging the rigor with which standardized procedures for mapping words to colors are applied to challenging the legitimacy of any such procedures.

(See also *acquisition, brain, category, evolution, relativity, vision*)

Bibliography

Berlin, Brent, and Paul Kay
   1969   Basic Color Terms: Their Universality and Evolution. Berkeley and Los Angeles: University of California Press.

De Valois, Russell L., I. Abramov, and G. H. Jacobs
   1966   Analysis of Response Patterns of LGN Cells. Journal of the Optical Society of America 56:966–977.
Garro, Linda
   1986   Language, Memory and Focality: A Reexamination. American Anthropologist 88: 128–136.
Heider, Eleanor Rosch
   1972   Probabilities, Sampling and the Ethnographic Method: The Case of Dani Colour Names. Man 7:448–466.
Kay, Paul, and Willett M. Kempton
   1984   What Is the Sapir-Whorf Hypothesis? American Anthropologist 86:65–79.
Kay, Paul, and Luisa Maffi
   2000   Color Appearance and the Emergence and Evolution of Basic Color Lexicons. American Anthropologist 101: 743–760.
Kay, Paul, and Chad K. McDaniel
   1978   The Linguistic Significance of the Meanings of Basic Color Terms. Language 54:610–646.
Lenneberg, Eric H., and John M. Roberts
   1956   The Language of Experience: A Study in Methodology. Memoir 13 of International Journal of American Linguistics.
Lucy, John A., and Shweder, Richard A.
   1979   The Effect of Incidental Conversation on Memory for Focal Colors. American Anthropologist 90:923–931.
MacLaury, Robert E.
   1997   Color and Cognition in Mesoamerica: Constructing Categories as Vantages. Austin: University of Texas Press.
Saunders, B. A. C., and J. van Brakel
   1997   Are There Non-trivial Constraints on Colour Categorization? Brain and Behavioral Sciences 20:167–228. [The paper is accompanied by thirty-one peer commentaries.]

■ *Marcyliena M. Morgan*

Community

The speech community is a theoretical concept central to the study of language in culture and society. Its focus is on when and how speakers use their language system. In linguistic anthropology, speech community refers to speakers who participate in interactions based on social and cultural norms and values that are regulated, represented, and recreated through discursive practices. Because they are constructed around culturally and socially constituted interaction, speech communities cannot be defined by static physical location and can be experienced as part of a nation-state, neighborhood, village, club, compound, on-line chat room, religious institution, and so on. Though speech communities may take any and all of these forms and more, it is not an infinitely malleable concept, changing shape, form, and meaning according to scholarly need or any new gathering of people. Rather, a speech community reflects what people do and know when they interact with one another. It assumes that when people come together through discursive practices, they behave as though they operate within a shared set of norms, local knowledge, beliefs, and values. It means that they are aware of these things and capable of knowing when they are being adhered to and when the values of the community are being ignored. Because a speech community is constructed around the knowledge of communicative practices as well as their implementation, it is fundamental in understanding identity and representation of ideology. Thus it is central to the discussion of linguistic concerns like mutual intelligibility, variation, and communicative competence, as well as cultural, political, and sociolinguistic concerns like language and gender, nationalism, transnationalism, ethnicity, social class, and so on. One's speech community can multiply during the life cycle, and, indeed, there are cases where a member exchanges one community for another, vowing never to speak using the same ideological system associated with the rejected speech community.

Linguistic anthropology's use of speech community was first formulated when ethnographic research centered exclusively on daily life and rituals, largely ignoring influence from other cultures and societies. In fact, Leonard

31

Bloomfield's description of speech community assumed a shared single language within a single community. Formal linguistics' definition of speech community was even more rigid, and an idealized notion of homogeneous language use was considered the norm. This idealization was also typical among dialectologists who considered linguistic homogeneity fundamental to the identification of regional speech and suggested that the geographical boundaries of lexical items represented the boundaries of speech communities. Yet research in urban areas and language contact situations, especially pidgin and creole language studies and bilingual and multilingual societies, quickly revealed the limits of a definition focused exclusively on language theory rather than language in social life. Through the arguments and research of scholars such as William Labov, John Gumperz, Dell Hymes, and Michael Halliday, it became clear that the focus should be on interaction as a social process. This is not to say that speech communities do not conflict over issues of linguistic diversity as well. For example, the case of African American English (AAE) in the United States suggests that many Americans remain conflicted over its existence and continued use. Some believe that those who speak AAE reflect the history and politics of U.S. race and class history and relations. Others reject this theory and argue that the AAE speech community is different by choice and simply wants to be outside of the larger speech community.

While it is true that all speech communities show some linguistic variation and what is socially and culturally acceptable and grammatical, it is also true that the current state of technological communication, globalization, and transmigration can challenge its viability as a useful concept. Yet this represents the challenge to the analyst who must work in a shrinking cultural and social world, rather than the concept itself. Speech community remains a resilient unit of analysis because the definition of language that binds it is based on the notion of diversity of language, varieties, and styles. What is shared among its members is knowledge of language ideology and attitude toward language use. This is evident in cyber chat rooms where the style of interaction constitutes the group of individuals. In this case, it is not cyber space alone that defines the speech community. Rather, it is the use and regulation of the codes of chat rooms whether in the form of symbols, turn taking, language restrictions, and topic focus – the rules of interaction constitute the identity of the chat room. This distinction has become increasingly important as people throughout the world gain access to people and cultures, including some knowledge of discursive practices.

With modernity, the accessibility of what were previously national and cultural boundaries has resulted in people from outside these cultures appropriating the language of speech communities to which they have no social or cultural relationship. In fact, cultural conflict can arise when those who are familiar with communities where they may not share membership, use a language or jargon for emphasis, play, or to align with an "outside" identity within the boundaries of their own communities. In this case the style of speaking may be readily identified as belonging to another community, but the value norms and expectations of the source community do not accompany it. What's more, the words and expressions may be used out of context and in ways considered inappropriate and offensive. Yet speech community is not a concept that unravels with conflict, complex situations, and shifts in identity. Instead of problematizing the notion of speech community, conflicts such as these highlight its efficacy in exploring the relationship between linguistics and identity, politics, and society. The concept of speech community binds the importance of local knowledge and communicative competence in discursive activities so that members can identify insiders from outsiders, those passing as members and those living in contact zones and borderlands.

(See also *competence, contact, crossing, gender, identity, ideology, style, switching, variation*)

Bibliography

Bloomfield, Leonard
  1933 Language. New York: Holt, Rinehart & Winston.
Gumperz, John
  1962 Types of Linguistic Community. Anthropological Linguistics 4:28–40.
  1972 Introduction. *In* Directions in Sociolinguistics: The Ethnography of Communication. John Gumperz and Dell Hymes, eds. Pp. 1–25. New York: Holt, Rinehart and Winston.
  1982 Discourse Strategies. Cambridge: Cambridge University Press.
Halliday, M. A. K.
  1978 Language As Social Semiotic: The Social Interpretation of Language and Meaning. London: Edward Arnold.
Hymes, Dell
  1972 On Communicative Competence. *In* Sociolinguistics. J. B. Pride and J. Holmes, eds. Pp. 269–293. Harmondsworth, Middlesex: Penguin Press.
  1974 Foundations in Sociolinguistics: An Ethnographic Approach. Philadelphia: University of Pennsylvania Press.
Labov, William
  1972a Language in the Inner City: Studies in the Black English Vernacular. Philadelphia: University of Pennsylvania Press.
  1972b Sociolinguistic Patterns. Philadelphia: University of Pennsylvania Press.
  1980 Is There a Creole Speech Community? *In* Theoretical Orientations in Creole Study. A. Valdman and A. Highfield, eds. Pp. 369–388. New York: Academic Press.

■ *Jack Sidnell*

Competence

T he term *competence* is generally used to describe the knowledge underlying a native-speaker's production and interpretation of a potentially infinite number of syntactically well-formed strings in a given language. The term was first used in this sense in *Aspects of the Theory of Syntax* by Noam Chomsky who distinguished it there from performance, understood not only as the actuation of competence but also as the workings of attention, memory, and perception. Competence then is an abstraction designed to clear away a set of complex and interacting variables so as to allow the linguist an uncontaminated perspective on linguistic form. In its Chomskian usage, competence is ahistorical and asocial and at the same time the fundamental object of study for linguistics. How are society and history excised from the generative view of language? First, knowledge of language (or rather, "knowledge of grammar") is said to consist primarily, although not exclusively, of generative rules as opposed to the products of learning and memorization. This view excludes from consideration the pragmatics of language learning and acquisition (e.g. input) and the social dynamics of language change. Second, this knowledge of generative rules is said to be largely unconscious. In this way speakers' indigenous understandings (metapragmatic reflections) are effectively excluded from consideration of the total linguistic fact. While non-linguists may not share a set of descriptive formalisms with linguists, they nevertheless exhibit varying degrees of language awareness (in some cases this may be bound up with occupation). Field linguists often encounter certain individuals who, though completely untrained in current generative theories of grammar, nevertheless are able to discuss language in terms of its structural principles with extraordinary acuity. "Linguistics" it would seem is an indigenous tradition in every community. The claim that knowledge of language is largely unconscious (except in the case of academic linguists) may thus strike many anthropologists as particularly ethnocentric and Victorian. Third, understood largely as a reflection of universal grammatical principles and language-specific parameter settings, competence fits neatly within the Chomskian vision of the "completely homogeneous speech community," with both sociolinguistic and cross-linguistic variation traditionally given second-billing to the discovery and description of formal linguistic universals. In each case, the conception of competence implicitly precludes an understanding of the embedding of language in the social world, history, and structured activities of its users. One may well ask whether the notion of competence remains relevant to a socially informed linguistics.

It should be noted that both linguists and linguistic anthropologists concerned with language use recognize that knowledge of language is a necessary but not sufficient condition for the production and interpretation of many (if not all) utterances. Consider in this respect an utterance such as *I live here*. The proper interpretation of such an utterance will depend not only on the recipient's knowledge of English grammar, allowing assignment of appropriate grammatical functions to individual lexical items, but also on the hearer's knowledge of the fact that the verb *live* can be used to mean 'inhabit.' Further removed from the linguistic domain are the kinds of knowledge that allow for the proper interpretation of *here*. How is a referent assigned to this deictic when it could conceivably refer to 'at the desk,' 'in this room,' 'in this house,' 'in this city,' 'in this country' ad infinitum. Clearly the predicate (*live*) suggests that *here* refers to a definable space in which human(s) might reside. So in making sense of this utterance speakers draw on their knowledge of the kinds of spaces humans typically inhabit. The example illustrates that the interpretation of any specific use of language in fact demands that hearers draw on many kinds of knowledge. Along these lines, Dell Hymes noted that a member of a speech community must know when to speak and when not to, what to "talk about with whom, when, where, in what manner." Speakers not only form grammatically acceptable strings but at the same time perform through them social actions in contextually appropriate ways. Hymes further suggested that just as syntax exerts control over aspects of phonology and morphology, so too pragmatics might have some influence on aspects of language structure. If this is so, grammatical description and an understanding of competence should be part of a theory of language uses and functions. It is precisely this concern with language function that led some linguists to a significantly different view of the relation between competence and performance and to seriously re-evaluate the role of theory and explanation in linguistic argumentation. In generative theories of grammar, synchronic variation, which could not be adequately formalized in terms of transformational rules, had been assigned to the domain of performance. Thus, for example, the fact that some speakers occasionally say *They was going down there* is not taken as an indication that the speaker lacks adequate knowledge of person and number agreement in English. Within a sociolinguistic paradigm, on the other hand, speakers, in constructing such a sentence, are seen as making a choice as to which form to use (and also, potentially, whether to implement an agreement system or not). Over time such choices can lead to a system in which just one form is consistently used while the other becomes archaic or even extinct. In this way it is possible, as Vološinov anticipated, to turn the old dichotomy on its head and see competence (or Saussure's *langue*) as a reflection of a history of performances

(Saussure's *parole*). That is to say, synchronic grammar, which is itself a linguist's abstraction, is now understood as a partial reflection of a history of uses in context, and the relation between structure and use is understood in dynamic rather than static terms. Usage determines not only which form will win out in such cases – it also plays a role in the emergence of grammatical forms. Thus a linguistic element that begins its career as a contentive lexical item occurring in specific syntactic positions due to pragmatic constraints can over time lose its lexical meaning (a process sometimes referred to as "semantic bleaching") and come to indicate a purely grammatical relation. Such examples, of which there are many, illustrate the way in which change over time involves the reanalysis of existing forms – that is, a reworking of linguistic form within the competence of particular users. As such, competence is not some timeless set of generative abstractions and formalisms, but rather a highly dynamic system which undergoes continual modification. Recently Chomsky revised the distinction between competence and performance, and now prefers to speak of I(nternal) language and E(xternal) language. The change in terminology, however, involves no significant modification of the underlying abstraction (except a slight change of focus in the E-language/performance side of the dichotomy). Talmy Givón's twenty-year-old critique thus remains relevant – the abstraction devised as a point of methodological convenience has been elevated to a position of theoretical prominence in generative grammar. Ripped from its embeddedness in the social life of its users, language is reduced to "models of language" evaluated against one another in terms of their "economy," "simplicity," "efficiency," that is, in purely system-internal terms. In contrast, a socially informed perspective seeks to describe knowledge of language with a view to its fundamental role in communication between socially located actors in continuously changing human societies.

(See also *acquisition, community, evolution, grammar, indexicality, performativity, socialization, variation*)

Bibliography

Chomsky, Noam
    1965   Aspects of the Theory of Syntax. Cambridge, MA: MIT Press.
    1986   Knowledge of Language: Its Nature, Origin and Use. New York: Praeger.
Givón, Talmy
    1979   On Understanding Grammar. New York: Academic Press.
Hymes, Dell
    1972[1971]   On Communicative Competence. *In* Sociolinguistics: Selected Readings. J. B. Pride and Janet Holmes, eds. Pp. 269–285. Harmondsworth: Penguin.
Silverstein, Michael
    1981   The Limits of Awareness. Sociolinguistic Working Paper no. 84. Austin, TX: Southwest Educational Development Laboratory.
Vološinov, V. N.
    1986[1973]   Marxism and the Philosophy of Language. Trans. Ladislav Matejka and I. R. Titunik. Cambridge, MA: Harvard University Press.

■ *Marco Jacquemet*

Conflict

C onflict provides a unique opportunity to study the articulation of language and power. Conflict interrupts the normal course of social exchanges and can lead to interactional breakdowns and yet it provides a central force for the constitution of social relations. The process of managing conflict is fundamentally communicative and through conflict-related communicative performances (the Trobriander's yakala, Eskimo's song duels, U.S. adversarial cross-examinations), social networks are activated and social relationships reconfigured. From large-scale confrontations to family squabbles, conflict is constituted by the airing of more or less direct accusations for which speakers must take responsibility, which require answers, and which cannot be withdrawn without complicated negotiations. Conflict allows speakers' wills to power to be heard. Thus a full appreciation of this phenomenon depends on a thorough understanding of communicative practices.

Until recently, most legal anthropologists treated talk as a source of information about conflict rather than as a techno-political device used by participants in the conflict. From Malinowski to Hoebel to Gluckman, conflict – between social classes, ethnic groups, individuals, and society, or individual interactants – has always been one of the major concerns of sociocultural anthropology. Yet their studies yield very little knowledge of how people actually manage conflict in interaction. They suffer from an absence of detailed primary data, electing to present summaries, reports by informants, or reports from meetings held to resolve the conflict. In sum, these studies talked more about conflict than about conflict talk.

Conversely, conflict has been quite neglected in the study of language until recently. Even when language was considered a form of social action (as in sociolinguistics, speech act theory, or the ethnography of communication), it was analyzed for its conversational coherence and negotiated character, not for its disruptive potential. For instance, researchers concerned with interethnic communication viewed communicative breakdowns as the result of interactants' interpretative failure due to cultural misunderstandings.

To overcome the limitations of earlier research, contemporary work on conflict talk looks at language as a contested field, more like a battlefield where interactants are acutely aware of the power of their (and others') words. Under the influence of social theorists such as Michel Foucault, Pierre Bourdieu, or Raymond Williams, this new brand of conflict studies cross-pollinates an analysis of language with an analysis of power. Talk is thus analyzed not only for devices that ensure coherence and cohesion, but also for those mechanisms by which speakers/hearers achieve a sudden shift and undermining of context and bring about a breakdown of conversational coherence. This will to control and dominate is part of the local technology of power and as such is informed by strategies indexing asymmetrical social relationships and tactics seeking interactional dominance.

Among the many techno-political devices employed in this will to power, special attention has been recently given to those that evoke or establish particular kinds of contexts. From public oratory to legal arbitration to ritual wailing, researchers have been focusing on the disruptive but empowering quality of direct speech ("straight talk") associated with conflict. Two such devices of primary importance are contextualization strategies and meta-pragmatic awareness.

Contextualization strategies refer to communicative practices that both produce representations of the social world in accord with a given ideology and seek to persuade others to comply with these representations. Such strategies are found in all societies and usually consist of three parts: the decontextualization of an event from its occurrence in a particular space and time, its entextualization into a discourse with a more controllable set of truth-values, and the recontextualization of this discourse within a communicative frame set up to legitimize it (for instance, embedding an opponent's statement within one's own speech while inverting its referential value or adding a negative comment through intonational coloring – most instances of reported speech in argumentative situations conform to this strategy).

By metapragmatic awareness, I mean the awareness of how speech forms are used to establish specific participation frameworks: the indexical relationship between interactants, including the speaker's stance or attitudes; the social relations or relative status of the participants; and special attributes of particular individuals. In conflict, this awareness can turn vicious and manifest itself in a metapragmatic attack: a strategy of consciously and overtly calling attention to the specific use of linguistic mechanisms in the context of the interaction at hand for the purpose of interactional control. A metapragmatic attack can be used to comment on non-verbal behavior ("don't use that tone with me"), to draw attention to a particular word or style ("don't call me stupid" or "you sound like a broken record"), or to address the indexical relationship between speaker and hearer ("you don't know who you're talking to" or "you must call me sir"). An explicit accusation at the metapragmatic level produces a communicative break that escalates the stakes of the conflict. Metapragmatic attacks put an individual on the defense without having to level any specific accusations. They unravel the raw fabric of communicative interactions, exposing the disputants' maneuvers as they struggle for control, respect, and interactional dominance.

From the study of conflict talk we can draw some broader conclusions about the relationship between language and power. First, we must understand that most techno-political devices are intentionally staged, performative acts. People in positions of dominance stage these acts in order to perform their power (with of course some helpful aids, such as a dilution of responsibility in case their performance fails). Thus the outcome of any attempt to gain control over communicative resources is never predetermined. Second, the study of conflict talk forces us to look at communication as verbal hygiene, in which proper and correct, "clean" forms of talk are activated as techniques for achieving cohesion and solidarity in a context of postcolonial and national languages, linguistic minorities, and class or gender consciousness. Third, conflict talk teaches us to avoid a simplistic correlation between speech forms and power: its techno-political devices are deployed from all positions, from the core as well as from the periphery, from the superior as well as from the inferior. Different forms of domination produce different configurations of language use. Any linguistic form gains different meanings and has different social and political effects within specific institutional and ideological contexts. Finally, conflict talk forces us to address the issue of the relationship between language and social change. Conflicts over language use change the repertoire of social meanings associated with power relations. Through these fights, social relationships are interactionally transformed, opening the way for more profound social transformations. The struggle in the United States over sexist language and the generic masculine pronoun provides an example for this potential for change: linguistic awareness of gender bias renders problematic the generic use of the masculine pronoun, and this newly produced sensitivity can be exploited during conflict, since it provides powerful weapons for the fight. It would be naive to claim that awareness of sexist language in itself changes gender relations. However, by focusing speakers' attention on the inner workings of language, it opens a reflection on the social meanings of particular linguistic repertoires, and this in turn can lead to structural change.

(See also *act, control, indexicality, participation, performativity, power*)

Bibliography

Brenneis, Donald, and Fred Myers, eds.
  1984   Dangerous Words: Language and Politics in the Pacific. New York: New York University Press.
Briggs, Charles, ed.
  1996   Disorderly Discourse: Narrative, Conflict, and Inequality. Oxford: Oxford University Press.
Conley, John M., and William M. O'Barr
  1998   Just Words: Law, Language, and Power. Chicago: University of Chicago Press.

Duranti, Alessandro
   1994   From Grammar to Politics: Linguistic Anthropology in a Western Samoan
      Village. Berkeley: University of California Press.
Foucault, Michel
   1980   Power/Knowledge. New York: Pantheon Books.
Grimshaw, Allen, ed.
   1990   Conflict Talk: Sociolinguistic Investigations of Arguments in Conversa-
      tions. Cambridge: Cambridge University Press.
Hirsch, Susan F.
   1998   Pronouncing and Persevering: Gender and the Discourses of Disputing in
      an African Islamic Court. Chicago: University of Chicago Press.
Jacquemet, Marco
   1996   Credibility in Court: Communicative Practices in the Camorra Trials. Cam-
      bridge: Cambridge University Press.
Schieffelin, Bambi, Kathryn A. Woolard, and Paul V. Kroskrity, eds.
   1998   Language Ideologies: Practice and Theory. Oxford: Oxford University
      Press.
Watson-Gegeo, Karen A., and Geoffrey White, eds.
   1990   Disentangling: Conflict Discourse in Pacific Societies. Stanford, CA:
      Stanford University Press.

■ *Christine Jourdan*

Contact

The phenomena that are described by the term *contact* in linguistic anthropology are found in association with cultural contacts between groups of people sharing, or not sharing, cultural assumptions about social life and understandings about language. Far from being anomalous, contact, both linguistic and cultural, is a normal state of affairs, given that cultural groups and languages do not live in isolation. Cultural formations are not static either, but contact with other groups brings about changes at a pace faster than those produced by inner cultural dynamics. As one of the most salient effects of contact, change is the essence of languages and cultures and testifies to the vitality of linguistic communities. It also reveals the adaptive nature of culture. Therefore, by definition, a theory of contact should include a theory of change, social and linguistic, or, rather, a theory of changes.

The challenge for anthropologists and for linguists studying contact-induced change has been to understand the mechanisms of change and the processes that govern it. Linguists and sociolinguists studying language change in contact situations have focused on language interference (i.e., on the study of the structural and non-structural factors that impede or promote interference), interlanguage, bilingualism, multilingualism, language shift, obsolescence, and on the genesis of pidgin and creole languages. Anthropologists working on cultural contacts have focused on cultural borrowing, diffusion, reinterpretation, syncretism and acculturation, but also on biculturalism and multiculturalism, and more recently on cultural creolization and on the effect of globalization on local cultures.

The history of peoples and their languages is best understood through their contact history. In order to understand how linguistic and cultural changes come into play, and more importantly why, one has to know the sociolinguistic history of speakers and actors, if only because linguistic and cultural contacts vary along different axes: duration of contact; intensity; respective status and political might of the cultural groups in a contact situation; ideologies and space. These axes allow social groups and individuals voluntary or imposed access to other cultural or linguistic groups, and will affect

41

cultural and linguistic changes differently. Permanent exposure to otherness through contact with neighboring groups may lead to an exacerbated sense of group identity that is often symbolized through added linguistic differences (as in the Amazon basin or in Melanesia). On the other hand, and for pragmatic reasons, it is often associated with multilingualism, which, in some cases, may lead to some dialect leveling. Some forms of contact, such as colonization and forced displacements of population, are extreme types that, through imposition of new ideologies and modes of life, have severely altered, and often destroyed, the pre-existing linguistic and cultural balance of power between neighboring groups. They have often brought about the birth of new languages (such as pidgins and creoles), but also the death or attrition of others. Under colonization, or any other forms of hegemonic conditions, the cultural anchoring of languages is challenged and often shattered, leading individuals and groups to adopt the language spoken by the dominant power, or, and it is often the same one, to adopt the language that will allow them to survive socially. All these types of contact lead to some measure of cultural and linguistic interference, borrowing, and change that are often analyzed in terms of loss, or in terms of spuriousness.

Students of contact-induced linguistic changes have searched for the typological constraints that allow for interference and borrowing across languages, and have sought to explain the nature of the changes in relation to the social conditions of enaction, particularly those surrounding the transmission of language between generations, or to other groups. Normal transmission, i.e., without cultural breaks, seems to lead to language maintenance with light or heavy restructuring depending on the nature of contact, and may lead to bilingualism and to shift. Linguistic and cultural breaks (such as the ones found on plantation settings in the colonial Caribbean) are likely to foster the loss of the vernaculars and the genesis of pidgin and creole languages. By their very nature these conditions lead to shift. Students of contact-induced cultural changes do not agree on the characteristics of these changes, on whether they are qualitatively different from the ones taking place outside of contact, on whether they affect cultures differently, or, again, on whether they affect some aspects of cultures and not others. Of course, such analyses are predicated on the reification of culture by anthropologists, allowing them to privilege culture traits over processes or representations. This privileging of culture traits stresses the malleability of cultures in terms of recombinable elements, in a way that is quite akin to the search for structural changes that is associated with the study of linguistic interference. The efflorescence of cultural contact studies that took place in the 1940s and 1950s in the United States found some resonance in the studies of linguistic acculturation, and assimilation (of immigrants, particularly) that followed. Fishman's linguistic assimilation model is a case in point. All proved to be tautological because of their totalizing view of culture that made acculturation almost inevitable, and almost always unidirectional, with diffusion (the corollary of acculturation) taking place from the dominant group to the dominated one.

Globalization is the new form of contact that social scientists are grappling with, and it is fast becoming a synonym, albeit very imprecise, for rapid social change. Its epistemological premise stems from that of World System Theory and it has all the flavor of old acculturation models. Globalization is a form of social change that is often presented as homogenizing. Yet this is not the case. The anthropological linguist recognizes in globalization the kinds of contact-induced ideological and experiential pressures that are likely to lead to rapid sociocultural formations, and particularly to the genesis of creole languages. That is, to the formation of new cultural forms. Playing with disciplinary boundaries, and with the epistemological hurdle represented by the borrowing of models across disciplines, one may propose that the model of linguistic creolization can be enlarged and applied to the social sphere, where it can help us understand the type of contact-induced changes brought about by globalization. Remembering the superstrate and substrate influences at work in the creation of pidgins and creoles, some similar parallels can be drawn with the processes at work during globalization. For instance, the complementarity of the substrate and the superstrate could reveal how and why, despite the onslaught of a generic world system of culture (the superstrate) onto local traditions (the substrate), the new cultural formations of Ibadan (Nigeria), Honiara (Solomon Islands), or Labastide-Murat (France) can be different from one another. Culturally, the new forms may appear very different from the substrate supplied by vernacular cultures, but in fact, very often, as I have shown for the Solomon Islands, cultural creolization allows for new shells to be filled with old meanings. The difficulty here will be to define the substrate. In fact, if we decide that these new cultural worlds are different from one another because the substrate influences are different, are we not saying that it is possible to define the substrate? This, of course, raises the question of the importance of the substrate in cultural and linguistic contacts, points to processes of identity maintenance and creation in contact situations leading to fast and rampant change, and defines the terrain of culture as a contested ground.

(See also *codes, crossing, endangered, grammar, identity, ideology, reconstruction, switching, syncretism, variation*)

Bibliography

Calvet, Louis-Jean
   1979   Linguistique et colonialisme: petit traité de glottophagie. Paris: Payot.
Fishman, Joshua
   1965   Language Maintenance and Language Shift: The American Immigrant Case within a General Theoretical Perspective. Sociologus 16:19–38.
Hannerz, Ulf
   1996   Transnational Connections: Culture, People, Places. New York: Routledge.
Jourdan, Christine
   1994   Urbanisation et créolisation aux Iles Salomon. Journal de la Société des Océanistes 99(2):177–186.

Kulick, Don
  1992 Language Shift and Cultural Reproduction: Socialization, Self and Syncretism in a Papua New Guinean Village. Cambridge: Cambridge University Press.
Linton, Ralph, ed.
  1940 Acculturation in Seven American Indian Tribes. New York: Appleton-Century-Crofts.
Silverstein, Michael
  1998 Contemporary Transformations of Local Linguistic Communities. Annual Review of Anthropology 27:401–426.
Thomason, Sarah G., and Terence Kaufman
  1988 Language Contact, Creolization, and Genetic Linguistics. Berkeley: University of California Press.
Tsitsipis, Lukas
  1998 A Linguistic Anthropology of Praxis and Language Shift: Arvanitika (Albanian) and Greek in Contact. Oxford: Clarendon Press.
Weinreich, Ulrich
  1979[1953] Languages in Contact. The Hague: Mouton Publishers.

■ *Allen D. Grimshaw*

Control

Social control is getting people to do things they would not choose to do were they completely free to decide, or not to do things they probably would do were they free to choose. While it is possible, of course, to control behavior physically or through denial of financial wherewithal or through non-verbal signals, such control for competent users of language is primarily accomplished through discourse, spoken or written. What resources are available for control (and resistance thereto) are determined by the sociological variables of relations of power and of affect between/among interactants, and the valence to interactants of outcomes sought.

A sampling of the many dimensions upon which language-based control moves may vary follows.

(1) *Intentionality and ends:* When a child asks a grown-up to cut up her meat, she probably wants to be able to eat. When an older sibling warns a younger one to eat more slowly, she may want to keep her brother from choking – but she may also want to demonstrate her authority. She may unintentionally cause an audience to see her as bossy. Control moves through talk can have multiple goals, both conscious and unconscious; the talk may produce a variety of outcomes – not all of which will be accessible to all interactants. The great variety of possible goals of talk contributes to deniability of socially disapproved motives for control – or to possibilities for unwarrantedly claiming societally endorsed motives for what are actually raw displays of power.

(2) *Directness–indirectness:* Indirect speech acts such as "Isn't it cold in here?" when one wants a window closed, or a thermostat turned up, or an offer to bring a sweater.

(3) *Instrumentality selection:* English has a large number of labels for verbs that name ways of talking intended to control others' behavior (e.g., *cajole, entreat, hint, nag, persuade*). Actors of lower power don't ordinarily *order* those of higher power, nor do those of higher power *beg* those with less. But considerations of affect or of the perceived importance of an end sought by someone of lower power may generate unexpected behaviors. What we do to make sensible strangenesses we hear reveals our knowledge of rules for

competence in social control accomplishment. This sense-making is greatly facilitated by our sometimes conscious, sometimes not so conscious, attunement to shifting characteristics of contexts identified by Erving Goffman as "keys" and "keying."

(4) *Intensity/degree:* How likely are signs such as "Private," "No Trespassing," "Restricted Area – Intruders May Be Shot" (or their spoken equivalents) to deter potential trespassers – independently of the presence of higher and more formidable fences? If a social actor has committed an offense, would they rather be *admonished, berated, chastised, chewed out, chided, harangued, rebuked, reprimanded, reproached, scolded,* or *tongue-lashed*?

(5) *Paralinguistic cues and related dimensions:* There are both individual and cultural differences in the meanings attributed to production of speech varying in such features as (a) paralinguistic/prosodic aspects such as amplitude, hesitation, intonation, rhythm, stretching, stress, tempo, voice quality and so on, (b) register, (c) sequencing, (d) phonology, (e) lexical selection, and a variety of kinesic/proxemic behaviors including (f) gestures, (g) gross bodily movements, (h) gaze management, and (i) proxemic orientation. These and other features collectively define/identify what Dell Hymes has called "key," viz., "the tone, manner, or spirit in which an act is done." Utterances thus varying may be seen to differ in key as between *mock* and *serious* or *perfunctory* and *painstaking*. Within speech communities such variation signals how seriously an "order" or "entreaty" is to be taken. Across speech communities, unfamiliarity with subtleties of key can generate communicative non-success and tension.

(6) *Powerfulness–powerlessness:* Studies of language in the courtroom show that witnesses who produce powerful speech, epitomized by assured affirmative or negative responses to questions ("yes" or "no") are seen as more credible than those who employ hedges, hesitation forms, polite forms, question intonation, tag questions ("You know about tag questions, don't you?"), and intensifiers. Not surprisingly, control attempts by actors who speak with assertive assurance are most likely to be successful.

(7) *Positive–negative/reward–punishment:* "Grandpa will take you two for ice cream if you let him finish this piece on control" as opposed to "Stop fighting or you'll both be grounded" is one obvious example.

(8) *Modes of control:* Basil Bernstein has labeled "positional" ("Because [I/your mother] said so") as opposed to "personal" ("Because it's too close to dinner time and you won't eat your supper" or "Because tomorrow is a school day") parental responses to children's queries about why they can't have something to eat or watch the rest of a television show.

(9) *Words of autonomous power/words as arbitrary symbols:* Medieval Europeans believed in the efficacy of a curse of damnation – particularly if it came from a senior cleric. Modern Americans don't believe in magical words, incantations, charms, spells ("Abracadabra," "Open Sesame," "Shazam"[?]). Why then do we "knock on wood" and tell interlocutors, "Don't even think of it" or "I don't want to hear it"? The ability to produce the right words for ritual is, in some religions, more important than the state of the producer's

soul. Word taboos are a very nearly universal feature of even the most modern societies – just as rules about the employment of sacral languages and not vernaculars in religious contexts have been for millennia. Words *can* hurt, and some individuals have onomatomania (irrational fear of a particular word). The notion that words have autonomous power has often been made more complicated by beliefs about the special qualities of written text as opposed to spoken.

(10) *Relevant social differentiation:* Compare "Get th' fuck outta my face!" and "Please leave me alone" or "No!", "Don't do that!", "I'd think twice before doing that," and "That's probably not a good idea," and consider differences in "languages of control" available to different social strata, genders, age groups, and so on, interacting with similarly differentiated interlocutors.

(11) *Spoken–written discourse:* Schieffelin has shown how the invention and introduction of an evidential construction to refer to printed religious material among the Kaluli (Papua New Guinea), translatable as "known from this source/not known before," has not only granted authority to this written text and to the literate themselves but has also been associated with the introduction of higher status for the new role of interpreter of Christianity where prior stratification rested on quite different bases. Written text gains part of its authority because of its accessibility only to some and its close association with modernity, Christianity, and truthfulness. It may also be seen as more powerful than speech because of its relative permanence and availability for documentation, whether of contractual obligations or of commitment to love (comparisons of the weight of written text and of oaths before audiences need to be made). In modern, "secular" America, "swearing on the Bible" is seen as somehow more binding than simply giving one's word. The greater efficacy and lesser fallibility accorded written text with emergent literacy is inextricably inter-implicated with just noted beliefs about intrinsic power of words.

Contemporaries from "critical linguists" of various stripes to practitioners of various sorts of structuralism or deconstruction have looked for ways in which to uncover the manipulation which goes on in (primarily) written text. These researchers conclude that language is used to control behavior; most conclude that "emancipation" from that control is possible, but not to be taken for granted. Kress and Hodge see control processes as axiomatic and treat them as linear (i.e., social structure > ideology > language in use > social control). Their model treats social structure and ideology as givens and control-outcomes as dependent on the manipulation of choices among linguistic options such as active or passive voice and the presence or absence of agents (on which two matters see Trew's examination of ideological slanting of newspaper coverage). Control efforts can be so subtle that they can be revealed only by practices of "interpretation-interruption." Most of us have experienced the control which can be accomplished by written text.

(See also *gesture, inference, literacy, orality, plagiarism, power, register, turn*)

Bibliography

Bailey, F. G.
  1983 The Tactical Uses of Passion: An Essay on Power, Reason, and Reality. Ithaca, NY: Cornell University Press.
Bernstein, Basil
  1971 Class, Codes, and Control, Vol. 1. Theoretical Studies Towards a Sociology of Language. London: Routledge & Kegan Paul.
Fowler, Roger, Bob Hodge, Gunther Kress, and Tony Trew
  1979 Language and Control. London: Routledge & Kegan Paul.
Goffman, Erving
  1974 Frame Analysis: An Essay on the Organization of Experience. New York: Harper and Row Colophon.
Grimshaw, Allen D.
  1981 Talk and Social Control. In Social Psychology: Sociological Perspectives. M. Rosenberg et al., eds. Pp. 200–232. New York: Basic Books.
  1989 Collegial Discourse: Professional Conversation among Peers. Vol. 32 in the series Advances in Discourse Processes. Norwood, NJ: Ablex Publishing Corporation.
Hymes, Dell
  1974 Foundations in Sociolinguistics: An Ethnographic Approach. Philadelphia: University of Pennsylvania Press.
Labov, William, and David Fanshel
  1977 Therapeutic Discourse: Psychotherapy as Conversation. New York: Academic Press.
Lerer, Seth
  1991 Literacy and Power in Anglo-Saxon Literature. Lincoln: University of Nebraska Press.
Schieffelin, Bambi B.
  1996 Creating Evidence: Making Sense of Written Words in Bosavi. *In* Interaction and Grammar. Elinor Ochs, Emanuel A. Schegloff, and Sandra A. Thompson, eds. Pp. 435–460. Cambridge: Cambridge University Press.

■ *Ben Rampton*

Crossing

L *anguage crossing*, or just *crossing*, refers to the use of a language or variety that, in one way or another, feels anomalously "other." Precisely who it is that experiences this feeling – whether it's the speaker, the interlocutor(s), or both – will vary, and sometimes you can "pass," using language selection to project an identity that nobody suspects or challenges. But because at some level or other it involves a sense of movement across quite sharply felt social or ethnic boundaries, crossing generally runs into questions about its legitimacy, and when speakers code-cross, you either have to deal with this – when, for example, someone laughs in your face – or, alternatively, you can confine your crossing to moments and events where the routine flow of everyday social order is uncertain or relaxed. Moments and events where normal social relations are suspended can vary a great deal in their scale and duration, and you can often get away with switching into a conspicuously out-group language both in micro-activities like greetings and self-talk, and in larger activities and genres like games, jocular abuse, and musical performance. The key point is, though, that others don't think that you truly, seriously, mean or believe in the identity you're projecting.

In interaction, the fact that the language being spoken isn't easily acknowledged as an uncontroversial part of the speaker's habitual repertoire usually generates extra inferential work for interlocutors trying to cope with insistent interactional questions like "Why that now?" and "What next?" Crossing sets up a dense symbolic dialogue between the speaker's Self and the images of the Other evoked through the special code selection, and the relationships between them range from contempt or fear to amusement and desire – the voice or language one is putting on might, for example, be some relic from an inheritance that's attributed to one but that one is keen to leave behind, or, alternatively, it might be part of someone else's that one dearly wants for oneself.

Crossing is often surrounded by a great deal of explicit local commentary and evaluation, but it is its recurrence as a spontaneous practice within daily life that makes it especially rich as a site for relatively tacit processes of ideological formation and dispute. When a relatively unexpected language code gets used, it usually inserts images of a particular social type into the flow of interaction, and it both instantiates and sparks off heightened displays of the participants' orientations to one another, to the representations, and to the relationship between them. This in turn reveals a great deal to the analyst about (1) how individuals negotiate their group alignments and (2) how the meanings of group identity are themselves ratified or redefined. In some empirical accounts we can see insidious affirmations of stratification by race, ethnicity, class, gender, sexuality, etc., whereas in others we can glimpse unconventional language choices that destabilize hegemonic biological and cultural essentialisms and look for new solidarities to replace them.

In terms of established sociolinguistic concepts, language crossing can first be seen as a form of code-switching, though there are several ways in which the study of crossing usually differs from traditional treatments. Code-switching research has tended to look for conventional syntactic patterns in the mixed speech of relatively well-established in-groups, which itself reflects the wider view that (1) language study is centrally concerned with systematicity in grammar and coherence in discourse and (2) these properties come from community membership, that is, people learn to talk grammatically and coherently from extensive early experience of living in fairly stable local social networks. Admittedly, the conventionalization of crossing practices is itself an important issue for future research, quite likely, for example, to throw light on language change; for the time being, however, there is as much emphasis in crossing on emergence, improvisation, and the (partial) denaturalization of convention. In addition, in an age where ethnicities are turned into commodified lifestyle options and aerials can count as much as roots, the crossing concept is capable of addressing language practices where, ostensibly, the consumer's personal taste and purchasing power matter as much as or more than their early socialization.

Seen from a second angle, crossing has a lot in common with Richard Bauman's (much wider) notion of artful "performance." Neither are rigidly set apart from ordinary speech, but with varying degrees of intensity both invite a break with routine habits of interpretation. Both objectify ways of speaking, bringing stylistic resources into the spotlight for reflexive evaluation and critique, and Mikhail Bakhtin's "double-voicing" is intensely relevant to both.

Looked at from a third angle, crossing's defining interest in the use of a language that doesn't obviously belong to the speaker means that the study of it addresses some of the same empirical concerns as research on second and foreign language learning and teaching. Here, though, there are sharp methodological differences, and one of crossing's most important contributions may be to help interrogate second language research in its role as an ideological apparatus nourishing massive commercial, state, and imperial enterprises in foreign language teaching.

Descriptively, the analysis of language crossing initially requires close attention to (1) the semiotic texture of the linguistic product itself, (2) the details of its local treatment and occasioning, (3) the interaction of these situated details with the images of the social world that the product symbolically calls into play, and (4) the established and emergent ideologies of language and social life that crossing contests, contributes to, and/or is assessed against. At the same time, (5) it is essential not to lose sight of the extra indeterminacy of meaning that is often crossing's hallmark. Once descriptive exigencies like these are addressed, analysis can turn to questions about the social and historical distribution of particular kinds of crossing practice, questions that are vital if we are to clarify crossing's value as a window on social contestation and change, and to develop our understanding of its political, social, and linguistic significance.

(See also *codes, community, identity, improvisation, individual, register, style, switching, syncretism, variation, voice*)

Bibliography

Bakhtin, Mikhail
  1984 Discourse in Dostoevsky. *In* Problems of Dostoevsky's Poetics. Mikhail Bakhtin, ed. Pp. 181–269. Minneapolis: University of Minnesota Press.
Basso, Keith
  1979 Portraits of "the Whiteman": Linguistic Play and Cultural Symbols among the Western Apache. Cambridge: Cambridge University Press.
Bauman, Richard, and Charles Briggs
  1990 Poetics and Performance as Critical Perspectives on Language and Social Life. Annual Review of Anthropology 19:59–88.
Hewitt, Roger
  1986 White Talk Black Talk. Cambridge: Cambridge University Press.
Hill, Jane
  1998 Language, Race, and White Public Space. American Anthropologist 100(3):680–689.
Pratt, Mary Louise
  1991 The Arts of the Contact Zone. Profession 91:33–40.
Rampton, Ben
  1995 Crossing: Language and Ethnicity among Adolescents. London: Longman.
  1998 Language Crossing and the Redefinition of Reality. *In* Codeswitching in Conversation: Language, Interaction and Identity. Peter Auer, ed. Pp. 290–320. London: Routledge.
  1999 Sociolinguistics and Cultural Studies: New Ethnicities, Liminality and Interaction. Social Semiotics 9(3):355–374.
Rampton, Ben, ed.
  1999 Styling the Other: The Performance and Representation of Outgroup Identities. Journal of Sociolinguistics 3/4 (special issue).

■ *Carol Padden*

Deaf

Deaf or deafness is conventionally a term referring to the absence of the ability to hear and is also used as a noun to refer to individuals who do not hear. The term has filtered into popular language as a term for inattention or neglect ("to turn a deaf ear to the pleas of the needy"), reflecting a long history of pathological connotations for this term. In this way, *deaf* is used along with words like *blind* and *blindness* to refer to individuals who cannot access the world directly and instead require adaptive means. The last thirty or forty years, however, have seen use of the term to refer to a cultural community of individuals who do not hear. Deafness, as well as its lesser impairments of moderate to mild hearing loss, is a condition that in varying degrees is said to be shared by approximately 8.6% of the population, or approximately 20 million individuals in the United States. Of this large category, which includes individuals with noise-induced deafness or decline in hearing due to age, there is a durable subset estimated at somewhere between 200,000 to 300,000 deaf individuals who use the term *deaf* to mark an identification with a cultural group that shares a common sign language. The broader population of individuals with hearing loss view deafness as a chronic condition with few surgical options, requiring prostheses such as hearing aids or sound-enhancing technology. The deaf community, on the other hand, is made up of individuals who have usually acquired deafness at birth or shortly after, and have for the most part spent most of their lives with the condition. For this group, deafness is not only a sensory condition, but also a way of life characterized by membership in a signing community, participation in educational programs for the deaf (such as one of many residential boarding schools that educated many deaf adults), and a network of social organizations, clubs, and affiliations where sign language is used.

The signing deaf community in the United States is linked with other signing deaf communities throughout the world, not by use of a common language, but through participation in common kinds of educational and social associations. American Sign Language is used in the United States and English-speaking parts of Canada, and is increasingly used as the international language at deaf professional conferences. There are numerous other national sign languages as well, possibly as many as there are spoken languages, though their geographies are not identical. The geography of sign languages largely follows the distribution of deaf education throughout the world in large part because deaf graduates of schools often settle nearby in order to form a community with each other, and sometimes to take employment at the schools. Because England and the United States have not shared deaf education systems, the two nations have very different sign languages. France, on the other hand, exported a member from one of its school for deaf children to help found the first deaf school in the United States in 1814. As a result, French Sign Language became a language of instruction at the American school. The blending of French Sign Language with the several local sign languages in existence in colonial America yielded a modern American Sign Language that shares some common vocabulary with French Sign Language, but the two languages have become separate and not mutually intelligible. As deaf education spread throughout the world between 1750 and 1850, new schools were founded in colonial countries: Episcopalian ministers from England founded schools in Ireland, Australia, and New Zealand. Nuns, on the other hand, founded deaf girls' schools in Ireland, resulting in a parallel existence of two different sign languages: the boys used signs from English Sign Language and the girls used French Sign Language. Marriages of deaf Irish men and women after leaving schools often resulted in partners with different sign vocabularies. With the relaxing of gender segregation in Ireland there came a unification project blending the vocabulary of the two sign languages to become the new sign language of Ireland. The pattern of spreading of deaf education across the globe, following philanthropic and missionary efforts, has resulted in a geography of sign languages sometimes matching national boundaries, though not always, as in the case of Ireland and in Switzerland, where there is a co-existence of two sign languages: French Swiss Sign Language and German Swiss Sign Language.

This global geography of sign languages is linked by national and international associations of deaf people who share ways of talking about themselves, their languages, and their condition. Deafness is seen less as a debilitating condition and more as an expression of community with other deaf people. Because the condition of deafness is relatively rare, deaf people have always co-existed with hearing people, either as parents, as siblings, or as children. There are an estimated 200 different inherited conditions that may result in deafness at birth or a decline in hearing through childhood. The possibility that these conditions may be transmitted is slightly higher between two individuals who are deaf, but the overall incidence of deaf children with deaf parents is very low (slightly under 10%). Most deaf people are born to hearing parents and have hearing siblings and hearing children. The fragility of transmission and the limited likelihood that deafness will be transmitted to future generations is built into the community in a number of ways: the community frequently has newcomers, or individuals who learn a sign language later in life, either because the condition came on later in life or because of a delay in meeting deaf people and sign language due to educational choice. Because of the permeability of the deaf community by hearing individuals who may or may not sign (e.g., hearing parents who communicate orally with deaf children), the community incorporates its dealings with the dominant society as part of its core set of beliefs: ways of talking about self and other, about sign and spoken language, about signing and speaking, about having deaf or hearing children. In its very fabric, deaf communities incorporate the presence of hearing people in their lives as part of its rhetoric and common beliefs.

The incidence of deafness is frequent enough to sustain sign languages and social networks, but not frequent enough to allow institution-building. Few deaf people have built their own schools; most are built for them by philanthropists or missionaries. Nor do they form neighborhoods or towns. Instead, deaf communities exist as durable social connections around the social institutions of the community: the deaf schools, the deaf clubs which are increasingly being replaced by deaf professional associations of varying kinds, reflecting the pattern of labor in the community, and the rising deaf professional middle class resulting from civil rights and disability movements allowing deaf people to hold professional jobs. Because of the dominant presence of hearing people in deaf people's lives, deaf people often talk about themselves in relativist terms. The dominant mode of self-explanation from about the middle of the nineteenth century to the middle of the twentieth is one of lack of hearing and the illnesses that contribute to the condition. It was frequent in short biographies for deaf people to describe themselves to each other and to hearing people in terms of how they acquired the condition. Common causes of deafness through this period were childhood diseases of measles, mumps (which causes high fevers and damage to auditory nerves), and spinal meningitis. An estimated 50% of all unknown causes of deafness are believed to be genetically related, resulting in a smaller presence of individuals who have inherited the condition and are more likely to have deaf parents. The deaf education literature of this time also distinguished between "pre-lingual" and "post-lingual" deafness, or those who acquired deafness before the age of 2, or before spoken language could be acquired, and those who acquired deafness later in life, when spoken language was already a first language. Deaf people were categorized in terms of whether they had acquired a spoken first language. The distinction was mirrored in self-descriptions that deaf people gave of themselves.

More recent self-descriptions have dropped the reference to illnesses or afflictions that gave rise to deafness and have focused more on familial connections to deafness, including whether or not the individual has deaf parents. The focus shifted away from when spoken language was acquired to when sign language was, either at birth or shortly after, marking the individual as a native signer, or later in life, as a newcomer to the culture and community. New definitions of deafness focus more on knowledge of cultural norms, cultural behaviors, and cultural practices. As a result, *deaf* has come to take on a distinctly cultural tone that seeks to make less privileged the pathological definition of the condition.

(See also *acquisition, identity, ideology, individual, orality, signing*)

Bibliography

Baynton, Douglas
    1996 Forbidden Signs: American Culture and the Campaign against Sign Language. Chicago: University of Chicago Press.

Davis, Lennard
    1995 Enforcing Normalcy: Disability, Deafness, and the Body. London: Verso.

Holt, Judith, Sue Hotto, and Kevin Cole
    1994 Demographic Aspects of Hearing Impairment: Questions and Answers. 3rd ed. Washington, DC: Center for Assessment and Demographic Studies, Gallaudet University.

Lane, Harlan
    1984 When the Mind Hears: A History of the Deaf. New York: Random House.

Padden, Carol
    1990 Folk Explanation in Language Survival. *In* Collective Remembering. David Middleton and Derek Edwards, eds. Pp. 190–202. London: Sage.

Padden, Carol, and Tom Humphries
    1988 Deaf in America: Voices from a Culture. Cambridge, MA: Harvard University Press.

Plann, Susan
    1997 A Silent Minority: Deaf Education in Spain, 1550–1835. Berkeley: University of California Press.

■ *Laura R. Graham*

Dreams

Although Westerners tend to think of dreams as reflecting uniquely personal experiences, dreams are also shared within communities. This sharing moves individual experience outward and entails converting "inner" experience into culturally conventional forms that can be publicly accessed and interpreted. Translating dream experiences into publicly circulating forms may be, as Ludwig Wittgenstein argued for inner processes generally, requisite for the establishment of their ontological reality. Narratives, and other expressive practices through which dream experiences are shared, select and shape dream images. At the same time, publicly circulating expressions may even influence the individual's dream experience itself.

In the relatively recent anthropological consideration of the public nature of dreams, language and performance are emerging as central themes. Concern with the social uses of dreams, processes of dream-sharing, and attention to the communicative contexts in which dreams are expressed, shifts what had been a prevailing focus on content and content analysis. Moving from beneath the shadow of dominant Freudian perspectives, current dream research attends to questions of *how* dreams are expressed or publicly represented, and ways in which dream expressions circulate within communities. Research is also concerned with *what* circulates in various cultural forms as dream and with dream metadiscourse.

This shift in focus entails a methodological reorientation. Researchers pay close attention to how dreams are expressed and used in and across social situations, attending particularly to dream expression as "naturally occurring discourse" – that is to reports that occur in the context of social interaction – rather than to specifically elicited texts. Language and performance-centered research does not eschew elicitation, however. It differs from earlier approaches by taking contextually situated discourse as the starting point for analysis. Elicitation and text-centered analysis are often incorporated at later stages, to illuminate specific issues.

Language and performance are central in recent anthropological considerations of dreaming because narratives and other discursive forms, such as song, are primary means of dream-sharing. Language and performance-centered studies move beyond referential discourse to consider formal properties of the language of dream narratives, the creative interplay between dream narratives and other forms of publicly circulating discourse and performance, and potential relations between the public circulation of dream expressions, individual subjectivity, and actual dream experience.

Among the formal linguistic devices scholars have noted in dream narratives are extensive use of evidentials, quotative particles, unique tense and aspect marking, and special verb forms. These linguistic devices suggest cultural perceptions of dreams. They are also constitutive of these perceptions. For example, Barbara Tedlock argues that the use of quotative particles in Quiché Maya dream accounts is evidence of a "free soul" that detaches itself from the dreamer in sleep and experiences a reality that is not associated with the individual's personal experience. Dream reports may be sprinkled with the quotative "he/she/it says," which is used in relating anecdotes and mythic narratives that do not deal with personal experience. For Quiché, the "I" of the dream is often not the "I" of narrator. However, when a dream is unambiguously positive, it is always shared without the quotative. In Cuzco, Quechua, dream (and myth) narratives employ the tense suffix -*sqa*, which marks narrated events not directly experienced by the narrator in a normal state of mind. Similarly, Kagwahiv Indians of Brazil employ a distinctive evidential past-tense marker that indexes unwitnessed past events. Among the Zuni and Quiché, dream narrators use verb forms that evidence distinct ontological and psychological orientations toward dreams. Whereas Zuni use intransitive verbs to indicate the experience as a state of being, Quiché use transitive verbs to denote that the dreamer acts upon something while dreaming.

Context may also influence discourse form. Among the Sambia of Melanesia, for example, dreams may be reported in three distinct types of social situation. Each situation has its own mode of discourse that permits pragmatic choices for disclosure.

Many language and performance-centered analyses emphasize relations and interactions between dream representations and other discursive practices within communities. These studies stress that dream expressions and other narratives are part of a community's discursive field whose constituents interact and are mutually influential. Dream and myth, in particular, appear to co-mingle in many cultures. The relationship may even be formally marked, as noted above. Among the Xavante of central Brazil, where forms of dream representation vary according to gender and life-cycle phase, elder men may infuse dream narratives with myth and other expressive forms. The dream performance I analyzed is highly intertextual, consisting of myth narrative, song, and dance. Intertextuality in dream-sharing serves multiple pragmatic ends, such as the invocation of interpretive frames and display of cultural knowledge.

A language-centered explanation for the affinity between myth and dream may be that in some cultures the realities of myth and dream can only be publicly accessed through referential discourse. Dream and myth narratives referentially portray fantastic images and events that capture intense public interest and stimulate further circulation. Greg Urban, who suggests this hypothesis, observes that ceremonies contrast with myth and dreams for the southern Brazilian Xokleng. The difference between dreams and myth, on the one hand, and ceremony, on the other, lies in public accessibility. Unlike myth and dream, ceremonies are publicly experienced and sensorily accessible. Ceremonies do not form the topic of discursive representation or metacommentary, as do dreams. Individual dream experiences can only be made accessible to others through semantico-referential discourse.

Bruce Mannheim reports a different relationship between myth, ritual, and dreams for Cuzqueño Quechua. Their dream lexicon and interpretive codes have experienced a near total replacement since colonial times. In contrast, mythic and ritual systems have remained relatively stable over time. The difference, according to Mannheim, lies in the fact that dream interpretations encode only the semantic dimension of language whereas myths and rituals draw meaning from broader and more persistent interpretive systems, including grammar.

Although spoken narrative is a primary means of dream-sharing, dream experiences may be expressed in various forms. Singing, or singing and dancing, is a significant form of dream expression and dreams are frequently cited as the source of creative inspiration in song composition. Song and dance, among other actions, are ways of "performing" dreams. In contrast to the Xokleng, where dreams are only accessible to others through narrative, the Xavante and Temiar enact movements and sounds that are said to be experienced in dreams. For the Xavante, sharing individual dreamed songs is a powerful means of promoting sociability among young men. In giving a dreamed song to the members of his group, a young man gives an intimate subjective experience to others who, later in collective performance, transform the individual's dream into collective experience.

Dreams are a source of creativity and innovation for a culture's expressive repertoire. At the same time, those dream experiences that are culturally selected for public circulation become stylized into recognizable expressive forms. Repeated sharing of these cultural types influences the public shape of future dream expressions. Publicly circulating forms may even influence how dreams are experienced by individuals and how dream experiences are presented to consciousness. Ultimately, it is impossible to know the dream experiences of others, and possibly even one's own, without filtering them through language-centered thought processes and translating them into culturally appropriate forms for sharing.

(See also *genre, improvisation, individual, interview, music, narrative, particle, performativity, reflexivity*)

Bibliography

Graham, Laura
  1994 Dialogic Dreams: Creative Selves Coming into Life in the Flow of Time. American Ethnologist 21(4):719–741.
  1995 Performing Dreams: Discourses of Immortality among the Xavante of Central Brazil. Austin: University of Texas Press.
Herdt, Gilbert
  1987 Selfhood and Discourse in Samida Dream Sharing. *In* Dreaming: Anthropological and Psychological Interpretations. Barbara Tedlock, ed. Pp. 55–85. Cambridge: Cambridge University Press.
Krake, Waud
  1990 The Dream as Deceit, the Dream as Truth: Dream-narrative Markers and the Telling of Dreams in Parintintin Kagwahiv. Paper presented at the annual meeting of the American Anthropological Association, Chicago, November 20–24.
Mannheim, Bruce
  1987 A Semiotic of Andean Dreams. *In* Dreaming: Anthropological and Psychological Interpretations. Barbara Tedlock, ed. Pp. 1132–1153. Cambridge: Cambridge University Press.
Price-Williams, Douglass, and Lydia N. Degarrod
  1989 Communication, Context, and Use of Dreams in Amerindian Societies. Journal of Latin American Lore 15(2):195–209.
Roseman, Marina
  1991 Healing Sounds from the Malaysian Rainforest: Temiar Music and Medicine. Berkeley: University of California Press.
Tedlock, Barbara
  1987 Zuni and Quiché Dream Sharing and Interpreting. *In* Dreaming: Anthropological and Psychological Interpretations. Barbara Tedlock, ed. Pp. 105–131. Cambridge: Cambridge University Press.
Tedlock, Barbara, ed.
  1987 Dreaming: Anthropological and Psychological Interpretations. Cambridge: Cambridge University Press.
Urban, Greg
  1996 Metaphysical Community: The Interplay of the Senses and the Intellect. Austin: University of Texas Press.

■ *Robert E. Moore*

Endangered

E ndangered languages are linguistic varieties spoken by relatively few people (perhaps most of them elderly), and/or in relatively few communities (perhaps even in a single, relatively small one), and/or on relatively infrequent occasions. They are languages whose future as anyone's primary (or even secondary) medium of day-to-day communication seems seriously in doubt – languages that in former times would have been identified as "moribund" or "dying."

Though the term "endangered languages" is of recent (post-1980) origin, research on languages like these has been carried on for a considerable period of time. Indeed, the whole tradition of "Americanist" anthropology has unfolded at least since the time of Franz Boas under the assumption that the linguistic varieties and cultural practices of central interest and concern (usually, those of Native American peoples) are in the process of disappearing once and for all, and need urgently to be documented for posterity (a familiar notion of "salvage" ethnography or linguistics).

Leonard Bloomfield commented in 1927 on the special problems of doing fieldwork in rapidly contracting language communities; but it was Morris Swadesh who, in 1948, applied the term "obsolescent" to these kinds of linguistic varieties, and this designation served the purposes of most researchers until the late 1980s.

By the mid-1970s a number of studies had begun to appear in the scholarly literature under a variety of rubrics, including "language obsolescence," language "replacement" and "shift," "de-acquisition," and sometimes, simply, "language death." These are not all synonyms, of course: "de-acquisition" suggests a focus on native-speaker competence (and the wide range of fluencies that can be observed), while "language shift" can occur whenever the members of a local speech community begin pervasively to abandon the use of one linguistic variety in favor of another, regardless of whether or not the language being abandoned continues to be spoken elsewhere.

Indeed, "language death" might be best understood as referring to the special case of "language shift" that obtains when a given local speech community abandons (whether under obvious duress or not) the use of a form of speech that for whatever reason is not being spoken anywhere else (what difference a "dialect" makes – as opposed, say, to a "language," or a variety that is perhaps the last actively spoken representative of a language family or phylum – has never been made clear, but is obviously an important issue).

A central concern in the linguistic literature on language obsolescence and death has been to establish what, if any, the structural or grammatical consequences of contraction and obsolescence are. Do languages that are in the process of "dying" or falling out of use display in their linguistic structure any characteristic, telltale signs of their imperiled status (simplification of inflectional paradigms, perhaps, and/or loss of vocabulary, and/or loss of productive processes of lexical and syntactic derivation)? Efforts at comparison across cases of language shift and death have yielded relatively few clear answers to such questions. Some languages seem to survive intact for a time, only to "die with their [grammatical] boots on," simply disappearing upon the death of a last fully fluent, even impeccably competent, speaker (the Yana dialect spoken by the fabled Ishi comes immediately to mind here), while others seem to undergo a kind of progressive (regressive?) simplification – reminiscent in several respects of pidginization – in the speech of two or more generations of partially fluent speakers and "semispeakers."

Exactly when the phrase "endangered languages" first appeared in print is difficult to establish. Since about 1990, concerns about endangered languages have reached a wide public through a number of feature-length stories in newspapers of record. Over the same period, the issue has been the focus of a number of high-profile contributions in academic and scholarly journals. As of mid-1999 there is at least one active listserv on the Internet devoted exclusively to discussions of endangered languages, and there are many more listserves and websites with specific regional, language, and/or cultural foci that deal extensively with endangered languages and with closely related issues (carmen.murdoch.edu.au/lists/endangered-languages-l/; cougar.ucdavis.edu/nas/terralin/home.html; sapir.ling.yale.edu/elf). In June 1999 the MacArthur Foundation awarded two of its Prize Fellowships to linguists working on language renewal projects (in the U.S. Southwest and Brazil, respectively), raising the public "profile" of the issue even higher.

The "endangered languages" discussion has clearly emerged from post-1960s "environmentalist" discourse; in the scholarly literature and mass media alike, analogies are repeatedly drawn, equating the disappearance of "whole languages" with the disappearance of whole "worldviews" (and "whole cultures"), on the one hand, and with the disappearance of plant and animal species, on the other. In this context, then, "a species" – or "a language" – becomes an object of contemplation and begins to partake of some of the qualities of the Kantian Sublime.

Analogies like these, despite the strategic value they may have in attempts to garner public attention and support for cultural and linguistic renewal efforts, may sometimes carry unfortunate ideological entailments. Remorse over the loss of languages *qua* scientific objects, over the "loss to science," in other words, may be keenly felt – "academic linguistics," as Michael Krauss has many times been quoted as saying, "may go down in history as 'the only science that has presided over the disappearance of the very subject to which it is devoted' " – but its relevance to what is happening "on the ground" in communities where ancestral languages are rapidly falling out of use (and even memory) is less clear.

If the study of obsolescent languages as lexicogrammatical systems – from the point of view of (Saussurean) *langue*, in other words – has yielded relatively few generalizations that could not also be made about structural (diachronic) change in language more generally, studies that have focused on the speech community and on speech as a form of practice – Saussurean *parole* – show much greater promise, even if far fewer studies of this latter sort have been carried out in any serious or sustained way to date.

Given this, it is difficult not to greet the contemporary emphasis on languages as "endangered" with some ambivalence, in spite of the obvious urgency of the work – including especially work that helps people in these communities find ways of preserving and maintaining ancestral forms of speech. Indeed, the emphasis to date in the "endangered languages" discussion has been on languages *qua* grammatical systems (and/or systems of nomenclature), as artifacts – valuable as such though they may be – of cognition: something akin to the Elgin Marbles, perhaps, in the realm of conceptualization.

Still missing from much of the contemporary literature on "endangered languages" is an anthropologically sophisticated understanding of language obsolescence and "death" as complicated social, cultural, and historical processes that usually unfold within small speech communities during periods of socioeconomic and political transformation (accompanied, virtually always, by societal bi- or multilingualism of an increasingly unstable sort). Much more ethnography needs to be done before "losses" can be properly counted, or even understood.

(See also *acquisition, community, competence, contact, media, performativity, register, variation, writing*)

Bibliography

Bloomfield, Leonard
    1927 Literate and Illiterate Speech. American Speech 2:432–439.
Dorian, Nancy
    1981 Language Death: The Life Cycle of a Scottish Gaelic Dialect. Philadelphia: University of Pennsylvania Press.
Dorian, Nancy, ed.
    1989 Investigating Obsolescence: Studies in Language Contraction and Shift. Cambridge: Cambridge University Press.
Gal, Susan
    1979 Language Shift: Social Determinants of Linguistic Change in Bilingual Austria. New York: Academic Press.

Hale, Ken, et al.
 1992 Endangered Languages. Language 68(1):1–42.
Hill, Jane H.
 1983 Language Death in Uto-Aztecan. International Journal of American Linguistics 49(3):258–276.
Hinton, Leanne
 1994 Flutes of Fire. Essays on California Indian Languages. Berkeley, CA: Heyday Books.
Kulick, Don
 1992 Language Shift and Cultural Reproduction. Cambridge: Cambridge University Press.
Silverstein, Michael
 1998 Contemporary Transformations of Local Linguistic Communities. Annual Review of Anthropology 27:401–426.
Swadesh, Morris
 1948 Sociologic Notes on Obsolescent Languages. International Journal of American Linguistics 14:226–235.

■ *Kathleen R. Gibson*

Evolution

T
wo great theoretical divides impact debates on the evolution of language. One differentiates those who posit that sharp, relatively unbridgeable, qualitative gaps separate human and animal minds from those who see continuities between animal and human mental faculties. The second differentiates those who consider that human linguistic abilities reflect general cognitive and neurological capacities from those who consider linguistic abilities to be qualitatively different from other mental capacities.

The human qualitative uniqueness position is epitomized by Descartes' postulates that animal behavior is instinctive but human behavior is rational, and by Morgan's Canon that one should always assume that animal behaviors are controlled by the simplest possible mental faculties. In recent decades, scholars of this persuasion have proposed that only humans possess consciousness and varied mental capacities, including symbolic and syntactic capacities. The contrasting continuity position was first fully elaborated in modern scientific terms by Charles Darwin, who proposed that mental differences between animals and humans are matters of degree, not of kind. It persists today among many primatologists and evolutionary biologists.

These dichotomous views have distinctly different implications for the evolution of language. Human uniqueness theories readily lend themselves to concepts that humans possess qualitatively unique, genetically determined, language-specific, neural structures. Continuity theories lend themselves to interpretations that language emerged from quantitative increases in neural tissues and that the same neural structures may contribute to different human behaviors.

Comparative neuroanatomical and behavioral evidence lend support to continuity positions. No unique anatomical structures are known to exist in the human brain. In contrast, evidence for quantitative differences between animal and human brains is solid and indisputable. The human brain is approximately three times as large as the average great ape brain. Several major neural structures including the neocortex, cerebellum, and some portions of the limbic system are also about three times as large in humans as in apes, and the basal ganglia, hippocampus, and diencephalon are about twice as large. Behavioral studies indicate that great apes possess rudiments of nearly all behaviors once thought to be uniquely human, including symbolism and syntax, but that many human behaviors have expanded in response to neural enlargement. Specifically, humans possess greater mental constructional skills (mediated by the neocortex) and greater procedural learning skills (mediated by the basal ganglia, the cerebellum, and the pre-motor cortex).

Mental construction is ability to join two or more perceptions, objects, actions, or concepts in order to create new, more information-rich, constructs and to embed these new constructs into still higher-order constructs. Humans and great apes exhibit mental constructional abilities in varied behavioral domains. In each domain, human skills exceed those of the apes. In the motor realm, mental construction evidences itself when positions of several body parts are simultaneously coordinated to construct gestural, tool-using, dance, or gymnastic postures, and when dance and gymnastic routines are constructed from a predetermined sequence of postures. Similar mental constructional skills allow humans to produce individual speech sounds by varying the configuration of the tongue, lips, and other vocal organs and to construct words and sentences from sequences of vocal tract configurations.

In conceptual domains, mental construction evidences itself in tool-use, art and architecture, language, and social behavior. Chimpanzee tool-using behaviors demand the construction of relationships between a tool, such as a hammerstone, and the object of the tool-use, such as a nut or another stone. Humans, however, construct tools of varied components. Even simple tools, such as spears with stone points, require an initial manufacture of the tool components (stone points, wooden shafts, binding materials) and the conjunction of separate components to form the final product. Thus individual components are "embedded" or subsumed within the final tool. Human artistic and architectural products utilize similar processes of manufacturing diverse components that are then embedded in a larger final object.

In the social realm, mental constructional skills are evident in behaviors that require an understanding of the thought processes of other humans or animals (theory of mind). Dennett has delineated several orders of theory of mind. These involve different levels of mental constructional skills and different levels of embedding. Hence, a first-order construct takes the form "Y believes that Q . . . ," while a third-order construct takes the form "Y wants Q to believe that Y believes. . . ." Great apes engage in deceptive behaviors that suggest the presence of some abilities to understand the thought processes of others. Only humans appear capable of higher-order constructs such as "I think that Susan thinks that Bill thinks that she is smart."

Ape versus human linguistic endeavors exhibit mental constructional differences similar to those in other behavioral domains. Apes can use simple visual symbols and combine two symbols according to syntactic rules. Humans routinely construct multiword utterances containing embedded phrases and clauses. Thus a great ape can create a construct such as "give milk," but humans can construct linguistic utterances such as "Please remember to put milk in the kitty's dish before you leave for the basketball game."

Many motor and conceptual constructs are unique one-time events. Others become routines after much practice and repetition allow them to be executed rapidly and automatically with little conscious thought (procedural learning). Young apes and humans, for instance, practice intensively until finally mastering culturally specific tool-use techniques, and human infants practice movements of the vocal tract until they can effortlessly pronounce their native language. Humans also learn to automatically generate symbolic gestures and syntactic structures, to automatically recite some factual information (e.g., the alphabet, the days of the week), and to automatically reproduce culturally specific rituals and songs. Without these expanded procedural learning abilities, human culture and language could not exist.

To conclude, language depends on mental constructional and procedural learning capacities that also underlie other human behaviors. These capacities exist in apes in more rudimentary form, and they depend on the processing capacities of varied neural structures that have enlarged in human evolution. These findings lend support to continuity theories of language origins.

(See also *acquisition, brain, category, grammar, individual, intentionality, socialization, turn, writing*)

Bibliography

Byrne, Richard
  1995 The Thinking Ape. Oxford: Oxford University Press.
Dennett, Daniel
  1991 Consciousness Explained. Boston: Little, Brown.
Gibson, Kathleen, and Tim Ingold, eds.
  1993 Tools, Language and Cognition in Human Evolution. Cambridge: Cambridge University Press.
Hurford, James, Michael Studdert-Kennedy, and Chris Knight, eds.
  1998 Approaches to the Evolution of Language. Cambridge: Cambridge University Press.
King, Barbara, ed.
  1999 The Evolution of Language: Assessing the Evidence from the Non-Human Primates. Santa Fe, NM: School for American Research.
Lock, Andrew, and Charles Peters
  1996 Handbook of Symbolic Evolution. Oxford: Clarendon Press of Oxford University Press.

■ *Aaron V. Cicourel*

Expert

E xpertise can be described by reference to the differential way sources of potential information are perceived and understood by novices and experts, particularly in the way they use language to authenticate their status vis-à-vis one another. In clinical medicine, for example, despite using almost identical technical language, medical history and physical examination information can be interpreted and processed differently by novices and experts even when recognizing certain symptoms or measures (wheezing, blood pressure readings, pulse rate, heart murmur) as relevant markers of medical problems. A central issue is the language of questions and answers and their interpretation. The language of elicitation procedures directly affects the kind of memory representations that are likely to be accessed. The language of the medical record is essential for framing the patient's symptoms, medical history, physical examination, and treatment plan.

Attributing minimal or mature expertise to someone assumes training and experience associated with a title and a prior credentialing process that usually includes official certification by a governmental agency and/or professional association. The designation of someone as a "novice" or "expert" can include ritualized activities or ceremonies and particular forms of address and clothing. Identifying symbols or outward appearances, therefore, can allow or restrict access to particular spaces and equipment or artifacts. Speech events often are the primary resource for understanding activities in task-oriented environments whose organizational constraints and expected oral and written representations become the basis for inferring and attributing expertise to someone. Language, therefore, is central to an understanding of novice and expert behavior.

Language use also plays a crucial role in activating a "hidden" but essential aspect of expertise: the ubiquitous constraints of memory and the ability to access a knowledge base that will be perceived as "authoritative." The content of a novice or expert's working memory, for example, includes the ability to access, delete, and restrict one's attention to locally available information in order to activate long-term memory representations that will be relatively uncluttered and contain relevant information. Novices' perception of the local task environment can produce information overload that compromises the activation of appropriate memory representations and the ability to use appropriate oral and written communication.

In professional settings, experts and novices are difficult to compare because the recipients of their functions are often not aware of how to distinguish one from another, and the actors so designated by organizational criteria do not always make their organizational status and knowledge backgrounds clear to clients or patients. Within an organizational setting, therefore, personnel may be keenly aware of status differences that signal variations in expertise, but recipients are often not aware of such differences and any potential consequences. Novices acquire early on the ability to simulate "expertise" to clients or patients despite not having the knowledge and experience to match their use of language.

Novices are often trained alongside the expert, as when a student pilot is first accompanied by an experienced instructor or a master plumber observes the apprentice attempt to repair or install the pipes of a water heater. Student lawyers perform before instructors in a mock court and are supervised when preparing a legal brief. In law firms, a novice lawyer will accompany an experienced member of the firm when the latter seeks and examines relevant documents, takes depositions, and represents a client in court. A third- or fourth-year medical student may interview a patient already seen by an attending but must explain her or his findings and recommendations (diagnosis and treatment plans) to an expert. A curious aspect of the training of residents is that they may not be observed directly by attendings, yet their oral presentation of the case to the expert is essential for revealing their acquisition and appropriate use of newly acquired expertise. The expert or attending, therefore, relies on the resident's language about the patient's symptoms or problems and a tentative diagnosis and treatment plan to assess the novice's competence.

Novices simulate expertise by projecting a sense of authority or control over information and motor skills and especially by the way they use particular words, asking questions while trying to achieve a poised demeanor and speech delivery to mask any anxiety or uncertainty about what is happening. In medicine, for example, first- and third-year residents can project the appearance of adequate knowledge background but can differ considerably in their ability to reach a viable differential diagnosis. The client or patient may feel they are being "dominated," but it can be difficult for the client or patient to be capable of challenging the authority of the person who assumes or is designated as the responsible person. The notion of domination, however, remains empirically illusive.

The empirical illusiveness of concepts like authority, power, and domination should make the reader wonder about the way research is conducted in medical settings. One source of data is to record novices and experts with clients or patients. Another strategy is to examine interaction between experts and novices, and with clients or patients in socially organized or institutional settings, in order to contextualize the sources of data while studying the status and role relationships that exist therein.

I tried to understand aspects of the process of acquiring expertise by spending months observing and recording in a particular medical service. I then asked a few attendings to listen to recordings of their residents in order to pinpoint aspects of the experts' views about the novice's use of language and reasoning during the medical interview and physical examination. I was present during the novice's interview and during the account given to the attending after the novice's encounter with the patient. I also observed the attending if he or she accompanied the resident back to the patient, presumably because something did not seem appropriate to the expert or if the novice asked for help in understanding the case.

I also tried to understand the acquisition of expertise by attending the microbiology/infectious disease classes required of medical students to learn something about relevant concepts and about the laboratory exercises students were assigned. I also spent several months observing and recording the deliberations of attendings, residents, and occasionally medical students during microbiology rounds each morning at University Hospital. On such occasions I would try "appropriate" language use while participating in examining blood samples in small bottles, smelling petrie dishes, and sometimes looking at slide specimens that residents were asked to describe. I also spent many months over a period of several years observing Infectious Disease Grand Rounds each week, where special cases were discussed and where microbiological and clinical evidence were presented. Such occasions often involved asking a novice (resident) to step up to a microscope and identify the organism on a slide while the audience observed a video depicting the same organism.

(See also *acquisition, body, codes, competence, control, healing, ideology, indexicality, orality, performativity, power, register, socialization*)

Bibliography

Ainsworth-Vaughn, Nancy
  1998 Claiming Power in Doctor-Patient Talk. New York: Oxford University Press.
Cicourel, Aaron V.
  1995 Medical Speech Events as Resources for Inferring Differences in Expert-Novice Diagnostic Reasoning. *In* Aspects of Oral Communication. Uta M. Quastoff, ed. Pp. 364–387. Berlin and New York: Walter de Gruyter.
Goss, M. E. W.
  1961 Influence and Authority among Physicians in an Outpatient Clinic. American Sociological Review 26:39–50.
Hutchins, Edwin
  1995 Cognition in the Wild. Cambridge, MA: MIT Press.

Lave, Jean
   1977   Cognitive Consequences of Traditional Apprenticeship Training in West
      Africa. Anthropology and Education Quarterly 8:177–180.
   1988   Cognition in Practice. Cambridge: Cambridge University Press.
Mishler, Elliot
   1984   The Discourse of Medicine. Norwood, NJ: Ablex.
Rogoff, Barbara
   1990   Apprenticeship in Thinking: Cognitive Development in Social Context.
      New York: Oxford University Press.
Turner, Bryan
   1987   Medical Power and Social Knowledge. London: Sage.

■ *Michael Silverstein*

Functions

Functionalism in the study of language and other sociocultural formations has generally been a teleologic or teleonomic exercise. The particular sociocultural form being considered is interrogated for its
instrumental role in some dynamic tendency – whether (1) of users of language and cultural forms, (2) of social structure as a self-regulative system,
or (3) of a pre-linguistic or pre-sociocultural order to be found in human
"nature" or in sociocentric "infrastructure."

(1) In user-focused functionalisms, the "functions" of language involve
intentionalities, purposes, and strategic plans; these mental (intensional) states
are thought to be made manifest in the way that sending and receiving verbal messages achieves or accomplishes various kinds of interpersonal adjustments of the intensional states of the participants involved. Thus language
and other behaviors "function" to reveal the mental states of one participant
to another, principally propositionally modeled representations of states-of-
affairs in various worlds, and participants' intensional states with respect
to them. (Notice also that even communicative "ease" and "difficulty" are
basically degree descriptions of language in these terms.)

One might think here also of ordinary language philosophy and its development in speech act philosophy. Language is said to be used by senders of
messages for the purpose of making senders' intentions – apparently both
"actual" and "conventional" – manifest to addressees. Critical attempts to
turn such a functionalist program to cross-cultural empirical ends has revealed the many ways in which it is no more than a Western philosophical
construction.

(2) In a functionalist perspective focused on social structure, the framework construes events of communicating as the means of re-enforcing the
interpersonal social arrangements of categories of people in society, recruited
to communicative roles. Thus the language forms used in communicative
events are referred to such a typology of events of language use. Language
use here thus "functions" institutionally as the primary channel of social organization. One might think here of British structural-functionalism, which,

71

insofar as acknowledging that people communicate, sees events of interpersonal naming, joking, circumspection in verbal usage, etc., as role diacritics of an essentially autonomous social structure of positionalities, timelessly maintained (or at least maintainable) by such linguistic, as by other, social behaviors. Here, too, lies much of the "ethnography of speaking" (or of communication), in which the speech event, principally the public, ritual speech event, is assumed to have a function insofar as maintaining a structural-functional order.

It should also be noted in this connection that what in the disciplinary discourse of linguistics is – ironically – called "formalism" to distinguish itself from "functionalism" (of our type [1]), is actually a structural-functional perspective on language. From Ferdinand de Saussure through Leonard Bloomfield to Noam Chomsky and his followers, it has concentrated on the autonomy of language as an internally organized form. Thus the "function" of forms is to be integrated into the whole. Autonomous language form constitutes, moreover, a primary institutional fact in its own order, whether or not we want to call this order "mental" in this special sense. (This contrasts with the role-diacritic structural-functionalism, concerned as it is with social structure and social organization, characterized just above.) In the writings of Chomsky, structural-functional "formalism" has necessitated the claim that linguistic formedness is, in essence, its own function, the fact of formedness now being ultimately biologized and termed an autonomous faculty or "mental organ." Here, perhaps, is the deeper connection to "structuralist" thought in anthropology that sees culture as an autonomous, ahistorical, pan-specific fact of human mentality; both are a kind of "upward reduction."

(3) This leads, by contrast, to the two varieties of classically "reductive functionalism," the psychobiological and the sociocentric. Language and all other aspects of meaningful human social action are seen as merely an epiphenomenal packaging for functional tendencies that exist and can be defined in more basic orders of phenomena independent of the semiotic properties seeming to inhere in language alone, reflexive intensionality (language being its own meta-semiotic) the central one among them.

Thus in a reductively "functional" approach of one sort, one purports to discover in the individual human psychobiology that asymmetries in the syntactic form of case-marking code-and-conceal – but, when analyzed, reveal – the egocentrically focused cognitive capacity of humans; or it discovers that there is a universal and pre-sociocultural affective calculus of "face" (and "threats" to it) coded-and-concealed, and, thus, analytically, revealed, cross-culturally in the very language forms of degrees and kinds of "politeness." (This approach easily lends itself to meshing with the program of "evolutionary psychology" and human ethology, since aggressive animal nature, red in tooth and claw, can thus be seen to lurk behind every *tu* and *vous*!)

Again, at the level of a sociocentric system, sociocultural forms, including language, become codings-and-concealings ("mystifications" is the technical term) that can be analytically penetrated to reveal their relation to a stadial, evolutionary scenario about the fundamental dimensions of the constitution of interpersonal relations in the means of production of economic value. See Pierre Bourdieu or Michel Foucault or any of the other extra-disciplinary writers on linguistic anthropology who use completely unanalyzed notions of "capital" – "real" as well as "symbolic" – and "power" as ether- or phlogiston-like properties of sociality in order to "reduce" communicational textuality and subjectively meaningful action to what seems to them to lie beneath.

All of these three kinds of older functionalisms – many, alas, still practiced though involving comparable teleological mystifications – present views of language constructed out of perhaps familiar folk ideologies of language in particular and of humans and their social formations more generally. At the same time, they do, in fact, duplicate in one or another way the various folk functionalisms of the very users of language whom we encounter as our interlocutory partners in trying to understand something of what we might mean by the term "functions of language." In the Malinowski-era Trobriands, language, properly formed and properly whispered over axes and other garden implements, puts some principle into the soil that made the yams grow big and fat. In the United States, language, properly formed by the decision of an infant's legal guardian(s) as communicated by a named licensee of the state and inscribed in the form of a (birth) certificate, actually creates the properly existent – because properly named or baptized – individual social person.

In contemporary theory, by contrast, the only viable notions of "functions" of language take the semiotic, or sign's-eye, view of the matter. Linguistic anthropology studies emergent real-time sign-structures called "texts" (and their parts) in relation to their "contexts" of occurrence, including larger "co-textual" structures of which they constitute aspects. Such contextualization-functions are studied as varieties of what one calls indexicality, how one thing signals the spatial, temporal, or causal co-presence of another. The role or "function" of language in social life is all based on the fact that linguistic – and dependent cultural – texts project (index) the metaphorically "surround-ing" contexts in which they by degrees "appropriately" occur, as well as project (index) the contexts that, by their occurrence, they have "effectively" brought into being. All the rest is a development of this fundamental fact.

(See also *codes, competence, genre, grammar, indexicality, maxim, performativity, reflexivity*)

Bibliography

Brown, Penelope, and Stephen C. Levinson
   1987   Politeness: Some Universals in Language Usage. Cambridge: Cambridge University Press.
Grice, Paul
   1989   Studies in the Way of Words. Cambridge, MA: Harvard University Press.

Hymes, Dell H.
  1974 Foundations in Sociolinguistics: An Ethnographic Approach. Philadelphia: University of Pennsylvania Press.
Nichols, Johanna
  1984 Functional Theories of Grammar. Annual Review of Anthropology 13:97–117.
Scherer, Klaus R., and Howard Giles, eds.
  1979 Social Markers in Speech. Cambridge: Cambridge University Press.
Searle, John R.
  1969 Speech Acts: An Essay in the Philosophy of Language. Cambridge: Cambridge University Press.
Sherzer, Joel
  1977 The Ethnography of Speaking: A Critical Appraisal. *In* Georgetown University Round Table on Languages and Linguistics. Muriel Saville-Troike, ed. Pp. 43–57. Washington, DC: Georgetown University Press.
Silverstein, Michael
  1987 The Three Faces of "Function": Preliminaries to a Psychology of Language. *In* Social and Functional Approaches to Language and Thought. Maya Hickmann, ed. Pp. 17–38. Orlando, FL: Academic Press.
Sperber, Dan, and Deirdre Wilson
  1986 Relevance: Communication and Cognition. Cambridge, MA: Harvard University Press.
Williams, Glyn
  1992 Sociolinguistics: A Sociological Critique. London: Routledge.

■ *Mary Bucholtz*

Gender

L inguists have traditionally distinguished "grammatical gender" (the classification of nouns based on linguistic morphology) from "natural" or "biological gender" (the division of human beings into binary categories based on anatomical morphology). The latter category has been problematized by a considerable body of work in gender theory that demonstrates that gender in this sense is a social construct rather than a biological given, whose "naturalness" is achieved in large part through discourse. The term *social gender* would therefore be a more accurate label for this phenomenon. Moreover, linguists have long recognized that grammatical gender and "natural" gender do not usually coincide (e.g., *Fräulein* 'young woman' in German is grammatically neuter), and linguistic anthropological research demonstrates that a language's gender categories are social resources rather than fixed grammatical structures. Thus attempts to read linguistic structure directly for information about social gender are often misguided. Information about social gender is best sought not in the abstract linguistic system but in how the system is put to use in practice.

The importance of discursive practice is ubiquitous in the much-discussed notion of "women's language" as a gender-marked linguistic variety. "Women's languages" have been cited in communities as divergent as the Lakhota Sioux, the Japanese, and middle-class European Americans. Accounts of non-European languages in particular tend to emphasize the sharp differentiation of female and male speakers, thereby exoticizing these communities, but in fact such "languages" rarely involve entirely different grammatical systems, instead hinging on relatively minor differences of lexicon, phonology, or morphosyntax. In both Lakhota and Japanese, for example, verbal suffixes frequently described as gender-marked basically indicate the speaker's epistemic or affective stance toward her or his assertion. The link between linguistic form and gendered meaning is indexical: it is forged through repeated associations between gender and stance. Although the gender ideologies associated with these linguistic forms are relatively rigid, actual practice is much more flexible, and speakers may use linguistic forms associated with

75

the other gender to index particular stances (thus women may use "men's" forms to index authority or casualness, and men may use "women's" forms to index affection or diffidence).

Speakers can also exploit the underlying gender ideology of such linguistic forms to forge particular kinds of identities: young Japanese women may use men's language to display their affiliation with modernity, while Japanese male transvestites may use traditional women's language to signal their transgressive gender identities. It is important to recognize that such cases of gender crossing more often serve to critique hegemonic gender arrangements than to mark straightforward identification with the other gender: working-class African American drag queens who use stereotypes of middle-class European American women's language in their performances do so not because they want to be white women but in order to challenge dominant ideologies of race, class, gender, and sexuality.

The complexity of gender identity is evident in other forms of gender transgression as well. Within so-called "third sex" categories in a number of cultures – among them the Lakhota *winkte*, the Indian *hijras*, the Nigerian *'yan daudu*, and the Brazilian *travestis* – biological males engage in cross-gender symbolic practices, including cross-dressing, physical self-alteration and, in the realm of language, manipulation of linguistic gender and stereotypical women's speech. Hence transgendered individuals may refer to themselves and others who share their identity with feminine gender markers.

Although these identities are often celebrated for seeming to transcend the gender dichotomy, it would be erroneous to claim that individuals who violate gender norms have freed themselves from cultural ideologies. Indeed, those who display transgressive identities often experience considerable stigmatization and persecution. And although they challenge binary gender systems, they necessarily draw on these systems as resources in identity construction. For example, a hijra may refer to herself with feminine linguistic morphology while engaging in linguistic practices, such as sexual insult, that are strictly taboo for Indian women. Transgendered identities certainly disrupt gender hegemony, but they do not displace it. For this reason, and because the groups that are often included within the category differ in substantive ways, the label *third* sex is misleading.

If these categories do not eliminate gendered subject positions, however, they at least demonstrate the possibility of shifts between positions. For instance, speakers do not generally rely solely on feminine linguistic forms in referring to themselves or others, but rather use both feminine and masculine gender markers in order to achieve specific discursive effects. Thus a narrator may alternate between feminine and masculine forms to refer to an individual whose gender identity or practice changes during the course of the narrative.

Linguistic studies of gender transgression are part of a larger movement within linguistic anthropology to localize gender-based research, for language and gender studies have tended to favor generalization over contextualization. The call for ethnographically specific research has led to an emphasis on the *practice* and *performance* of gender over the traditional foci of *difference* and *dominance*. Earlier research often took a comparative approach, seeking to explain gender differences in language use. In the dominance perspective, patriarchal privilege was held to be the source of such differences, while the difference perspective viewed the female and male genders as separate cultures and explained gender difference as cultural difference. The impasse between these two positions was more apparent than real, and both shared a tendency toward universalizing explanations: thus while women were thought to speak differently from men, these explanations required that they speak similarly to each other as members of the same category, women. Such models overlooked differences among women based on race, ethnicity, sexuality, social class, nationality, and local factors.

Penelope Eckert and Sally McConnell-Ginet's ethnographically grounded model of the *community of practice* has redirected energy to the in-depth investigation of communities constituted not in sameness but in diversity, made up of individuals who are temporarily unified through shared engagement in activity and thus are able to shift identities from moment to moment. Such an approach de-emphasizes gender (and any other single dimension of the self) as a primary explanatory category in favor of fluid, situated, and activity-based identities.

(See also *body, community, crossing, functions, identity, indexicality, participation, particle, power, register*)

Bibliography

Bucholtz, Mary, A. C. Liang, and Laurel A. Sutton, eds.
   1999 Reinventing Identities: The Gendered Self in Discourse. New York: Oxford University Press.

Eckert, Penelope, and Sally McConnell-Ginet
   1992 Think Practically and Look Locally: Language and Gender as Community-Based Practice. Annual Review of Anthropology 21:461–490.

Goodwin, Marjorie Harness
   1990 He-Said-She-Said: Talk as Social Organization among Black Children. Bloomington: Indiana University Press.

Hall, Kira, and Mary Bucholtz, eds.
   1995 Gender Articulated: Language and the Socially Constructed Self. New York: Routledge.

Inoue, Miyako
   In press Vicarious Language: The Political Economy of Gender and Speech in Japan. Berkeley: University of California Press.

Kulick, Don
   1997 The Gender of Brazilian Transgendered Prostitutes. American Anthropologist 99(3):574–585.

Livia, Anna, and Kira Hall, eds.
   1997 Queerly Phrased: Language, Gender, and Sexuality. New York: Oxford University Press.

Maltz, Daniel N., and Ruth A. Borker
  1982 A Cultural Approach to Male-Female Miscommunication. *In* Language and Social Identity. John J. Gumperz, ed. Pp. 196–216. Cambridge: Cambridge University Press.
Ochs, Elinor
  1992 Indexing Gender. *In* Rethinking Context: Language as an Interactive Phenomenon. Alessandro Duranti and Charles Goodwin, eds. Pp. 335–358. Cambridge: Cambridge University Press.

■ *Richard Bauman*

Genre

T he concept of genre has played a significant role in linguistic anthropology since the inception of the field, part of the philological foundation of the Boasian program. The centrality of texts in the Boasian tradition demanded discrimination among orders of texts, and generic categories inherited from the European (especially German) study of folklore served this classificatory purpose. Genre received little critical or theoretical attention in the field, however, until the latter part of the 1960s, under the convergent impetus of ethnoscience, with its analytical focus on indigenous (emic) systems of classification; structuralism, in both its morphological and structural-symbolic guises; and the ethnography of speaking, in which genre served as a nexus of interrelationships among the constituents of the speech event and as a formal vantage point on speaking practice. More recently, the influence of Mikhail Bakhtin's approach to genre as the compositional organizing principle of utterances has given further prominence to the concept of genre in the work of linguistic anthropologists.

Current approaches center on a conception of genre as one order of speech style, a constellation of systemically related, co-occurrent formal features and structures that serves as a conventionalized orienting framework for the production and reception of discourse. More specifically, a genre is a speech style oriented to the production and reception of a particular kind of text. When an utterance is assimilated to a given genre, the process by which it is produced and interpreted is mediated through its intertextual relationship with prior texts. The invocation of a generic (i.e., genre-specific) framing device such as "Once upon a time" carries with it a set of expectations concerning the further unfolding of the discourse, indexing other texts initiated by this opening formula. These expectations constitute a framework for entextualization, that is, for endowing discourse with textual properties: boundedness, internal cohesion, coherence, availability for decontextualization and recontextualization, and so forth.

The formal relationship implied in the notion of generic intertextuality has pragmatic and thematic correlates as well. The situated production of generically informed discourse indexes prior situational contexts and their constituent elements (e.g., settings, participant roles and structures, scenarios, goals and outcomes, etc.) in which other tokens of the generic type have been employed; genre thus transcends the bounded, locally produced speech event. From this perspective, genre appears as a set of conventional guidelines for dealing with recurrent communicative exigencies – greetings, for example, as a means of establishing interactional access. It would be misleading, however, to assume – as some have done – that there is a one-to-one correlation between genres and speech events. While particular genres may be primarily identified with specific situational contexts of use – for example, curing chants with healing rituals – it is of the very nature of genre to be recognizable outside of such primary contexts. Thus a curing chant may be performed in another context for entertainment, for the pleasure afforded by the chanter's display of virtuosity, or in still another as pedagogical demonstration in the instruction of a novice curer.

In like manner, each genre will be distinguished by its thematic or referential capacities, as a routinized vehicle for encoding and expressing particular orders of knowledge and experience. This thematic orientation to the world is thus part of the indexical field implicated in relationships of generic intertextuality.

Scholars differ on the question of how much of the speech economy of a community is encompassed by genre. Insofar as the concept of genre emphasizes conventionality and textuality, however, there is an operational tendency to restrict the notion to those discursive forms and practices for which conventional expectation and textual boundedness, cohesion, and coherence are relatively and recognizably more apparent.

While generic intertextuality is a means of foregrounding the routinized, conventionalized formal, pragmatic, and thematic organization of discourse, the same relational nexus also suggests that generic convention alone is insufficient to account for the formal-pragmatic-thematic configuration of any given utterance. This is so because the fit between a particular text and the generic model – or other tokens of the generic type – is never perfect. Emergent elements of here-and-now contextualization inevitably enter into the discursive process, forging links to the adjacent discourse, the ongoing social interaction, instrumental or strategic agendas, and other situational and extrasituational factors that interact with generic orienting frameworks in shaping the production and reception of the utterance. These in turn will influence the ways in which the constituent features of the generic framework – formal, pragmatic, thematic – are variably mobilized, opening the way to generic reconfiguration and change. Thus generic intertextuality inevitably involves the production of an intertextual gap. The calibration of the gap – its relative restriction or amplification – has significant correlates and effects. Certain acts of entextualization may strive for generic orthodoxy by hewing as closely as possible to generic precedent and assimilating the utterance to conventional practices for the accomplishment of routine ends under ordinary circumstances. By contrast, widening of the intertextual gap allows for the adaptation of generic frameworks to emergent circumstances and agendas. Such adaptive calibration may involve manipulation of any of the formal, functional, and thematic elements by which an utterance may be linked to generic precedents. It may also extend to the assimilation of a text to more than one generic framework, drawing upon and blending the formal and functional capacities of each of the genres thus invoked, as when the lowered pitch, falling intonation, measured stress, and moral content of their instructor's speech might lead a student to inquire of a classmate whether they had just heard a lecture or a sermon.

The calibration of intertextual gaps offers a useful vantage point on the ideology and politics of genre. Within any speech community or historical period, genres will vary with regard to the relative tightness or looseness of generic regimentation, but certain genres may become the object of special ideological focus. Prescriptive insistence on strict generic regimentation works conservatively in the service of established authority and order, while the impulse toward the widening of intertextual gaps and generic innovation is more conducive to the exercise of creativity, resistance to hegemonic order, and openness to change. These factors will be closely tied as well to hierarchies of value and taste (which genres are evaluated as relatively higher, better, more beautiful, more moral) and to the social regimentation of access to particular generic forms (who can learn them, master them, own them, perform them, and to what effect).

(See also *codes, expert, heteroglossia, indexicality, inference, register*)

Bibliography

Bakhtin, Mikhail M.
> 1986[1979]   The Problem of Speech Genres. *In* Speech Genres and Other Late Essays. Caryl Emerson and Michael Holquist, eds. Pp. 60–102. Austin: University of Texas Press.

Bauman, Richard
> 1992   Contextualization, Tradition, and the Dialogue of Genres: Icelandic Legends of The Kraftaskáld. *In* Rethinking Context: Language as an Interactive Phenomenon. Alessandro Duranti and Charles Goodwin, eds. Pp. 77–99. Cambridge: Cambridge University Press.

Ben-Amos, Dan, ed.
> 1976   Folklore Genres. Austin: University of Texas Press.

Briggs, Charles L.
> 1992   Generic versus Metapragmatic Dimensions of Warao Narratives: Who Regiments Performance? *In* Reflexive Language: Reported Speech and Metapragmatics. John A. Lucy, ed. Pp. 179–212. Cambridge: Cambridge University Press.

Briggs, Charles L., and Richard Bauman
> 1992   Genre, Intertextuality, and Social Power. Journal of Linguistic Anthropology 2(2):131–172.

Gossen, Gary
    1972 Chamula Genres of Verbal Behavior. *In* Toward New Perspectives in
    Folklore. Américo Paredes and Richard Bauman, eds. Pp. 145–167. Austin:
    University of Texas Press.
Guenthner, Susanne, and Hubert Knoblauch
    1995 Culturally Patterned Speaking Practices: The Analysis of Communicative
    Genres. Pragmatics 5(1):1–32.
Hanks, William F.
    1987 Discourse Genres in a Theory of Practice. American Ethnologist 14(4): 668–
    692.
Hymes, Dell
    1973 Ways of Speaking. *In* Explorations in the Ethnography of Speaking.
    Richard Bauman and Joel Sherzer, eds. Pp. 433–451. Cambridge: Cambridge
    University Press.
Urban, Greg
    1984 The Semiotics of Two Speech Styles in Shokleng. *In* Semiotic Mediation.
    Elizabeth Mertz and Richard J. Parmentier, eds. Pp. 311–329. Orlando, FL:
    Academic Press.

■ *John B. Haviland*

Gesture

Gesture usually starts with a dubious, if not downright bad, reputation. No matter how "dramatic" someone's occasional beau geste may be, it nonetheless remains "just a gesture," and thus liable to the suspicion of being only "token," or, worse, "empty." Often the bodily movements or gesticulations that routinely accompany speech just as routinely pass unremarked or dismissed as irrelevant in studies of language. When gesture *has* risen to analytical consciousness, the result has too often been a contrastive or "subtractive" account, in which gesture is what is left over after other phenomena that fall under some principled description are subtracted. Not surprisingly, such treatments frequently produce mutually contradictory views of the gestural residue. One family of approaches treats gesture as involuntary bodily leakage (whether mildly systematic, or largely anarchic) that "betrays" inner states and attitudes that intentionally communicative channels may be trying to hide. Here gesture is reduced to a kind of nervous tick, a sweaty palm that, unlike the treacherous tongue, cannot lie. Another family of approaches considers gesture to be scattered and only partly conscious bodily accompaniments to true language (whether spoken or otherwise), largely involuntary excrescences of the speaking process itself as it struggles to render inchoate or imagistic thought into the digital linearity of language. Here the emphasis is on gesture "for the speaker," and any communicative function it may have (except for the observing psychologist) is analytically irrelevant. For another class of theories, gesture is primitive "attempted" language, grounded in presumed universal iconicity, and thus the first resort of would-be communicators who do not share a linguistic code. Some theorists detect in this sort of imagined pantomime a credible basis for a kind of substitute for language, assuming that a gestural lingua franca can draw on a set of mimicable actions ("eating" perhaps) plus some transparent indexical referential devices (pointing is a popular candidate) to launch a basic system of extra-linguistic communication. Other gesture theorists place an almost diametrically opposite emphasis on *codified* and *culture-specific* gestural substitutes for spoken language: compacted, gestured holophrases known as "emblems." Examples include the "OK" sign formed with a ring made by the thumb and forefinger (a handshape which can have quite different meanings from one community to another), various gestures for "[s/he's] crazy," or the gesture in American English simply known as "the finger." All are signals which interlocutors must *learn* both to produce and to interpret. Because the messages encoded often have negative content, on such a view, the silent and even furtive corporeal modality of gesture may be particularly appropriate for their transmission.

Contrasting with these subtractive approaches is a view that integrates attitudes and movements of the body (including gaze), first, into the full repertoire of interactive human communicative resources and, second, into the expressive inflections of language itself. One influential typology of gesture distinguishes different varieties according to their "language like" properties on the one hand and their relative integration with or emancipation from speech on the other. At one end of the spectrum are "gesticulations," movements especially of the hands that occur only in coordination with verbalization and are relatively uninterpretable in isolation from speech. At the other are full-fledged sign languages, in which the gestural channel serves as the vehicle for language itself. Ranging in between are such phenomena as nonce pantomimes (meant to signal on their own, but nonconventionalized); culture-specific emblems that function as complete, quotable utterances in their own right, independent of or substitutable for speech; or "substitute" sign languages that replace speech in whole or in part under circumstances that require silence.

Studies of gesture as *part of* language produce such observations as the following:

a. Verbal and gestural performances are mutually synchronized: when a gesture appears to be linked in meaning to a word or phrase (sometimes called the gesture's "lexical affiliate"), the gesture either coincides with or just precedes the relevant speech fragment. Some researchers have used this fact to motivate a theory in which both speech and gesture originate in a single conceptual source, whose joint "expression" in the different modalities produces the observed synchronicity.

b. Gesture lends itself to "morphological" analysis, in which gestural gestalts are decomposed into distinct articulations (hand shapes, for example, or certain patterns of movement which are also among the formal primitives attributed to developed sign languages). Aspects of this morphology may be systematically deployed to express semantic inflections overlaid on the meaning of the gestalt. (In some communities, for example, a high pointing gesture suggests relative distance.)

c. There is complete semiotic parallelism between gestures and other linguistic signs. For example, links between gestural forms and their meaning may be classified according to the familiar Peircean trichotomy of icon (an "hourglass" motion to suggest a particular human body shape), index ("pointing toward" a referent), and symbol (a purely conventional "thumbs up" gesture, for example). The semiotic parallel between gesture and the rest of language extends to the characteristic linguistic reflexivity (imagine "quoted" gestures, or, for example, meta-discursive negation via gesture), its "arbitrariness," and its indexical links to contexts of speaking, which display the characteristic range from relatively entailing to relatively creative. (A good example is the semiotic complexity of pointing, which identifies referents by often complex indexical links as well as by characterizing elements in hand shapes or the form of other body parts. Pointing is typically susceptible to Bühlerian "transposition" in the same way as spoken deictics. Furthermore, pointing may acquire a cultural metapragmatic evaluation, as in the European injunction "It's not polite to point.")

d. In acquisition, it appears that universally gesture and spoken or other linguistic forms emerge together (whether shared or parallel processes are at work). Gestural routines in which stylized movements play central communicative roles appear before the first recognizable words. Moreover, the so-called "one word stage" is ordinarily characterized by the production not of "words" alone but of combined gestural and verbalized holophrases at the earliest stages of language learning. Phenomena such as gestural "babbling," or the spontaneous language-like "home sign" systems that arise in contexts where deaf children are not exposed to a pre-existing sign language attest to the insistence of manual and other bodily "expressions" in human communication, waiting in the cognitive wings to be summoned on stage by appropriate social and interactive contexts.

(See also *codes, deaf, iconicity, indexicality, participation, signing, vision*)

Bibliography

Armstrong, David F., William C. Stokoe, and Sherman E. Wilcox
  1995 Gesture and the Nature of Language. Cambridge: Cambridge University Press.
Goldin-Meadow, Susan, and Carolyn Mylander
  1998 Spontaneous Sign Systems Created by Deaf Children in Two Cultures. Nature 391:279–281.
Haviland, John B.
  1993 Anchoring, Iconicity, and Orientation in Guugu Yimithirr Pointing Gestures. Journal of Linguistic Anthropology 3(1):3–45.
Kendon, Adam
  1988 Sign Languages of Aboriginal Australia. Cambridge: Cambridge University Press.
  1997 Gesture. Annual Review of Anthropology 26:109–128.
Krauss, Robert M., Palmer Morrel-Samuels, and Christina Colasante
  1991 Do Conversational Hand Gestures Communicate? Journal of Personality and Social Psychology 61(5):743–754.

McNeill, David
  1992   Hand and Mind: What Gestures Reveal about Thought. Chicago: University of Chicago Press.
Morris, D., P. Collett, P. Marsh, and Marie O'Shaughnessy
  1979   Gestures, Their Origin and Distribution. New York: Stein and Day.
Petitto, L.A., and P. Marentette
  1991   Babbling in the Manual Mode. Science 251:1483–1496.
Schegloff, Emanuel
  1984   On Some Gestures' Relation to Talk. *In* Structures of Social Action: Studies in Conversation Analysis. J. M. Atkinson and J. Heritage, eds. Pp. 266–296. Cambridge: Cambridge University Press.

■ *John W. Du Bois*

Grammar

I f the term *grammar* elicits in the average anthropologist a reaction of fear and loathing, perhaps the "ugly grammarian" needs a new image – or, more precisely, the role grammar currently plays within anthropology needs explaining. Many anthropologists have become alienated from grammar ever since certain linguists convinced them that a new field called linguistics was taking over. Henceforth, work on grammar would preferentially be abstract, idealized, decontextualized, technical, and self-referential – and, incidentally, devoid of implications for culture. If grammar is exclusively technical, then only technicians need apply. If grammar describes only internal relationships among linguistic categories, then it cannot illuminate anything outside itself. If grammar is universal, then it cannot tell us anything of ethnographic interest about how one local culture differs from another.

But there are other ways to see grammar, even to coax grammar into throwing light on anthropological questions. Actually, such optimism has always guided the work of linguistic anthropologists, as they have consistently found ways to make grammar speak to the theoretical concerns of the day. Confirming grammar's pervasive and multiplex interpenetration with culture, the yield has often been rich. Today anthropologists who "mind their grammar" can tap a broad array of newly elaborated conceptual tools and theoretical perspectives for understanding grammar in culture and practice. Just as important, the technical requirements for doing anthropologically interesting work with grammar are within the reach of the general anthropologist. Grammar needs anthropology as much as anthropology needs grammar. Anthropologists can help illuminate how social actors use grammar to enact culture, for example. The anthropological voice was never really silent in the twentieth century, and its continued insistence that language is intrinsic to culture, and culture to language, has recently born fruit in an extraordinary revitalization of research in linguistic anthropology.

To study grammar is to study culture – because, as Sapir reminds us, grammar is culture. Culture is a dangerous word nowadays, and linking it with grammar may not improve its image. But this concept may be turned to advantage if we undertake a re-vision of grammar, and consequently of culture, in light of Sapir's idea of the "carrying-power" of pattern as its "propensity to embrace new experiences or cultural elements within its framework." Pattern derives from practice. Just as linguists must abstract away from specific acts of speaking to capture grammatical pattern, anthropologists abstract away from the behavioral flux to capture cultural pattern.

Re-conceiving grammar as *patterned speaking* allows us to revisit the traditional anthropological approaches to grammar, and to situate them now within the modern conception of discourse, taken broadly as the use of language and other symbolic systems in social life. Grammar comes to life in discourse, where its pervasive mediating role touches virtually every aspect of social life.

Grammar goes everywhere. In a given speech community the same grammar promiscuously participates in acts as diverse as intimate persuasion, work, gossip, sanction enforcement, religious speculation, joking, aesthetic play, and a host of other ways of living. Paradoxically, it is grammar's abstractness that frees it to move across domains to mediate the organization of so many and so varied aspects of social life. Grammar mediates, and thus partly organizes, knowledge, information, social relations, texts, institutions, interactional practice, and more.

Grammar organizes knowledge and cognition. Grammar is both reflection and instrument of a community's specific scheme for categorizing its phenomenal environment. Whorf showed how grammar's "obligatory categories" lead speakers to certain "forced observations," as when your grammar obligates you, whenever you use a verb, also to choose an evidential marker. Obligatory categories are always few yet pervasive, and thus influential. They continually demand attention to the distinctions they encode.

Grammar organizes social relations. Here obligatory categories may directly index status – for example, forcing continual monitoring, via overt grammatical encoding, of the speaker's status relative to the addressee's (as in the "power and solidarity" discrimination enforced by pronoun or agreement systems in many languages). Even where social relations are *not* classified via obligatory grammar, the very absence of coding may reflect local ideologies of egalitarian self-presentation.

Grammar organizes information. The speaker who seeks to impart new information must relate it to shared background to make it interpretable. Grammar provides an architecture for the structured differentiation of new information from given information. Local grammars evolve diverse yet comparable solutions, resolving competing universal and local culture-historical demands to legislate seemingly self-evident local organizations of information.

Grammar organizes texts, contributing to the rich structure of parallelism in poetry, oratory, and even conversation. Grammatical parallelism iconically diagrams culturally presupposed equations, manifesting otherwise unspoken classifications for young learners to grasp. Grammar's role reaches beyond the present text's internal structure to access meanings embedded in distant prior texts – understood as cultural resources invokeable within a community of textual culture – and grammatically reshape them to fit the present context.

Grammar organizes interaction. The structure of participation in talk is mediated in part by grammatical structures – combined with intonational, gestural, and other cues – that shape turn organization, nominate speech event participant roles, invoke speech event sequence expectations, and so on.

Admittedly, culture is a risky word these days. But if we conceive culture as *pattern that gives meaning to social acts and entities* and recognize that grammar *is* culture, we can start to see precisely *how* social actors enact culture through patterned speaking and patterned action.

On this re-vision of language and culture, the abstracting power of grammar serves not to generate an infinite unordered list of sentences, unconnected and unconnectable to what surrounds them, but to bridge the gulf that might separate us, one participant from another, present from past, social actor from cultural resource. Whether we engage in collaboration or conflict, grammar embraces abstraction to let us engage across particularities. If the pattern concept of culture (or grammar) were to elude us and social life fragment into a litany of isolated behaviors (or isolated sentences), we would lose our capacity to engage with others in the creation of meaning. The exceptionally fluid, encompassing, and creative forms assumed by grammar, seen in its natural ecology of dialogic interaction, provide a glimmer of a more general model of culture that can encompass convergence and contestation, sociality and individuality, systematicity and change, in which the mediating structures of patterned speaking and patterned action make possible the dynamic constitution and evolution of multiplex social life.

(See also *codes, community, competence, functions, ideology, participation, particles, poetry, reconstruction, socialization, syncretism, variation*)

Bibliography

Du Bois, John W.
    1987   The Discourse Basis of Ergativity. Language 63:805–855.
Duranti, Alessandro
    1994   From Grammar to Politics: Linguistic Anthropology in a Western Samoan Village. Berkeley: University of California Press.
Gumperz, John, and Stephen C. Levinson, eds.
    1996   Rethinking Linguistic Relativity. Cambridge: Cambridge University Press.
Lucy, John A.
    1992   Language Diversity and Thought: A Reformulation of the Linguistic Relativity Hypothesis. Cambridge: Cambridge University Press.
Mannheim, Bruce
    1991   The Language of the Inka since the European Invasion. Austin: University of Texas Press.

Ochs, Elinor, Emanuel Schegloff, and Sandra A. Thompson, eds.
    1996 Interaction and Grammar. Cambridge: Cambridge University Press.
Sapir, Edward
    1994 The Psychology of Culture. Reconstructed and edited by Judith T. Irvine. Berlin: Mouton de Gruyter.
Schieffelin, Bambi B., Kathryn A. Woolard, and Paul V. Kroskrity, eds.
    1998 Language Ideologies: Practice and Theory. Oxford: Oxford University Press.
Silverstein, Michael
    1977 Cultural Prerequisites to Grammatical Analysis. *In* Georgetown University Round Table on Languages and Linguistics. Muriel Saville-Troike, ed. Pp. 130–151. Washington, DC: Georgetown University Press.
Whorf, Benjamin Lee
    1956 Language, Thought, and Reality. John B. Carroll, ed. Cambridge, MA: MIT Press.

■ *James Wilce*

Healing

L anguage is central to diagnosis and healing around the world. Healing functions ascribed to language transcend clinical or public ritual
processes; they include not only curing disease but also healing illness
(restoring persons to life contexts). Healing discourse is thus oriented to pragmatic and moral "stakes."

Just how language might heal is controversial. Are healers' words placebos,
increasing hope and thus improving prognosis? Or do healers persuade
patients to experience the world and their condition differently? What rhetorical features (e.g., imagistic words that seem to make Jesus present to heal,
or the self-authenticating claims of a human healer) persuade so well? Or is
healing effected by the mutual attunement of embodied interactants in healing events (or across a series of events that, together, achieves incremental
healing)? Perhaps metaphor is the key insofar as it links bodily experience
with myth, influencing sensation, imagination, and action as much as mental
operations.

It may not be referential content that turns speech events into healing events
but, for example, the way the narrative structure of a healing encounter builds
and releases tension. Healers' voices may need to be "beautiful" to heal. The
aesthetics of sound, poetry, rhythm, and imagery in shamanic chant and in
group singing effects cures for Yolmo people (Nepal). For the Amazonian
Suyá, curing songs work when they name the right animal to evoke some
attribute needed to counterbalance its opposite in the sick person. Finally,
"indexicals" (like a vocal quality that "makes present" a powerful spirit and
not just a human medium) and "metaindexicals" ("We hereby make present
that mythic time when healing was possible") may alter patients' bodily
awareness.

Diagnosis is integral to curing and contributes to the drama of healing;
especially when revealed by a spirit, diagnosis itself may empower or re-
assure. Language mediates diagnostic practices from biopsychiatry to Bang-
ladeshi divination. But whereas herbalists and doctors treat speech as an
instrument for probing realities they take to be external to speech, exorcistic

91

and divinatory speech draws attention to itself, working performatively or magically in both diagnosis and cure.

Healing systems are genres that change over time and relate to larger cultural processes as well as to each other. Thus physical healing, inner healing, and deliverance (exorcism) – three genres of Catholic Charismatic healing – have distinctive discursive and phenomenological structures but are also interconnected. As structures entailing typifications of experience, narrative genres that are "self-centering" and therapeutic for some may tell others that their experience is beyond both genre and help. Participant structures vary greatly across such healing genres as Spiritism, shamanism, and group therapy. Patients, curers, spirits, family members, and others are charged with more or less responsibility in different genres. Australian Aboriginals who help (but ignore the words of) close companions when "it is the sickness itself speaking" are exclusively authorized to recount the sickness and its cure. Middle-class Americans may expect self-expression of trauma to be therapeutic, whereas others put hope in a healer's words and – because words "do things" – consider verbalization of suffering to be dangerous. Whereas some genres cure the self by centering it, a linguistic decentering of the self is crucial to others. Where possession cults are culturally salient, people may try to cure a person's first incident of possession but later see possession as a sign of a cure, or at least a sign that – in order to be well – the affected must participate in the possession cult and speak (dance, act, etc.) under a spirit's influence.

Typifications of language and healing relate to broader ideologies. What is language that it might heal? Suyé curing songs are viewed as substances blown and rubbed into patients' bodies. To look at language and healing together is to allow ideologies that treat language as embodied to challenge our own tendency to make it the proper object of (disembodied) cognitive science. Particular ideologies and social formations influence which discourse features are considered curative. Examples include written narratives of traumatic events that help the writer reorganize the memory; metaphors that aptly capture illness experience but increasingly introduce agency; glossolalia as a sign but also a vehicle of the healing work of the Spirit; and playful use of dramatic and rhythmic speech features to alter unhealthful patterns of thought and embodied habit. These value-laden visions of healing incorporate notions of language, affect, personhood, and bodies. A complete account of language and healing would examine how discourses constitute illness, disease, and medicine in broader terms. It is within a whole linguacultural-ideological system that "the inability to put feelings into words" may, for instance, be pathologized – labeled "alexithymia," and expected to lead to "somatization" – while expressing distress in psychological terms may be privileged. The language-and-healing relationship itself reflects power, and the case described exemplifies what Foucault calls an "incitement to discourse."

Must language be clear in order to heal? Warao Amazonian curing traditions attribute efficacy to features such as vocables not meant to be understood by patient or audience. To claim that vocables and artfully ambiguous narratives heal highlights the limits of persuasive referential clarity. But alternation between clear and obscure speech also creatively indexes Warao shamans' authority. Power relations are reproduced when Warao shamans' speech (mostly in an esoteric register) is strategically clear just when they declare their own authority, but also when doctors interrupt patients' narratives or fail to use laymen's terms to instruct patients so that they can manage their illnesses. Mexican Spiritists might not share an analytic preoccupation with power that individuates and dramatizes the healing relationship. Corporate healing rituals defy personalistic analysis; their efficacy lies not in an intense, private, verbal relationship, but in empathic resonance in groups co-constructing testimonies of transcendence. Corporate rituals such as Sinhalese exorcisms, however, dramatize power relations, even when genres of humor central to exorcising demons serve secondarily (for middle-class Sinhalese) to index participants' (lower) class status. Language, thus, may heal one but "hail" or address others, from deities to bystanders and critics.

(See also *act, body, genre, indexicality, music, narrative, performativity, poetry, power, prayer, reflexivity, register*)

Bibliography

Crapanzano, Vincent
  1996 "Self"-Centering Narratives. *In* Natural Histories of Discourse. M. Silverstein and G. Urban, eds. Pp. 106–130. Chicago: University of Chicago Press.
Csordas, Thomas J.
  1994 The Sacred Self: A Cultural Phenomenology of Charismatic Healing. Berkeley and Los Angeles: University of California Press.
Desjarlais, Robert R.
  1992 Body and Emotion: The Aesthetics of Illness and Healing in the Nepal Himalayas. Philadelphia: University of Pennsylvania Press.
Finkler, Kaja
  1994 Sacred Healing and Biomedicine Compared. Medical Anthropology Quarterly 8(2):178–197.
Kapferer, Bruce
  1991 A Celebration of Demons: Exorcism and the Aesthetics of Healing in Sri Lanka. Oxford and Washington, DC: Berg/Smithsonian Institution.
Kirmayer, Laurence
  1993 Healing and the Invention of Metaphor: The Effectiveness of Symbols Revisited. Culture, Medicine and Psychiatry 17(2):161–195.
Laderman, Carol, and Marina Roseman, eds.
  1996 The Performance of Healing. New York: Routledge.
Lévi-Strauss, Claude
  1963 The Effectiveness of Symbols. *In* Structural Anthropology. Pp. 186–205. New York: Basic Books.

Sansom, Basil
  1982 The Sick Who Do Not Speak. *In* Semantic Anthropology. D. J. Parkin, ed. Pp. 183–196. ASA Monographs 22. London: Academic Press.
Seeger, Anthony
  1986 Oratory Is Spoken, Myth Is Told, and Song Is Sung, but They Are All Music to My Ears. *In* Native South American Discourse. J. Sherzer and G. Urban, eds. Pp. 59–82. Berlin: Mouton de Gruyter.

■ *Vyacheslav Ivanov*

Heteroglossia

H
eteroglossia means the simultaneous use of different kinds of speech or other signs, the tension between them, and their conflicting relationship within one text. The term was coined (from the Greek stems meaning "other" and "speech": ἑτερο-+γλοσσ-+ια) by Mikhail Bakhtin in his theoretical work on the novel in the period from 1934 to 1935, and has become extraordinarily popular in literary and anthropological works since the 1980s. Bakhtin had in mind both the stylistic and social differences within the language of any modern developed society, as well as the intention of writers to recreate them in prose, particularly in the novel, a medium that could operate with different artistic images of languages and styles (Joyce's *Ulysses*, each chapter of which was written in a different linguistic style, serves as an example). Heteroglossia is opposed to monoglossia (the dominance of one language), typical of an ancient city such as Athens, and to polyglossia (the co-existence of two languages, for instance of English and French in medieval England). The spoken language of a modern society may seem to be more or less unified, but there are not only different social dialects (such as the variations of New York English studied in modern sociolinguistics), but also individual differences among speakers. This peculiarity is reflected in the way a writer of novels characterizes each of their heroes. In a novel a main hero usually speaks in a way that is differentiated from the other characters. Each of the heroes may have his or her own stylistic sphere. A representative case of heteroglossia is found in the ironic use of speech forms, particularly in parody. In several places in *Ulysses*, Joyce suggests a parody of the new Irish drama: "It's what I am telling you, mister honey, it's queer and sick we were, Haines and myself, the time himself brought it in. . . ." In the chapter "Nausicaa," a woman's magazine style takes over; in the chapter "Eumaeus," a parody of provincial journalese is introduced. In other parts of the novel there is a grotesque mixture of several styles, as in a mockery of learned English in the speech of the ghost of Bloom's grandfather.

Conflicting tendencies are hidden in the semantic potential of almost every word and they may be realized in everyday speech. But particularly pronounced features occur in the social contexts that make their ambivalence relevant for the whole society. This aspect of language in a totalitarian society was depicted in the image of Orwell's Newspeak. In a single utterance different speech attitudes may appear simultaneously. It was said that the Soviet Communist party leader Leonid Brezhnev used to say to his family at night: "It's time for me to go read Marx." Without knowledge of the real context, a stranger might have heard in this sentence the genuine intention of a Marxist official to reread in his spare time the works of the founder of the movement (comparable, perhaps, to a rereading of the Bible by a priest). But what Brezhnev actually intended was his cynical hatred for this old-fashioned duty that had become a senseless ritual. To him Marx's works were terribly dull and could cause one to become drowsy. Thus what he really meant was his desire to go to bed. Even if this joke were not real and belonged to the realm of Soviet folklore of the period, it was quite symbolic because it showed the complete deterioration of the former communist creed, in which Marx had acquired the role of substitute apostle. A similar problem, but in connection to a real religion (and not its fake substitute, to which Soviet ideology deteriorated), has been discussed by Bakhtin in his study of Rabelais and the folk culture of the Middle Ages and the Renaissance. In this work, finished by 1945, Bakhtin (as Jacques Le Goff would do later) has discovered semiotic heteroglossia characteristic of the medieval European culture. It was characterized by the potential use of signs and words pertaining to the sphere of the official Church culture and of those which belonged to unofficial folklore. The latter used parody of the official language as well as another set of symbols pertaining to the carnival tradition. As rites involving the inversion of official symbols seem to be universal (according to the anthropological works of Edmund Leach and Victor Turner), semiotic heteroglossia utilizing grotesque carnival images may belong to the most important features of almost all known societies. In this particular case, heteroglossia may be seen at the purely linguistic level as well as on a higher level of signs encoded with verbal expressions. Thus in a medieval Old Czech mystery studied from a similar point of view by Roman Jakobson, Latin songs coexist with grotesque jokes in Old Czech. Heteroglossia (very often called by different terms having the same meaning), as a parallel or simultaneous use of different signs and images belonging to partly opposed or conflicting spheres, may be a feature common to all cultures.

(See also *competence, crossing, humor, ideology, indexicality, poetry, style, syncretism, theater, translation, voice*)

Bibliography

Bakhtin, Mikhail
   1968   Rabelais and His World. Hélène Iswolsky, trans. Cambridge, MA: MIT Press.
   1981   Discourse in the Novel. *In* The Dialogical Imagination: Four Essays by M.

Bakhtin. M. Holquist, ed. Caryl Emerson and Michael Holquist, trans. Pp. 259–422, 428. Austin: University of Texas Press.

Burgess, Anthony
  1973 Joysprick. An Introduction to the Language of James Joyce. Pp. 93–109. New York: Harcourt Brace Jovanovich.

Howard, Jacqueline
  1994 Reading Gothic Fiction: A Bakhtinian Approach. Oxford: Clarendon Press.

Jakobson, Roman
  1985 Medieval Mock Mystery. *In* Selected Writings VI. Early Slavic Paths and Crossroads. Part 2. Medieval Slavic Studies. Pp. 666–690. Berlin/New York/Amsterdam: Mouton de Gruyter.

Jordan, Robert M.
  1995 Heteroglossia and Chaucer's "Man of Law's" Tale. *In* Bakhtin and Medieval Voices. Pp. 81–93. Miami: University of Florida Press.

Leach, Edmund
  1961 Rethinking Anthropology. Monographs in Social Anthropology 22. London: Athlone Press.

Le Goff, Jacques
  1977 Pour un autre Moyen Age. Pp. 223–334. Paris: Gallimard.

Morson, Gary Saul, and Caryl Emerson
  1990 Mikhail Bakhtin. Creation of a Prosaics. Stanford, CA: Stanford University Press.

Turner, Victor
  1969 The Ritual Process: Structure and Anti-Structure. Chicago: Aldine.

■ *William O. Beeman*

Humor

H umor is a performative pragmatic accomplishment involving a wide range of communication skills including, but not exclusively involving, language, gesture, the presentation of visual imagery, and situation management. Humor aims at creating a concrete feeling of enjoyment for an audience, most commonly manifested in a physical display consisting of displays of pleasure, including smiles and laughter.

The basis for most humor is the setting up of a surprise or series of surprises for an audience. The most common kind of surprise has since the eighteenth century been described under the general rubric of "incongruity." Basic incongruity theory as an explanation of humor can be described in linguistic terms as follows: A communicative actor presents a message or other content material and contextualizes it within a cognitive "frame." The actor constructs the frame through narration, visual representation, or enactment. He or she then suddenly pulls this frame aside, revealing one or more additional cognitive frames which audience members are shown as possible contextualizations or reframings of the original content material. The tension between the original framing and the sudden reframing results in an emotional release recognizable as the enjoyment response we see as smiles, amusement, and laughter. This tension is the driving force that underlies humor, and the release of that tension – as Freud pointed out – is a fundamental human behavioral reflex.

Humor, of all forms of communicative acts, is one of the most heavily dependent on equal cooperative participation of actor and audience. The audience, in order to enjoy humor, must "get" the joke. This means they must be capable of analyzing the cognitive frames presented by the actor and following the process of the creation of the humor.

Typically, humor involves four stages, the *setup*, the *paradox*, the *dénouement*, and the *release*. The setup involves the presentation of the original content material and the first interpretive frame. The paradox involves the creation of the additional frame or frames. The dénouement is the point at which the initial and subsequent frames are shown to co-exist, creating tension. The release is the enjoyment registered by the audience in the process of realization and the release resulting therefrom.

The communicative actor has a great deal to consider in creating humor. He or she must assess the audience carefully, particularly regarding their pre-existing knowledge. A large portion of the comic effect of humor involves the audience's taking a set interpretive frame for granted and then being surprised when the actor shows their assumptions to be unwarranted at the point of dénouement. Thus the actor creating humor must be aware of and use the audience's taken-for-granted knowledge effectively. Some of the simplest examples of such effective use involve playing on assumptions about the conventional meanings of words or conversational routines. Comedian Henny Youngman's classic one-liner "Take my wife . . . please!" is an excellent example. In just four words and a pause, Youngman double-frames the word *take*, showing two of its discourse usages: as an introduction to an example, and as a direct command/request. The double framing is completed by the word *please*. The pause is crucial. It allows the audience to set up an expectation that Youngman will be providing them with an example, which is then frustrated with his dénouement. In this way the work of comedians and the work of professional magicians is similar.

Humans structure the presentation of humor through numerous forms of culture-specific communicative events. All cultures have some form of the *joke*, a humorous narrative with the dénouement embodied in a *punchline*. Some of the best joke-tellers make their jokes seem to be instances of normal conversational narrative. Only after the punchline does the audience realize that the narrator has co-opted them into hearing a joke. In other instances, the joke is identified as such prior to its narration through a conversational introduction, and the audience expects and waits for the punchline. The joke is a kind of master form of humorous communication. Most other forms of humor can be seen as a variation of this form, even non-verbal humor.

Sigmund Freud theorized that jokes have only two purposes: aggression and exposure. The first purpose (which includes satire and defense) is fulfilled through the hostile joke, the second through the dirty joke. Humor theorists have debated Freud's claims extensively. The mechanisms used to create humor can be considered separately from the purposes of humor, but, as will be seen below, the purposes are important to the success of humorous communication.

Just as speech acts must be *felicitous*, in the Austinian sense, in order to function, jokes must fulfill a number of performative criteria in order to achieve a humorous effect and bring the audience to a release. These performative criteria center on the successful execution of the stages of humor creation.

The setup must be adequate. The actor must either be skilled in presenting the content of the humor or be astute in judging what the audience will assume from their own cultural knowledge, or from the setting in which the humor is created. The successful creation of the paradox requires that the alternative interpretive frame or frames be presented adequately and be plausible and comprehensible to the audience. The dénouement must successfully present the juxtaposition of interpretive frames. If the actor does not present the frames in a manner that allows them to be seen together, the humor fails.

If the above three communicational acts are carried out successfully, tension release in laughter should proceed. The release may be genuine or feigned. Jokes are such well-known communicational structures in most societies that audience members will smile, laugh, or express appreciation as a communicational reflex even when they have not found the joke to be humorous. The realization that people laugh when presentations with humorous intent are not seen as humorous leads to further question of why humor fails even if its formal properties are well structured.

One reason that humor may fail when all of its formal performative properties are adequately executed is – *homage* Freud – that the purpose of the humor may overreach its bounds. It may be so overly aggressive toward someone present in the audience or to individuals or groups they revere; or so excessively ribald that it is seen by the audience as offensive. Humor and offensiveness are not mutually exclusive, however. An audience may be affected by the paradox as revealed in the dénouement of the humor despite their ethical or moral objections and laugh in spite of themselves (perhaps with some feelings of shame). Likewise, what one audience finds offensive, another audience may find humorous.

Another reason humor may fail is that the paradox is not sufficiently surprising or unexpected to generate the tension necessary for release in laughter. Children's humor frequently has this property for adults. Similarly, the paradox may be so obscure or difficult to perceive that the audience may be confused. They know that humor was intended in the communication because they understand the structure of humorous discourse, but they cannot understand what it is in the discourse that is humorous. This is a frequent difficulty in humor presented cross-culturally, or between groups with specialized occupations or information who do not share the same basic knowledge.

In the end, those who wish to create humor can never be quite certain in advance that their efforts will be successful. For this reason professional comedians must try out their jokes on numerous audiences and practice their delivery and timing. Comedic actors, public speakers, and amateur raconteurs must do the same. The delay of the smallest fraction in time, or the slightest premature telegraphing in delivering the dénouement of a humorous presentation, can cause it to fail. Lack of clarity in the setup and in constructing the paradox can likewise kill humor. This essay has not dealt with written humor, but many of the same considerations of structure and pacing apply to humor in print as to humor communicated face-to-face.

(See also *control, genre, gesture, improvisation, metaphor, performativity, poetry, theater, truth*)

Bibliography

Beeman, William O.
　1981　Why Do They Laugh? An Interactional Approach to Humor in Traditional Iranian Improvisatory Theatre. Journal of American Folklore (special issue on folk theater, Thomas A. Green, ed.) 94(374):506–526.
Freud, Sigmund
　1963　Jokes and Their Relation to the Unconscious. Trans. James Strachey. New York: Norton.
Norrick, Neal R.
　1993　Conversational Joking: Humor in Everyday Talk. Bloomington: Indiana University Press.
Oring, Elliott
　1992　Jokes and Their Relations. Lexington: The University Press of Kentucky.
Sacks, Harvey
　1974　An Analysis of the Course of a Joke's Telling in Conversation. *In* Explorations in the Ethnography of Speaking. Richard Bauman and Joel Sherzer, eds. Pp. 337–353. Cambridge: Cambridge University Press.
Willeford, William
　1969　The Fool and His Sceptre: A Study in Clowns, Jesters and Their Audience. Evanston, IL: Northwestern University Press.

■ *Bruce Mannheim*

Iconicity

I conicity is a relationship between a sign and its object (often a linguistic pattern or another sign) in which the form of the sign recapitulates the object in some way. Charles Sanders Peirce defined an icon as a "sign by virtue of its own quality and [a] sign of whatever else partakes of that quality." Even the most "natural" looking icon, though, is mediated through social convention and subject to the historically specific interpretative habits of its users. Consider the skull-and-crossbones, which used to mark poisons. Some children interpreted the icon through an alternate set of conventions to mean "pirate food," and a concerted effort was made to replace it with another conventional icon, "Mister Yucky."

Peirce identified three main subtypes of icons: images, diagrams, and metaphors. Images "partake of the simple qualities" of their objects. They may be graphic, optical, perceptual, mental, or verbal – as W. J. T. Mitchell has observed – but what they have in common is that the form of the sign reflects its object directly and concretely. Sound images include verbal signs that are sometimes referred to as "sound symbolic" or "onomatopoeic." Diagrams are signs that represent the relations of the parts of their objects by analogous relationships among their own parts. It is commonplace in narrative, for example, for the order of narrative to diagram the order of narrated events. Metaphors are signs that represent "a parallel in something else," often through a vaguely sensed affinity. Constellations of words in which a similarity of form evokes a similarity of meaning, such as the *sl*-words in English (slip, slide, slush, sleaze, etc., described by Dwight Bolinger) are instances of metaphoric iconicity.

Iconicity has several key effects: It naturalizes one set of semiotic distinctions by referring it to another that is understood by the speakers to be more basic, essential, outside volitional control, or outside culture. It allows particular linguistic and cultural patterns to be referred to each other, such that they become mutually interpreting. Along the same vein, the alignment of structural forms across distinct cultural domains unifies cultural patterns; a song can be iconic of a textile. It fits the form of a speech event closely to the specific contours of its setting, making it compelling to the participants and providing cues that they use to interpret it. Finally, by bringing distinct cultural and linguistic structures into structural alignment it enhances their cognitive retention by individuals, as Dedre Gentner has shown. As a form of structural alignment, iconicity is important in both the transmission and persistence of cultural forms.

When signs are taken individually, they seem relatively unmotivated. When they are seen as parts of larger clusters – actions, patterns, texts, conversations, grammars, cultures – iconicity, and especially diagrammaticity, looms large in understanding how they cluster and interact, as pointed out by Paul Friedrich. All three Peircian subtypes of iconicity figure in ethnographic analyses, from the macro-organization of social systems to the micro-organization of the lexicon. The examples below illustrate the pervasiveness of iconicity in language-and-culture.

Naturalizes one set of semiotic distinctions by referring it to another: It is common for political systems to naturalize a particular social order by laying it out territorially and in calendrical time. For example, the Inka capital Cuzco (in the research of Zuidema, Sherbondy, and Bauer) was organized into a nested system of hierarchically ranked sightlines radiating from the ritual center. Each node was associated with a specific social segment, ranked according to its position in the system. The sightlines defined a set of irrigation districts, determining each group's rights to specific sources of water (and hence to specific agricultural lands). Social segments were associated with sacred places ranked along the same sightlines and were responsible for tending them on specific ritual occasions, sequenced by position on the system of sightlines. In short, the spatial organization of Inka Cuzco was a diagrammatic icon of the relationships among social segments, irrigation rights, and ritual responsibilities. Similarly, Richard Parmentier shows that social segmentation and hierarchy in Belau were made to seem natural and inevitable through diagrammatic iconicity.

"Click" (velar) sounds entered a Nguni speech of southern Africa, as discussed by Judith Irvine and Susan Gal, from neighboring Khoi languages, spreading through an Nguni speech register that expressed social distance and deference. Thus clicks came to be interpreted as icons of foreignness, both expressing the social distance implied by use of the respect register and naturalizing an essentialized social distance.

Allows particular linguistic and cultural patterns to become mutually interpreting: Among Kaluli in Melanesia, the *gisaro* ritual – discussed by Steven Feld and Edward L. Schieffelin – establishes a diagrammatic correspondence among a specific myth, the social orders of birds and humans, the ritual enactment of birdness by humans in the ritual. The tonal structure of song diagrams the calls of birds being enacted by ritual dancers. J. Becker and A. L. Becker showed that in Javanese the diagrammatic correspondence among melodic cycles, the organization of performance, and calendric cycles similarly unifies these domains. Barbara and Dennis Tedlock have shown that Quiché Mayan textiles can be read intertextually as diagrams of verbal texts-narratives and of divinatory performances, and vice versa.

The order of suffixes in the Southern Quechua verb (Mannheim) is a diagrammatic icon of the degree to which they express the subjective positions of participants in the speech event, such that the least deictic suffixes appear closer to the verb stem, with person and tense appearing near the end, and evidentials, which express the speaker's subjective orientation toward the message, appearing at the very end of the verb. In historical linguistics, morphological changes are partly predictable as shifts toward a diagrammatic economy of representation in which relationships among forms come to diagram their semantic relationships (Andersen), as Watkins has shown for the history of the Celtic person system.

Fits the form of a speech event closely to the specific contours of its setting: In lowland Ecuadorian Quichua narrative, iconic aspectual expressions punctuate narrative, creating a sense of verisimilitude linking the performance of the narrative with the events being described. In Nahuatl narrative, specific socially located "voices" are marked with characteristic intonations that allow listeners to track the voices across the narrative and connect the voices to their social locations. Roman Jakobson suggested that as a pragmatic principle of language, the default (or unmarked) setting is to treat the order of events in narrative as a diagrammatic icon of their order "in the world"; any non-default interpretation requires special narrative devices. Similarly, the hierarchy of conjoined nouns – by default – reflects the presupposed hierarchy of their referents.

In short, iconicity can inhere in virtually any aspect of language, culture, and society, making reference to the world assumed to be outside of language; to aspects of the social situation; to crystallized patterns elsewhere in the language or culture; to essentialized social domains; and from one piece of a text or of a social performance and another. One analytic goal of linguistic anthropologists and other ethnographers is to make these iconic linkages explicit.

(See also *ideophone, indexicality, media, narrative, orality, vision, writing*)

Bibliography

Andersen, Henning
    1980 Morphological Change: Towards a Typology. *In* Historical Morphology.
    Jacek Fisiak, ed. Pp. 1–50. The Hague: Mouton.
Benveniste, Emile
    1939 Nature du signe linguistique. Acta Linguistica Hafniensia 1:23–29.
Burks, Arthur W.
    1949 Icon, Index and Symbol. Philosophy and Phenomenological Research 9:679–
    689.
Friedrich, Paul
    1979 The Symbol and Its Relative Non-arbitrariness. *In* Language, Context, and
    the Imagination. Pp. 1–61. Palo Alto, CA: Stanford University Press.

Haiman, John
    1980   The Iconicity of Grammar. Language 56:515–540.
Irvine, Judith, and Susan Gal
    2000   Language Ideology and Linguistic Differentiation. *In* Regimes of Language:
        Language Ideologies and the Discursive Construction of Power and Identity.
        Paul Kroskrity, ed. Pp. 35–83. Santa Fe, NM: School of American Research
        Press.
Jakobson, Roman
    1965   Quest for the Essence of Language. Diogenes 51:21–37.
Nuckolls, Janis B.
    1996   Sounds Like Life: Sound-Symbolic Grammar, Performance, and Cog-
        nition in Pastaza Quechua. Oxford: Oxford University Press.
Peirce, Charles Sanders
    1955[1902]   Logic as Semiotic. *In* Philosophical Writings of Peirce. Justus Buchler,
        ed. Pp. 98–115. New York: Dover.
Tedlock, Barbara, and Dennis Tedlock
    1985   Text and Textile: Language and Technology in the Arts of the Quiché Maya.
        Journal of Anthropological Research 41:121–146.
Urban, Greg
    1991   A Discourse-centered Approach to Culture. Austin: University of Texas
        Press.

■ *Paul V. Kroskrity*

Identity

I dentity is defined as the linguistic construction of membership in one or more social groups or categories. Though other, non-linguistic criteria may also be significant, language and communication often provide important and sometimes crucial criteria by which members both define their group and are defined by others. Identities may be linguistically constructed both through the use of particular languages and linguistic forms (e.g., Standard English, Arizona Tewa) associated with specific national, ethnic, or other identities and through the use of communicative practices (e.g., greeting formulae, maintenance of mutual gaze, regulation of participation) that are indexed, through members' normative use, to their group. Language and communication are critical aspects of the production of a wide variety of identities expressed at many levels of social organization.

This typology of identity includes national, ethnic, racial, class and rank, professional, and gender identities. For hundreds of years, champions of nationalism and apologists for nation-states have used the notion of a shared language, and the common identity it was understood to represent, as a means of naturalizing political boundaries. Recent research on national identity by non-linguistic anthropologists, such as Benedict Anderson, has emphasized the importance of shared participation in literacy activities (like reading newspapers and popular novels) written in standardized, national languages, as a means of creating national identities. Ethnic and racial identities operate within nation-states as members (e.g., African- and Native American in the United States) deploy African-American Vernacular English or ancestral languages like Tewa as a means of expressing nested and/or alternative group membership both through these culturally distinctive linguistic forms and through the interactional use of discursive practices (e.g., indirection in African-American, traditionalism and purism in Arizona Tewa) that are valued within these ethnic/racial groups. Class and rank provide other examples of social identities that must be performed through use of appropriate linguistic forms. Members of the working class in urban neighborhoods, such as those of Belfast, often demonstrate a strong loyalty to class through their use of phonology and vocabulary that differ from the standardized forms endorsed and supported by the state. New Yorkers of the lower middle class display their recognition of the importance of language as an identity indicator by producing a wide range of pronunciation styles ranging from the local vernacular to the national standard. Kuna (Panama) chiefs, Samoan nobles, and the Arizona Tewa priestly elite all must display their high rank in part through specialized linguistic knowledge and communicative comportment. Professional identities are displayed in the use of specialized vocabularies of groups such as doctors and lawyers as well as in the routines of their disciplinary discourses (e.g., the medical interview, the Socratic dialogue that governs both the courtroom and the law school classroom). Gender identities are also established by the use of vocabulary and discursive practices which position the speaker with regard to cultural models of masculine and feminine speech behavior. The queer identities of gays and lesbians are communicatively produced in a similar fashion by redefining the gender opposition and indexing speech differences to an elaborated set of subculturally recognized gender identities and appropriate forms of display.

One thing this simplified typology of identities suggests is that even though it is conventional to talk about "language and identity," most of these different types of identity are neither exclusive nor singular. Though researchers sometimes focus on only one of these levels, individuals, as social actors, experience the multiplicity and interactivity of these levels, in their repertoires of identity. Distinctive ethnic identities of minority groups, for example, must be constructed from linguistic symbols and/or communicative practices that contrast with resources available for the construction of other ethnic identities or more generally available national identities. Women, in constructing professional identities, especially in fields formerly dominated by men, must simultaneously provide communicative evidence of professional competence and refuse compliance with inappropriate gendered stereotypes (e.g., expectations of accommodation, politeness). Some scholars have suggested that the use of language to communicate distinct identities has intensified in the contemporary, urbanized world as more interactional exchanges occur between relatively anonymous others or those who only know each other in a limited role or set of roles. Under circumstances where little is known about the other's biographical identity, interactants must provide in the here-and-now the communicative symbols by which they will be classified and assessed as persons. In so doing, individuals may engage in strategic communicative work that permits them to interactionally foreground or suppress specific identities. Though it is important to emphasize the role of communicative practices, like the strategic selection of codes from a linguistic repertoire or the patterned use of code-switching to signal discrete or hybridized identities, it is wrong to think that similar processes do not occur in smaller communities. In such societies, interaction typically occurs between people, often kin or fictive kin, who know each other in so many roles that they must interactionally establish which identity is situationally relevant.

The collective work in linguistic anthropology has contributed significantly to the appreciation of the role of linguistic and communicative microculture in the constructivist approach to identity that has emerged in anthropology and adjacent fields. But though this emphasis on identities, not as essentially given, but as actively produced – whether through deliberate, strategic manipulation or through out-of-awareness practices – both captures the agency of speakers and views language as social action, it has met with objection by some social scientists. They argue that the focus on an individual's freedom to manipulate a flexible system of identities fails to adequately take into account that some identities – most notably race and caste – are imposed and coercively applied. Though this perspective overstates the case by depicting political-economic factors as utterly determinative and top-down, this observation offers an admonition against any approach to identity, or identities, that does not recognize both the communicative freedom potentially available at the microlevel and the political economic constraints imposed on processes of identity-making.

(See also *agency, community, crossing, gender, ideology, indexicality, switching, variation, voice*)

Bibliography

Alonso, Ana Maria
   1994   The Politics of Space, Time and Substance: State Formation, Nationalism, and Ethnicity. Annual Review of Anthropology 23:379–405.
Anderson, Benedict
   1983   Imagined Communities: Reflections on the Origin and Spread of Nationalism. London: Verso.
Barth, Fredrik
   1969   Ethnic Groups and Boundaries. Boston: Little, Brown, and Company.
Basso, Keith H.
   1979   Portraits of "the Whiteman": Linguistic Play and Cultural Symbols among the Western Apache. Cambridge: Cambridge University Press.
Gumperz, John J., and Jenny Cook-Gumperz, eds.
   1982   Language and Social Identity. London: Cambridge University Press.
Irvine, Judith T., and Susan Gal
   2000   Language Ideology and Linguistic Differentiation. *In* Regimes of Language: Language Ideologies and the Discursive Construction of Power and Identity. Paul V. Kroskrity, ed. Pp. 35–83. Santa Fe, NM: School of American Research.
Kroskrity, Paul V.
   1993   Language, History, and Identity: Ethnolinguistic Studies of the Arizona Tewa. Tucson: University of Arizona Press.
Livia, Anna, and Kira Hall, eds.
   1997   Queerly Phrased: Language, Gender, and Sexuality. New York: Oxford University Press.

Ochs, Elinor
    1992   Indexing Gender. *In* Rethinking Context. Alessandro Duranti and Charles
        Goodwin, eds. Pp. 335–358. Cambridge: Cambridge University Press.
Zentella, Ana Celia
    1997   Growing Up Bilingual: Puerto Rican Children in New York. Malden, MA:
        Blackwell.

■ *Joseph Errington*

Ideology

L anguage ideology refers to the situated, partial, and interested character of conceptions and uses of language. It covers a wide range of concerns: the differential openness of language structure for metalinguistic objectification; the ways metalinguistic discourses can mediate social interests; the "naturalization" of social differences through construals of language as embodying identity and community. In these and other ways, "language ideology" is a rubric for dealing with ideas about language structure and use relative to social contexts.

I sketch here some intellectual trends and empirical issues in linguistic anthropology for which notions of language ideology have recently become salient. I discuss the notion first as part of linguistic anthropologists' responses to various critiques of received scholarly objectifications of "Language" and "languages." Then I sketch its role in the framing of language use as social practice, engaged in and construed from different perspectives in different contexts.

"Ideology" has become a central notion in critical studies of scholarly discourses on language, often ambiguous and conflicted, which have emerged in broader intellectual and political projects. In this regard it suggests self-reflexive awareness of the underlying comparability of "folk" and "expert" conceptions of language, and of the ways that covert interests can inform both. Both concerns can be read from influential critiques of post-Enlightenment conceptions of "language."

V. N. Vološinov, for instance, traced the "abstract objectivist" tendencies of Saussurean linguistics, and its eighteenth-century Romanticist antecedents, to Europe's early encounters with the rest of the world. In this way, he saw structural linguistics as having originated in and subserving a larger intellectual and political encounter with linguistic and cultural otherness. In broadly similar manner, Edward Said's influential critique of Orientalist colonial scholarship focused on the premises and effects of early comparative Semitic linguistics. The result is a powerful argument by example for recognizing covert political grounds of a scholarly tradition that, in one form or other, continues to be practiced throughout the formerly colonialized world.

110

Recognizing the interested partialness of such linguistic projects does not require the jettisoning of core descriptive notions as "discursive effects." Rather, it means explicating the sociohistorical grounds of their uses. One upshot has been the exploration of political and cultural contingencies that shaped the promotion of "dialects" into "languages" in parts of the world as different as Subsaharan Africa and Southeast Asia. Contemporary "facts" of linguistic and social difference are in this way understood as politically salient, invented linguistic traditions.

Concern for the ways social interests are inscribed in linguistic descriptions has also been stimulated by studies of Western societies, like Pierre Bourdieu's sociological account of academic institutions in France. He developed an influential critique of ambiguously descriptive "models of" and prescriptive "models for" the French language. He also assimilated language to a broad notion of "symbolic capital" in ways that resonate with assumptions and findings of variationist sociolinguistics. But it has been cogently questioned on empirical and theoretical grounds by anthropological linguists working in societies as close to France as Spanish Catalonia.

Increased interest in nationalism has similarly led linguistic anthropologists to study the rise and ideological grounds of secular, print-mediated national languages. In otherwise very different accounts, Ernest Gellner and Benedict Anderson have foregrounded the origins and effects of hegemonically standard languages. These comparative and theoretical issues have been recently recast within fine-grained work on language-linked enactments and conceptions of national and subnational identities (ethnic, class, gender, etc.).

Language ideology is relevant in these and other empirical studies that link verbal particulars to institutional contexts and interactional processes. In this regard, ideology stands in useful contrast to framings of talk as social practice to deal with situated interactional perspectives and social values, which can tacitly vary and shift between contexts and communities. This is a particularly important issue in scenes of social and linguistic contact, conflict, and change, where unrecognized and misrecognized differences in modes of interactional engagement arise.

Bilingualism and code-switching, language shift and language death, interference and borrowing, are all phenomena arising at such points of sociolinguistic encounter, and all require the social framing of patterned verbal particulars. Thought of as plural, often tacit, and sometimes conflictual, ideologically grounded perceptions of language use can be related to broader constellations of institutional forces, historical processes, and interests. Framed in these multiple ways, talk can be seen as a point of convergence between the immediacies of social life and the longer-term shaping of community, sameness, and difference.

In conclusion, the two spheres of research just sketched can be brought together under a still more abstract, semiotically keyed sense of language ideology. This is part of Michael Silverstein's explication of reflexive relations between languages as vehicles of structured semantic content, and objects of metadiscourse. By adducing the focal place of semantico-referential meaning in metadiscourse, he throws into relief the multiple indexical links between tokens and contexts of language use. This multiple spatio-temporal and social situatedness, and perceptions of such situatedness, can thus be brought under the semiotic profile inspired by Charles Peirce. The upshot is a concept of language ideology broad enough to speak to the foundational role of language in human life, and specifiable enough to help capture the perspectival complexities of languages in social contexts.

(See also *body, codes, contact, crossing, gender, grammar, identity, indexicality, names, power, socialization, syncretism, truth*)

Bibliography

Anderson, Benedict
    1991 Imagined Communities: Reflections on the Origin and Spread of Nationalism. 2nd ed. New York: Verso.
Bourdieu, Pierre
    1991 Language and Symbolic Power. G. Raymond and M. Adamson, trans. Cambridge, MA: Harvard University Press.
Gal, Susan, and Judith Irvine
    1995 The Boundaries of Languages and Disciplines: How Ideologies Construct Difference. Social Research 62(4):967–1001.
Schieffelin, Bambi B., Kathryn A. Woolard, and Paul V. Kroskrity, eds.
    1998 Language Ideologies: Practice and Theory. Oxford: Oxford University Press.
Silverstein, Michael
    1976 Shifters, Linguistic Categories, and Cultural Description. *In* Meaning in Anthropology. K. H. Basso and H. A. Selby, eds. Pp. 11–56. Albuquerque: University of New Mexico Press.
    1981 The Limits of Awareness. Sociolinguistic Working Papers 84. Austin, TX: Southwest Educational Development Laboratory.
    1996 Monoglot "Standard" in America: Standardization and Metaphors of Linguistic Hegemony. *In* The Matrix of Language: Contemporary Linguistic Anthropology. D. Brenneis and R. Macaulay, eds. Pp. 284–306. Boulder, CO: Westview Press.
Woolard, Kathryn
    1985 Language Variation and Cultural Hegemony: Toward an Integration of Sociolinguistic and Social Theory. American Ethnologist 12:738–747.
Woolard, Kathryn, and Bambi Schieffelin
    1994 Language Ideology. Annual Review of Anthropology 23:55–82.

■ *Dennis Tedlock*

Ideophone

Ideophones are words or phrases that do the work of representation by phonetic means. They are abundant in all known languages and constitute a counterforce to the arbitrariness of phonemes. It is naming that lies behind the Greek-derived term *onomatopoeia*, which simply means "to make names." Words described as onomatopoeic in English are called "picture words" in German (*Lautbilder*) and French (*mots images*). This reflects the fact that ideophones are often synesthetic, representing phenomena in sensory domains other than the auditory one.

The term *ideophone* first came into use among linguists specializing in African and especially Bantu languages. Most systematic studies of ideophones have been conducted by Africanists (for example, William Samarin and Lioba Moshi), and it was Samarin who developed a methodology for conducting such studies in the field. The early history of the interest in African ideophones is bound up with the history of attempts to construct stages of linguistic evolution. By now the study of ideophones has become a part of the Africanist subtradition in linguistics, independent of evolutionist theory. Serious studies of ideophones outside Africa are widely scattered; an important recent example is Janis Nuckolls' study of Quechua sound symbolism.

The marginal status of the study of ideophones has long been guaranteed by the central notion that languages are closed, conventional codes. In textbooks and introductory lectures, ever since Ferdinand de Saussure's lectures were published in his *Cours*, it has been customary to raise the issue of ideophones (under various names) only in order to dismiss it. It is argued that ideophones are rare, and that even the ones that purport to imitate non-linguistic sounds are arbitrary. The latter point is demonstrated by brief citations of cases in which different languages represent similar sounds in dissimilar ways. The focus is thus on the contrast between English *bow-wow* and French *ouaoua* rather than on the resemblance. But when allowances are made for differences in phonology, words that represent the same acoustic phenomenon can be quite similar between unrelated languages, as in *ky'alh*, the Zuni equivalent of English *splash*, and *xpurpuwek*, the K'iche' Maya rendition of the call of the bird whose English name is whippoorwill. Even linguists who engage in the serious study of ideophones often employ strategies that have the effect of limiting the role such phenomena might play in the general study of language. The narrowest limitation is achieved by restricting attention to words that include sounds not otherwise found among the phonemes of a given language. In the case of Zuni, this would mean separating words with a glottalized *ch'*, which is found only in verb stems that represent non-linguistic sounds, from verb stems whose representations involve glottalized consonants that have a wider distribution in Zuni. Thus *ch'uk'i-*, which evokes sounds like that of an eye popping out of its socket, would be classed as an ideophone, whereas *ts'ini-*, which evokes a tinkling sound, would not.

Some studies define as ideophonic only such words as can be placed in a separate syntactic class of their own. Alternatively, ideophones may be allowed to participate in classes that include non-ideophones, but the classes in question may be limited to such secondary ones as interjections, adjectives, adverbs, and particles. Such an approach may work in Bantu languages, where ideophones seem not to take the form of verbs, but in Amerindian languages they frequently do (as in the Zuni examples already given). As for nouns, an enormous problem is raised by birds and insects, whose names are frequently ideophonic in character. English examples include *killdeer, bobwhite, cricket,* and *katydid.* In Zuni, names of this kind include not only birds and insects, as with *kwiishahapak'o* for "robin" and *shonnalhik'o* for "housefly," but also mammals, as with *wahts'uts'ukya* for "chipmunk."

Reduplication, applied at the level of syllables or words or whole phrases, is a universal ideophonic phenomenon, as shown by Roman Jakobson and Linda Waugh. There are two major categories, one involving the repetition of an entire sound sequence and the other combining partial repetition with a change in a consonant or vowel. In K'iche', the routine call of the bird called *xar* (Steller's jay), represented as *xaw xaw xaw*, is interpreted as an indexical sign that a xar is nearby, but is otherwise regarded as meaningless. However, this bird sometimes makes a sound represented as *xaw xɪw*, with the second syllable completely unvoiced (indicated here by small capitals). This pair of syllables has the structure of a phonemic minimal pair, but it unites standard K'iche' phonemes with unvoiced versions of *i* and *w*, which are non-standard. It is interpreted as coming closer to human speech than the call involving simple repetition, and is consequently assigned greater meaning. It is an omen, warning of danger in the road ahead.

In English, ideophones referring to non-auditory domains are commonly constructed by means of partial reduplication (*willy-nilly, hoity-toity, roly-poly, heebie-jeebies, zigzag*). Words that are not ideophonic in themselves may be combined in phrases whose meaning derives from ideophonic repetitions (*row upon row, day after day, busy busy busy*) or partial contrasts (*here and there, black and blue, slip and slide*). Visual ideophones are ideographs turned inside out, in the sense that they are words whose sounds draw pictures instead of being pictures whose shapes evoke words. Concrete poems can be ideophonic and ideographic at one and the same time, as in the case of the poem by Carlo Belloli about trains that reads, "treni / i treni / i / iiiiiiiiiiii."

(See also *iconicity, indexicality, metaphor, meter, music, orality, poetry, writing*)

Bibliography

Belloli, Carlo
    1970   Untitled Poem. *In* Concrete Poetry: A World View. Mary Ellen Solt, ed. Fig. 81. Bloomington: Indiana University Press.
Hinton, Leanne, Johanna Nichols, and John J. Ahala (eds.)
    1994   Sound Symbolism. Cambridge: Cambridge University Press.
Jakobson, Roman, and Linda Waugh
    1979   The Sound Shape of Language. Bloomington: Indiana University Press.
Moshi, Lioba
    1993   Ideophones in KiVunjo-Chaga. Journal of Linguistic Anthropology 3:185–216.
Nuckolls, Janis B.
    1996   Sounds Like Life: Sound-Symbolic Grammar, Performance, and Cognition in Pastaza Quechua. Oxford: Oxford University Press.
Samarin, William J.
    1970   Field Procedures in Ideophone Research. Journal of African Languages 9:27–30.
    1971   Survey of Bantu Ideophones. African Language Studies 12:130–168.

■ R. Keith Sawyer

Improvisation

I mprovisation is an element of all performance genres that are not prescriptively notated, and is found in the performance genres of a wide range of cultures. Verbal genres that require improvisation include ritual, negotiation, gossip, greeting rituals, and conversation. Improvisation can be as basic as a performer's elaboration or variation of an existing framework – a song, ritual prayer, or traditional story. At the other extreme, in some forms of improvisation, the performers start without any advance framework and create the entire work on stage. Thus, improvisation is not an absolute, but a relative term, and is always in a dialectic with the pre-existing structures of verbal performance that, in large part, define a genre. A focus on improvisation is consistent with many recent trends in linguistic anthropology: the ethnography of speaking, the focus on verbal art and creativity, the emphasis on context rather than text.

This focus on performance is a late-twentieth-century development. In the first part of the twentieth century, ethnographic and folklore research focused on identifying "the text" of performance, in an attempt to identify and transcribe the invariant aspects of the performance text. These texts were often analyzed using tools and techniques originally developed to study written performance texts. However, unlike the study of performance texts – scores, scripts, and liturgies – the analysis of improvisational performance requires a fundamentally interactional semiotics, one that incorporates context, audience effects, performer creativity, and the balance of tradition and creativity.

In the 1960s and 1970s, some linguistic anthropologists and folklorists began a line of research called the *ethnography of speaking*. These researchers viewed folklore as a living, practiced tradition and thus explored the improvisational creativity of the performer, emphasizing that performance is a creative and emergent process. These researchers considered the dynamic interplay between the social, conventional, and ready-made in social life and the individual, creative, and emergent qualities of human existence.

Although many genres of verbal performance are extremely structured, linguistic anthropologists have documented variations even in the most formalized rituals. Thus all performances contain at least some degree of improvisation; a central concern of researchers is to document the relative contributions of tradition and individual agency in each performance and each genre. Terms such as *ritualization, routinization,* or *formalization* are used to describe the processes whereby verbal performances take on more structure. Conversely, even the most improvised performances involve structure and pre-determined materials. Research has focused on two types of structures within a genre: (1) short segments of formulaic speech and (2) scripted routines and overall performance templates. The former type, involving selection from paradigmatic sets of ready-mades, is quite common worldwide; examples include the parallel couplets of the island of Roti and the canonical Slavic epic poetry. The latter type – improvisation on a routine or within an overall template – is found in everyday conversational routines such as the *greeting rituals* studied by conversation analysts and in performance genres including storytelling, bridewealth negotiation, and marriage rituals.

Thus a fundamental empirical issue is the relative degree of improvisation and ritualization in a performance genre. Various analytic schemas have been proposed to allow researchers to characterize different genres of verbal interaction within a single framework. These analyses suggest that different types of verbal interaction, from ritual performance to ordinary conversation, must be characterized along a set of semiotic dimensions, rather than a single dimension from "ritualized" to "improvisational." The following are some of the dimensions along which different genres of performance can be contrasted:

Ossification. Ritualized genres are often in a dead language or use archaic speech forms, whereas improvised genres use contemporary registers.

Involvement of audience. More improvised genres tend to be more receptive to audience participation and interaction with the performers.

Resistance of genre to change. More improvised genres are more receptive to innovation.

Permanence of genre change. Although improvised genres are more receptive to change, those changes are more likely to be short-lived.

Cultural valuation. The more ritualized genres of a culture tend to be more culturally valued than the same culture's improvised genres.

Indexicality and metapragmatics. More improvised genres tend to require a more sophisticated use of indexicality, with speakers incorporating references to the specifics of the performance event. Likewise, they tend to require of the performer a more sophisticated use of metapragmatic techniques – the reflexive use of language to creatively regulate, or frame, the performance.

Breadth of genre definition. In a more improvised genre, a greater variety of performances will be considered to be tokens of the same event type (culturally defined). In a relatively ritualized genre, a much more narrow range of possible performances is considered to be an instance of the event type; a variation is simply viewed as an incorrect performance (often then losing its ritual effectiveness).

There are many promising areas for future research on these topics. Research is needed on how genres vary on these dimensions; to what degree the dimensions are interrelated; their cultural context, to develop a framework that can characterize the shifts in social purpose which co-vary with these dimensions; and the folk theories of performance within cultures, to determine how concepts of "improvisation" and "creativity" vary across culture and across genre.

(See also *genre, music, orality, oratory, performativity, prayer, theater*)

Bibliography

Bauman, Richard
   1977   Verbal Art as Performance. Prospect Heights, IL: Waveland Press.
Bauman, R., and J. Sherzer, eds.
   1974   Explorations in the Ethnography of Speaking. New York: Cambridge University Press.
Frost, Anthony, and Ralph Yarrow
   1990   Improvisation in Drama. London: Macmillan Press Ltd.
Nettl, Bruno, and Melinda Russell, eds.
   1998   In the Course of Performance: Studies in the World of Musical Improvisation. Chicago: University of Chicago Press.
Sawyer, R. Keith
   1996   The Semiotics of Improvisation: The Pragmatics of Musical and Verbal Performance. Semiotica 108(3/4):269–306.
   2000   Creating Conversations: Improvisation in Everyday Discourse. Cresskill, NJ: Hampton, Inc.
Sawyer, R. Keith, ed.
   1997   Creativity in Performance. Greenwich, CT: Ablex.
Schegloff, Emanuel A.
   1986   The Routine as Achievement. Human Studies 9:111–151.
Silverstein, Michael
   1993   Metapragmatic Discourse and Metapragmatic Function. *In* Reflexive Language. J. A. Lucy, ed. Pp. 33–58. New York: Cambridge University Press.

■ *William F. Hanks*

Indexicality

The term *indexicality* refers to the pervasive context-dependency of natural language utterances, including such varied phenomena as regional accent (indexing speaker's identity), indicators of verbal etiquette (marking deference and demeanor), the referential use of pronouns (I, you, we, he, etc.), demonstratives (this, that), deictic adverbs (here, there, now, then), and tense. In all of these cases, the interpretation of the indexical form depends strictly on the context in which it is uttered. To say that any linguistic form is "indexical" is to say that it stands for its object neither by resemblance to it, nor by sheer convention, but by contiguity with it. As Charles Peirce put it, an indexical sign stands in a relation of "dynamical coexistence" with its object. In other words, the indexical and what it stands for are in a sense co-present in the context of utterance.

Despite the broad scope of indexicality, the most familiar examples are natural language pronouns and deictics. If I utter "I want you to have this" while handing over a book to Madeleine, the forms "I, you, this" are indexical because they must be interpreted in relation to the situation of utterance. Thus the identical utterance form, if spoken in another situation, could pick out a different speaker and addressee, as well as a different object. Moreover, because indexicals encode little or no description of their referents, a form like "this" could as well be used to refer to a physical thing, an event ("this conference"), a period of time ("this Thursday"), or a place ("this is where I live"). In short, there is no inherent property of thisness, thatness, hereness or thereness that an object must display in order to be appropriately denoted by the corresponding indexicals. Instead, what indexicals encode are the relations between objects and contexts (e.g., proximal, distal, speaker, addressee, simultaneous, antecedent). It is this link to context that secures uniqueness of reference even without description. Part of what makes this possible is the directive function of indexicals, whereby they direct an addressee to look, listen, or take an object in hand. Similarly, the close association between indexicals and gestures (pointing, showing, handing over) helps to anchor them in the interactive field of utterance, what Karl Bühler called the "demonstrative field."

Most indexicals can be used either exophorically, in reference to objects in the speech setting, or anaphorically, in reference to objects mentioned in prior discourse. Similarly, most can be used alone (this), or elaborated with lexical description (this book). Deictic forms typically vary in referential scope according to the situation. Thus "here" can as well be used to denote a point on the speaker's own body, the immediate space of utterance, the area, building, region, country, hemisphere in which the utterance occurs, or indeed the entire earth. It is an empirical question how variable the scope of a given form in any language is, and how many degrees of remove from the utterance space are lexically distinguished in the language (cf. English *here/there* vs. French *ici/là/là-bas*). Another defining feature of indexicals is that they systematically shift in reported speech. So "I'll stay here with you" becomes "he said he'd stay there with me." Inversely, in verbatim quotation, the current speaker uses indexicals that are anchored not in the current context but in some other, as when George tells Terry what Jack said to Madeleine, saying "Jack told Madeleine 'Here, I want you to have this'." Notice that the indexicals in the embedded quotation refer not to George and Terry, as they would normally do, but to Jack and Madeleine. Thus, just as indexicals are anchored to utterance context, so, too, they may be transposed from the current context into other ones, recalled, imagined or merely projected. Indeed, these forms are among the most central resources in human languages for tracking references both within and across contexts.

In recent decades, there has been a growing interest in the study of indexicals, both referential and non-referential. This research has demonstrated that indexicality is a universal feature of human languages, that all referential-indexical systems (including pronouns, demonstratives, and deictics) share a number of specific properties, and that indexical relations are crucial to contextual inference, reflexivity, and semantic interpretation more generally. It has also become clear that processes of indexical anchoring are more subtle and complex than hitherto appreciated, and that they cannot be understood without relatively deep analysis of the social and cultural contexts of speech. At the same time, the formidable abstractness of indexicality as classically defined, and the sheer variety of things the term is applied to, raise the question of whether there is any significant unity to the category. Furthermore, the lack of an established methodology for studying the phenomenon has made it difficult to compare indexical forms or paradigms across languages. Ultimately, the concept of contiguity on which indexicality is based must be defined relative to local standards of co-presence and relevance. This implies that the universality of the phenomenon in human languages is offset by the highly culture-specific ways in which indexicals are structured and interpreted. These are among the central problems facing contemporary research on the topic, and it is only through fine-grained empirical work that they will be resolved.

(See also *body, crossing, functions, gesture, grammar, iconicity, inference, names, reflexivity, vision, voice*)

Bibliography

Benveniste, Emile
  1974   Le langage et l'expérience humaine. *In* Problèmes de linguistique générale. Vol. 2. Pp. 67–78. Paris: Gallimard.
Bühler, Karl
  1990[1934]   Theory of Language: The Representational Function of Language. D. F. Goodwin, trans. Amsterdam and Philadelphia: John Benjamins.
Goffman, Erving
  1981   Forms of Talk. Pp. 124–159. Philadelphia: University of Pennsylvania Press.
Hanks, William F.
  1990   Referential Practice: Language and Lived Space among the Maya. Chicago: University of Chicago Press.
Kaplan, David
  1978   On the Logic of Demonstratives. *In* Contemporary Perspectives in the Philosophy of Language. Peter A. French, Theodore E. Uehling, Jr., and Howard K. Wettstein, eds. Pp. 401–412. Minneapolis: University of Minnesota Press.
Levinson, Stephen
  1983   Pragmatics. Cambridge: Cambridge University Press.
Peirce, Charles S.
  1955   Logic as Semiotic: The Theory of Signs. *In* Philosophical Writings of Peirce. J. Buchler, ed. Pp. 98–119. New York: Dover Publications.
Putnam, Hilary
  1975   The Meaning of "Meaning." *In* Mind, Language and Reality. Philosophical Papers, Vol. 2. London: Cambridge University Press.
Schutz, Alfred
  1967   The Phenomenology of the Social World. G. Walsh and F. Lehnert, trans. Evanston, IL: Northwestern University Press.
Silverstein, Michael
  1976   Shifters, Linguistic Categories, and Cultural Description. *In* Meaning in Anthropology. K. Basso and H. Selby, eds. Pp. 11–55. Albuquerque: University of New Mexico Press.

■ *Barbara Johnstone*

Individual

For the most part, linguistic theory makes statements about languages rather than about speakers, conceptualizing its object of study in such a way as to exclude from consideration individual voices and individuals' choices. The idea that language is most clearly seen as an abstract system, located in the social realm, has its roots in the foundational texts of twentieth-century structuralism. But anyone who thinks about linguistic variation and change is forced to confront questions about the relationships between individual speakers and languages. Some nineteenth-century comparative linguists, asking the still troublesome "actuation question" about how changes in linguistic systems get started, argued that change begins in creative choices by individuals. In the twentieth century, linguistic anthropologists such as Edward Sapir, Dell Hymes, and Paul Friedrich repeatedly stressed the importance of thinking about language from the perspective of the individual as well as from the social perspective.

Underlying this view is the observation that language is fundamentally the property of the individual. This is true whether language is defined as competence (no two speakers have the same set of experiences from which to generalize, so no two speakers could possibly have exactly the same knowledge of language) or whether language is defined as discourse (even in settings in which ideological individualism – the valuation of individuality and its expression – does not play the role it does in Western societies, different people speak differently and say different things). Emile Benveniste argued, in fact, that it is precisely language that creates phenomenological individuality: language makes subjectivity possible via (universal) systems of grammatical person, forcing us to categorize the world into self and others.

Thinking about language from the perspective of the individual means re-examining conventional wisdom about how utterances come to be and how they are interpreted. For example, theories of pragmatics typically describe the process of interpretation as based in conventions shared by communities: people can interpret utterances if they can parse them into allowable patterns, if they have heard them before, or if they depart from familiar structures or formulas in conventional ways. But while conventionality is without a doubt crucial in interpretation – we far more often decide what an utterance means with reference to familiar patterns of structure and use than completely de novo – speakers can and do cope with linguistic novelty. This happens most obviously in the context of verbal artistry, in interlinguistic or intercultural communication, and in early childhood. However, since no two individuals could completely share sets of conventions, interpreting forms and strategies that are completely new is an aspect of all meaning-making. If we take this aspect of discourse as fundamental, we need a theory of pragmatics that sees its basic task as explaining how general cognitive strategies for interpretation are deployed rather than just how pre-existing conventions are accessed. Rules and conventions, in this view, are convenient shortcuts to interpretations, useful in cases of relatively conventional ways of meaning, rather than being the basic mechanism by which meanings are computed.

Standard accounts of linguistic variation and change are also framed on the abstract level of the speech community. Individuals are operationalized as bundles of demographic characteristics, and, in the traditional variationist view, an individual's linguistic behavior is implicitly seen as determined by these characteristics. (Women speak the way they do because they are women, working-class speakers because they are working-class, and so on.) Some more recent accounts supplement this model with the important observation that ideologies – beliefs about what social and linguistic facts mean – play a key mediating role. But social facts and linguistic facts, ideologies and ways of speaking, are also mediated by individual speakers. The actual mechanisms by which variation comes to have meaning and patterns of language use come to change can only be seen in situated choices (often unconscious but sometimes not) by individuals creating unique ways to sound, to be, and to respond to specific rhetorical exigencies.

Thinking about variation from the individual outward rather than from the social inward means thinking about how individuals create voices by selecting and combining the linguistic resources available to them, resources which may be relatively codified, shared, and consistent (such as a school-taught standard variety or a stylized, out-group representation of a non-standard variety) or which may be highly idiosyncratic, identified with particular situations or people rather than with groups ("the way my mother talks," for instance). Not all speakers have access to the same variety of resources. For example, the people in the relatively homogeneous, relatively isolated communities that were traditionally the focus of research by dialectologists, sociolinguists, and anthropological linguists may in some cases have had a relatively limited range of available ways of speaking and evaluating speech, and may accordingly have sounded more like one another and shared more norms for evaluating what variability meant. But completely homogeneous speech communities have always been a theoretical idealization, and even relatively homogeneous communities are less and less typical, so it is increasingly evident that our models need to describe speakers in more mobile, heterogeneous social worlds as well.

Working outward from the individual also helps in rethinking questions about other concepts developed with reference to abstract collectivities and ways of speaking: What is a language, for example? What is a speech community? What does it mean to be bilingual? It is being increasingly suggested that the questions that define linguistics can only be answered in full with reference to the particular, by recasting questions about the social as questions about the individual, questions about language as questions about discourse, questions about rules and constraints as questions about strategies and resources. Taking the perspective of the individual on language and discourse means shifting to a more rhetorical way of imagining how communication works, a way of thinking about communication that incorporates ideas such as strategy, purpose, ethos, agency (and hence responsibility), and choice. It also means a shift to the sort of methodological particularity that A. L. Becker calls "modern philology," in which work in the bottom-up, inside-outward cases-and-interpretations mode supplements work of the more traditional sort.

(See also *acquisition, community, contact, crossing, ideology, improvisation, intentionality, maxim, names, reconstruction, relativity, variation, voice*)

Bibliography

Becker, A. L.
   1995   Beyond Translation: Essays toward a Modern Philology. Ann Arbor: University of Michigan Press.
Cohen, Anthony P.
   1994   Self Consciousness: An Alternative Anthropology of Identity. London: Routledge.
Friedrich, Paul, and James Redfield
   1979   Speech as a Personality Symbol: The Case of Achilles. *In* Language, Context, and the Imagination: Essays by Paul Friedrich. Anwar S. Dil, ed. Pp. 402–440. Stanford, CA: Stanford University Press.
Hymes, Dell
   1979   Sapir, Competence, Voices. *In* Individual Differences in Language Ability and Language Behavior. Charles Fillmore, Daniel Kempler, and William S. Y. Wang, eds. Pp. 33–45. New York: Academic Press.
Johnstone, Barbara
   1996   The Linguistic Individual: Self-Expression in Language and Linguistics. New York: Oxford University Press.
Johnstone, Barbara, and Judith Mattson Bean
   1997   Self-Expression and Linguistic Variation. Language in Society 26:221–246.
LePage, Robert B., and Andrée Tabouret-Keller
   1985   Acts of Identity: Creole-based Approaches to Language and Ethnicity. Cambridge: Cambridge University Press.
Macaulay, Ronald K. S.
   1991   Locating Dialect in Discourse: The Language of Honest Men and Bonnie

Lassies in Ayr. New York and Oxford: Oxford University Press.
Milroy, James
   1992   Linguistic Variation and Change. Oxford and Cambridge, MA: Blackwell.
Sperber, Dan, and Dierdre Wilson
   1986   Relevance: Communication and Cognition. Cambridge, MA: Harvard University Press.

■ *John J. Gumperz*

Inference

Individuals engaged in a verbal encounter do not just rely on literal or denotational meaning to interpret what they hear. At issue is communicative intent – that is, what a speaker attempts to convey at a particular time and place in the interaction, not what an utterance means in the abstract. More often than not, listeners build on what they remember about preceding talk, their expectations about what is to follow, as well as on culturally specific background knowledge acquired through previous communicative experience, in order to fill in for what is left unsaid. I use the term *inference* or *conversational inference* to refer to the mental operations we engage in to retrieve such knowledge and integrate it into the interpretive process. The notion has become familiar to students of everyday communication through the writings of anthropologist Dan Sperber and linguist Deirdre Wilson, who argue that theories that treat meaning as directly transmitted via codes assuming a one-to-one relationship of sound to thought are inadequate to explain the facts of everyday discourse. Following philosopher Paul Grice, they suggest that everyday interpretive processes are akin to scientists' deductions from experimental evidence. From this perspective, talk can be treated as communicative practice, a form of goal-oriented human action, and as such its interpretation is contingent on power relations as well as culturally based typifications and premises. Consider the following illustrative example.

As I was driving home from the office one evening, my car radio was tuned to a classical music station. The announcer, a replacement for the regular host who was about to return, signed off with the following words: "I'VE enjoyed being with YOU these last two weeks." I had not been listening closely but the unexpected prosodic highlighting of "I've" and "you" in unmarked syntactic position (here indicated by capitals) caught my attention. It sounded as if the speaker were producing the first part of a formulaic leave-taking sequence. But since he did not follow up with the expected second part, "I hope YOU have enjoyed being with ME," I hypothesized he was relying on his audience to infer, from the way he had used prosody to contextualize his talk, that this is what he intended to convey or, to use Grice's term, implicate. Several points are worth noting here: (1) We rely on such inferencing both to interpret content and to construct the contextual premises or presuppositions in terms of which content is understood. (2) Although my interpretation goes beyond what was literally said, it is important to note that inferences here are directly grounded in linguistic form. (3) To the extent it builds on listeners' ability to perceive and recall interdiscursive relationships learned through shared communicative experience, the inferential process is by its very nature culture-bound. Culture, when seen in these terms, becomes a resource we rely on to participate in situated discursive practice. (4) Finally, the interpretation is not the only possible one; there are always many possible interpretations. The interpretive process yields plausible assessments that must then be either confirmed or defeated by what follows in the exchange. That is, it is the discursive exchange as a whole rather than an individual utterance that constitutes the basic unit of analysis. The following example illustrates this.

Two students sitting in a coffee shop are gossiping about their landlords: A: "But she's a FLAKE." B (fast tempo): "Ya know we should probably watch it. They're probably sitt'n there." A (overlapping B's last three words): "I know." B: "It's just nice going to cafes now and I feel like I don't have to avoid anybody." A (overlapping B's last three words): "THIS is the LIFE." To those familiar with American student culture, the exchange seems perfectly understandable; moreover, from the way the two respond, overlapping each other's turn, they seem in perfect agreement. But surface meaning of component utterances alone does not indicate how the talk coheres. Only if we assume that B's phrase about not having "to avoid anybody" indirectly indexes or evokes a normative principle – "do not gossip about people when there is a chance they can hear you" – does her reply make sense. When A replies with an overlapping "I know," we conclude that the two are engaging in shared inferencing. This is then confirmed at the end where the two jointly manage a change in theme to coffee shop life, again with overlapping turns. In other words, by focusing on the inferencing and the extent to which it is shared, we come to see the exchange as a cohesive whole that alludes to students' cultural worlds and the attendant tensions between the satisfactions of peer life and the adult world of landlords, where power and inequality are inevitably at work.

Comparative analyses of discursive practice following the above principles can account both for shared inferencing and the societal forces that affect it. If carried out in a representative sample of discursive encounters and human societies, such analyses should not just provide insights into how inferencing works. They should also show how and in what ways the inferential process is culture-bound. Cultural knowledge and power come to be seen as integrally involved in discourse. The ways in which they work are subject to empirical analyses that do not depend on a priori assumptions about ethnicity or group membership. In this way, discourse analyses may among other things show how communicative practices create and maintain cultural identity.

(See also *identity, indexicality, intentionality, maxim, power, reflexivity, truth*)

Bibliography

Clark, Herbert
  1992   Arenas of Language Use. Chicago: University of Chicago Press.
Duranti, Alessandro, and Charles Goodwin, eds.
  1992   Rethinking Context: Language as an Interactive Phenomenon. Cambridge: Cambridge University Press.
Garfinkel, Harold
  1967   Studies in Ethnomethodology. Englewood Cliffs, NJ: Prentice-Hall.
Grice, Paul
  1989   Studies in the Way of Words. Cambridge, MA: Harvard University Press.
Gumperz, John
  1982   Discourse Strategies. Cambridge: Cambridge University Press.
Hanks, William F.
  1996   Language and Communicative Practices. Boulder, CO: Westview Press.
Lucy, John A., ed.
  1993   Reflexive Language. Cambridge: Cambridge University Press.
Sperber, Dan, and Deirdre Wilson
  1986   Relevance. Oxford: Basil Blackwell.

■ *Alessandro Duranti*

Intentionality

In the philosophical tradition started by the Scholastics and later revived by Franz Brentano and Edmund Husserl, intentionality is the property of human consciousness of being directed toward or being about something (another term for this notion of intentionality is "aboutness"). This notion of intentionality should be distinguished from the commonsense notion associated with the doing of something on purpose (as in "I had no intention of hurting anybody") or according to a plan (as in "My intention was to write a book"). The substitution of the first concept with the second is a common source of theoretical confusion.

Husserl is responsible for the most thorough discussion of intentionality so far. In a line of argument that is reminiscent of Gottlob Frege's distinction between "sense" (*Sinn*) and "reference" (*Bedeutung*), Husserl distinguished between the intentional act (produced by the thinking, perceiving Subject) and the entity (or Object) about which the act occurs. Just like Frege had argued that it is possible to identify the same referent with different definite descriptions, each of which has a different meaning (for him, "sense") (e.g., we can identify Bill Clinton as "the President" or "Hillary's husband"), Husserl argued that a distinction is necessary between intentional acts and their Object (Frege's "reference"). While the Object may stay the same, the acts may change. For example, we can admire, despise, observe, or ignore the same person (or the same thing, idea, act, etc.). Husserl diverged from Frege in insisting that the meaning is always an act, that is, an intentional experience. The focus on acts as opposed to entities provided the foundations for Husserl's phenomenology: meanings are constituted in our consciousness through the different ways in which we engage with the world (whether real or imaginary). It is the ability to engage in such acts that makes us meaning-making individuals. It is the same ability that allows for communication to take place. For Husserl, sounds, gestures, or marks on a piece of paper become meaningful when they can be interpreted as produced by entities (e.g., human beings) who are judged capable of experiencing intentional acts, including the (rather complex) act of wanting their experiences (e.g., feelings, beliefs, wishes) communicated to others.

Intentionality plays an important role in J. L. Austin's theory of speech acts, Paul Grice's theory of meaning, and John Searle's theory of mind (an extension of his theory of speech acts). Intentionality is also seen as an important dimension for assessing children's cognitive development and evolution. Primatologists and other researchers have posited different levels of intentionality to distinguish between human intelligence and the intelligence of other species or that of machines. For example, Dorothy L. Cheney and Robert M. Seyfarth used Daniel Dennett's hierarchy of intentional systems for assessing the cognitive abilities of vervet monkeys. Zero-order intentional systems cannot have beliefs or desires. First-order intentional systems have beliefs and desires (e.g., "x believes/wants that p"), whereas second-order intentional systems have beliefs and desires about beliefs and desires (e.g., "x wants y to believe that p"), and so on. A third-order intentional system is needed for what Grice called "non-natural" meaning (typical of human communication): "for A to mean something by x ... A must intend to induce by x a belief in an audience, and he must also intend his utterance to be recognized as so intended."

Grice's and other rationalist accounts of human action typically rely on a commonsense view of people's beliefs and desires. For anthropologists, the crucial issue is whether it is possible to separate intentional acts from the cultural context in which they are produced. Since the route to interpretation relies on conventionality as much as on intentionality, it is possible, and in fact quite common, that an audience may respond to what they judge to be contextually relevant conventions, ignoring the issue of the speaker's intentions. Ethnographers have also shown that the view that one can know what goes on in another person's mind is not shared by all cultures, and a difference in power or authority, sometimes defined in terms of expertise, may grant some individuals or groups the right to interpret while depriving others of the right to reclaim their original intentions. Furthermore, when we abandon imagined exchanges and look at actual interaction, we learn that participants cannot always know what their actions or words are meant to achieve, as shown by John Heritage for the particle *Oh!* in English.

Another line of research on intentionality is informed by the critique of Husserl's paradigm by his students and collaborators. For example, Martin Heidegger – who had been Husserl's assistant – built on the phenomenological approach but reframed intentionality as a derived rather than primordial capacity of human beings. Our intentional acts – and, ultimately, what we call rationality and science – are founded on a pre-theoretical being-in-the-world as a structure of human concern (or "care") always projected ahead of itself and filled with objects that are first and foremost understood pragmatically, that is, in terms of their use. Heidegger argued that meaning does not come from our intentional acts but from temporality, that is, the finitude that characterizes human life. A number of poststructuralist theorists have built on some of Heidegger's intuitions, working on a concept of intentionality (sometimes called "cognition") as distributed through acts of participation in culturally constructed activities. Pierre Bourdieu's notion of *habitus* as a system of dispositions that guide people's intentionality in routinized activities is in this tradition. Other social scientists have highlighted the importance of tools (e.g., maps, measuring instruments) as well as the collaborative work of others in constituting what at first appear as individual intentional acts but under better scrutiny turn out to be collective (albeit not necessarily equally shared) accomplishments. Collaboration is certainly at work in development, when children learn to communicate through interactions with more competent members who guide, name, and reframe their intentional acts. The intersubjective construction of intentionality has been recently emphasized by linguistic anthropologists and other scholars who take seriously the view that language is a major resource for introspection and mutual monitoring.

(See also *agency, control, evolution, expert, maxim, names, participation, socialization, vision, writing*)

Bibliography

Cohen, Philip R., Jerry Morgan, and Martha E. Pollack
    1990   Intentions in Communication. Cambridge, MA: MIT Press.
Dennett, Daniel C.
    1987   The Intentional Stance. Cambridge, MA: MIT Press.
Duranti, Alessandro
    1993   Intentionality and Truth: An Ethnographic Critique. Cultural Anthropology 8:214–245.
Grice, H. P.
    1957   Meaning. Philosophical Review 67:53–59.
Heidegger, Martin
    1985   History of the Concept of Time. Prolegomena. Theodore Kisiel, trans. Bloomington: Indiana University Press.
Heritage, John
    1990–91   Intention, Meaning and Strategy: Observations on Constraints on Interaction Analysis. Research on Language and Social Interaction 24:311–332.
Hill, Jane H., and Judith T. Irvine
    1993   Responsibility and Evidence in Oral Discourse. Cambridge: Cambridge University Press.
Husserl, Edmund
    1970   Logical Investigations. J. N. Findlay, trans. New York: Humanities Press.
Rosen, Lawrence
    1995   Other Intentions. Santa Fe, NM: School of American Research.
Searle, John R.
    1983   Intentionality: An Essay in the Philosophy of Mind. Cambridge: Cambridge University Press.

■ *Charles L. Briggs*

Interview

Interviewing constitutes one of the most fascinating and poorly investigated realms of social scientific and linguistic inquiry. Practitioners in a range of disciplines rely on interviews, and the widespread use of interviewing by journalists, providers of social services, physicians, and employers, as well as the emphasis that politicians and corporations place on surveys, point to the central role that interviews play in creating the institutional structures of modern societies. For members of dominant sectors of society, interviewing simply becomes part of commonsense linguistic practice. Practitioners may also be reluctant to subject interviews to too profound a critique in view of their efficacy as means of imbuing social scientific discourses with authority. Although most researchers assume that interviews are relatively simple, straightforward, and well understood, the limited number of works that investigate the discursive foundations of interviewing in depth rather point to their complexity.

The major mode of structuring interviews is the recursive use of question–answer pairs, often with follow-up Q&A sequences (generally termed "probes"). The participation framework of interviews is organized around a central, asymmetrical opposition: the interviewer asks the questions, the respondent answers them, and the interviewer then signals when she or he considers the response adequate (by asking a new question). Formal or structured interviews are pragmatically distinct from informal, unstructured ones. The former involve the use of a predetermined set of questions, and their presentation by an interviewer is standardized as much as possible: questions are to be read as printed and presented in the same order. The standardization of responses may be maximized through the use of closed questions, in which the interviewee must choose between preselected alternatives. In survey interviews, professional social scientists write questions that reflect their research interests and chosen methodology. The researchers then hire a staff of interviewers, who are generally not social scientists, instruct them in how they are to present questions, and assign lists of interviewees that are produced by sampling techniques. Formal interviews are thus structured by an absent party, one who also controls rights to interpret the discourse, a fascinating sort of ventriloquism.

Informal interviews are generally conducted by the researchers themselves. While lists of questions are often prepared in advance, exact wordings and the order of presentation emerge in the course of the interview. Since the range of possible responses is less constrained, respondents are often invited to use a wider range of discursive forms (such as narratives). Unstructured interviews are generally associated with qualitative research and structured interviews with quantitative approaches; the work of William Labov and other sociolinguists suggests, however, that open questions posed during relatively unstructured phases of an interview may also be analyzed quantitatively. While formal interviewing constitutes an attempt to maximize reliability (that is, to reduce the effects of situational and interactional dynamics on data), open-ended methods stress validity, the accuracy of a given technique in measuring the phenomena in question. Critical perspectives suggest that reliability and validity are not only contradictory goals but are powerful textual constructions.

Recent attempts to incorporate issues of power and political economy into research on discourse suggest that studies of interviews can provide important perspectives on broader social questions. Michel Foucault played a key role in shifting the study of discourse to concerns with relations of power in broader institutional contexts. As Richard Bauman and Charles Briggs and others have argued, a vital part of the process of rendering discourse socially powerful is to gain control over its recontextualization – rights to determine when, where, how, and by whom it will be used in other settings. Interview discourse is maximally configured in terms of both form and content for recontextualization into the sorts of texts that the researcher anticipates creating – interviewees are granted very few rights over this process. In survey research, "instruments" (lists of questions) and techniques for "implementing" them maximize the social control of interviewers by the researchers who direct the study as well of interviewees by interviewers, creating hierarchies of discursive authority that also include individuals responsible for coding data. As Aaron Cicourel, Ann Oakley, and Américo Paredes suggested long ago, however, respondents often attempt to resist the discursive constraints imposed in both formal and informal interviews.

Drawing on research in linguistic anthropology, Pierre Bourdieu argues that forms of communicative competence constitute symbolic capital, the acquisition of which is constrained by such gate-keeping institutions as schools and professional societies. Interviews are used by members of dominant sectors in furthering their institutionalized needs, such as the compilation of census information and the use of surveying in enhancing consumption or devising political rhetoric. Dominated communities are common targets for interview projects.

Interviews currently form a crucial facet of the process of generating notions of both the public and political sphere. Implicit models of interviewing construct notions of public culture in individualist ways in that they view questions and answers as discrete units of information and interviewees as bundles of separable demographic characteristics, behaviors, and attitudes; groups and societies can then be pictured as statistical aggregates. Bourdieu and others have suggested that polling is thus as much a form of political imagination as a scientific measurement of "public opinion."

These perspectives are cross-cut by the recent interest in ideologies of language – explicit and implicit notions of communication, text, language, and speech held by scholars and laypersons alike. These ideologies play a key role in constructing hierarchies of communicative practices, texts, professional discourses, genres, and styles. In turn, the people, disciplines, and institutions are stratified by virtue of how they are linked to these ideologically charged forms; the process works the other way round as well. The complexity of interviews emerges, in part, from the manner in which multiple ideologies and practices intersect in the research process, rendering questions and answers as well as the texts that recontextualize them heterogeneous and complex. At the same time that interviews embody and impose dominant linguistic ideologies, they provide sites for constructing alternative identities and practices.

Exploring questions regarding discursive practices and language ideologies is thus not only requisite to constructing and interpreting interviews but also for showing how research that takes interviews as objects rather than simply as tools can yield insights into central issues in social theory.

(See also *community, control, genre, ideology, improvisation, participation, power, truth*)

Bibliography

Bauman, Richard, and Charles L. Briggs
  1990 Poetics and Performance as Critical Perspectives on Language and Social Life. Annual Review of Anthropology 19:59–88.
Bourdieu, Pierre
  1979[1972] Public Opinion Does Not Exist. *In* Communication and Class Struggle. Vol. 1. Pp. 124–130. New York: International General.
  1991 Language and Symbolic Power. Gino Raymond and Matthew Adamson, trans. Cambridge, MA: Harvard University Press.
Briggs, Charles L.
  1986 Learning How to Ask: A Sociolinguistic Appraisal of the Role of the Interview in Social Science Research. Cambridge: Cambridge University Press.
Cicourel, Aaron V.
  1974 Theory and Method in a Study of Argentine Fertility. New York: Wiley Interscience.
Foucault, Michel
  1980 Power/Knowledge: Selected Interviews and Other Writings, 1972–1977. Colin Gordon et al., trans. New York: Pantheon.
Labov, William
  1972 Some Principles of Linguistic Methodology. Language in Society 1(1): 97–120.

Mishler, Elliot G.
  1986   Research Interviewing: Context and Narrative. Cambridge, MA: Harvard University Press.
Oakley, Ann
  1981   Interviewing Women: A Contradiction in Terms. *In* Doing Feminist Research. H. Roberts, ed. Pp. 30–61. London: Routledge and Kegan Paul.
Paredes, Américo
  1977   On Ethnographic Work among Minority Groups: A Folklorist's Perspective. New Scholar 7:1–32.

■ *Niko Besnier*

Literacy

L iteracy can be roughly defined as communication through visually decoded inscriptions, rather than through auditory and gestural channels. Literacy as a human activity has lurked in the background of both anthropological and linguistic research throughout its history, thought about but not investigated systematically, borne in mind but marginalized. Social anthropologists have long speculated on the peculiar thinking processes, social structures, and cultural patterns that characterize literate individuals and groups. Until not long ago, linguists viewed literacy as what linguistics does not study, a reaction, in part, to the association in popular thinking of written language with prescriptive normativity. Only in recent decades have these speculations and negative definitions given way to systematic investigations and a more centralized focus in both disciplines.

Several identifiable currents underlie contemporary research on literacy in linguistic anthropology. First, attempts to deconstruct age-old statements about the fundamental differences between literate and pre-literate societies have led researchers to explore the vast patterns of diversity covered under the umbrella term "literacy." (And, of course, the same statement can be made about orality, which is often contrasted with literacy, as Alan Rumsey discusses in this volume.) For example, the pedagogical literacy that children practice at school and the literacy activities that their parents engage in at home can differ widely. Similarly, literacy in the workplace, during leisure time, in the courtroom, and at church all have particular characteristics, associations, and implications. Literacy varies widely in form and context across societies as well: contexts of use, levels of prestige, communicative norms, identities of users, and social dynamics all shape literacy in particular ways in each society or community. Each society or community is literate in ways that differ from the ways in which other societies or communities are literate. Research in the diversity and heterogeneity of literacy experiences is thus explicitly particularistic and ethnography-driven.

The drawback of this particularistic approach is that it is potentially too generalization-shy; at worst, it becomes an amalgamation of anecdotes collected by researchers marveling at the diversity of humankind. The second current in recent works on literacy saves it from these dangers: linguistic anthropologists strive to apprehend the meaning of reading and writing as social, cultural, and cognitive activities. This meaning may consist of symbolic relationships, associations, and connections between reading and writing, on the one hand, and other aspects of human existence, on the other. For example, ethnographers of literacy have demonstrated that for participants in literate communication, the activities that take place "around" literate communication (i.e., simultaneously, in the same social space, with the same people) provide a specific flavor to the literacy activity, a flavor that becomes part of its inherent meaning. Thus, for instance, literacy produced or consumed during religious ceremonies highlights the same aspects of the self, the same emotions, the same power and authority relations that are foregrounded in the religious ritual. These aspects of self, emotions, and relations are evident in the way that participants handle written texts (reading them, memorizing them, talking about them, touching them, etc.) and, often, in the form of the texts themselves. They become an integral part of the social and cultural meaning of the literacy activity.

Arriving at an understanding of this meaning therefore consists in searching for relationships and connections, which leads one to the third current identifiable in the linguistic anthropological investigation of literacy. Like all other communicative activities, most reading and writing activities are often "microscopic," i.e., they consist in messages exchanged over short periods of time between restricted numbers of persons, whose scope and consequences are minimal. (Of course, widely disseminated published writing is potentially more "macroscopic," but it is only one of many manifestations of literacy.) Despite their microscopic form, literate exchanges articulate the larger structures in which they are embedded. For example, when literate communities are embedded in a colonial context, or when they constitute different social classes or gender groups in a complex society, the differences in their literacy activities are no longer simply instances of the heterogeneity of literacy as a mode of communication. Rather, they become part of dynamics of domination and resistance, structure and agency, and reproduction and change. In such contexts, certain literacy activities are valued, exalted, and employed as gate-keepers restricting access to institutions and other organs of power. Other are devalued or simply not defined as literacy or communication at all. In other words, each act of reading and writing potentially reenacts in a moment-by-moment ("microscopic") fashion the macroscopic structures in which it takes place. Literacy, like many other social activities (even beyond the realm of communication), thus mediates between microscopic, person-centered, and agentive behavior and macroscopic, structural, overarching, and reproduction-centered institutions, ideologies, and similar categories. To use terminology now well established in anthropology from the work of Pierre Bourdieu, literacy activities are thus another form of *habitus,* and linguistic anthropological approaches to literacy take the investigation of how literacy-as-habitus functions as a central beacon in their endeavors.

In the works of Lucien Lévy-Bruhl, Claude Lévi-Strauss, Walter Ong, Jack Goody, and many others, literacy was foregrounded as a cornerstone that distinguished the "primitive" from the "civilized." Along with the rest of anthropology, students of literacy have re-examined the Orientalist and "othering" assumptions and consequences of such statements. Like all other products of human thinking, literacy is a complex and heterogeneous phenomenon, and certainly not one which we can privilege as a "cornerstone" that would help us distinguish between kinds of people, groups, cultures, and thinking activities. Like all other aspects of human existence, literacy is part of the complex web of activities through which humans organize themselves socially and culturally.

(See also *agency, endangered, ideology, media, orality, translation, truth, writing*)

Bibliography

Besnier, Niko
  1995 Literacy, Emotion, and Authority: Reading and Writing on a Polynesian Atoll. Studies in the Social and Cultural Foundations of Language 16. Cambridge: Cambridge University Press.
Goody, Jack
  1977 The Domestication of the Savage Mind. Themes in the Social Sciences Series. Cambridge: Cambridge University Press.
Heath, Shirley B.
  1983 Ways with Words: Language, Life, and Work in Communities and Classrooms. Cambridge: Cambridge University Press.
Lambek, Michael
  1993 Knowledge and Practice in Mayotte: Local Discourses of Islam, Sorcery, and Spirit Possession. Toronto: University of Toronto Press.
Messick, Brinkley
  1993 The Calligraphic State: Textual Domination and History in a Muslim Society. Comparative Studies on Muslim Societies 16. Berkeley: University of California Press.
Scribner, Sylvia, and Michael Cole
  1981 The Psychology of Literacy. Cambridge, MA: Harvard University Press.
Street, Brian V.
  1984 Literacy in Theory and Practice. Cambridge Studies in Oral and Literate Culture 9. Cambridge: Cambridge University Press.
Street, Brian V., ed.
  1993 Cross-cultural Approaches to Literacy. Cambridge Studies in Oral and Literate Culture 23. Cambridge: Cambridge University Press.
Street, Brian V., and Niko Besnier
  1994 Aspects of Literacy. *In* Companion Encyclopedia of Anthropology: Humanity, Culture, and Social Life. Tim Ingold, ed. Pp. 527–562. London: Routledge.

■ *Stephen C. Levinson*

Maxim

A maxim is an aphoristic principle of conduct. The term is now associated by anyone who studies language with H. P. Grice's "maxims of conversation," which in turn are held to follow from a "cooperative principle" that informs (rather than strictly governs) conversation. The "cooperative principle" states, "Make your conversational contribution such as is required, at the stage at which it occurs, by the accepted purpose or direction of the talk exchange in which you are engaged." To achieve this, Grice suggests that conversationalists follow four maxims named after the Kantian categories, which we may abbreviate as follows:

Quality: "Don't say what you believe to be false, and don't say that for which you lack adequate evidence."

Quantity: "Give sufficient information, but don't give too much information."

Relevance: "Be relevant (stick to the point, etc.)."

Manner: "Be perspicuous – avoid obscurities, be brief and orderly."

The imperatival wording is meant to suggest neither moral imperative nor legal requirement, but rather a recipe-like rational mode of conduct to achieve one's conversational goals.

Despite the fact that at first sight all this looks like poor sociolinguistics, the underlying idea remains extremely important. Grice was trained in Oxford "ordinary language philosophy," which held that many deep philosophical problems arise from equivocations in meaning; thus he learned from John Austin the trick of looking at how words are used in context. What he noted was that, for example, it would be odd to say "Sandra is either an anthropologist or a theologian" when you knew she was only an anthropologist – it would be true, but less than fully helpful. From the disjunction, we assume the speaker isn't sure. But how do we get from statements to unstated beliefs about speakers' states of mind? We can only do that if there are some principles linking what we say with what we should be thinking when we say it, and the maxims of conversation were a first guess at those principles. Grice believed that by spelling out these principles we could disentangle *meaning* from *psychology*, or convention from intention (although he also held that, ultimately, meaning conventions derive from special kinds of intentions). A much simpler theory of meaning should result.

Why was this important? Because for the first time we had a systematic way to talk about the *unsaid*. There are many professions built on exegesis of the unsaid, from theology to psychoanalysis to anthropology. But most of these see the professional as diviner and his powers as based on a mixture of long apprenticeship and inspiration. Instead, Grice offered us a glimpse of a science of the unsaid. Unsaid messages could arise in at least two ways. First, by following the maxims, the speaker raises expectations that the maxims are being adhered to. So when in answer to your question "Is Sandra an academic?" I reply "She is either an anthropologist or a theologian," you think that I'm sure she is at least one or the other (Quality), I'm sure she is not both (Quantity), and I'm sure she is an academic but unsure which kind (Relevance). Second, by flagrantly "flouting" the maxims, the speaker can trigger more open-ended inferences: if I were to say "Sandra is an excellent theologian" when you know that I know she is nothing of the kind but just an anthropologist, I would suggest that there is some passing analogy between the way Sandra practices her profession and theologians practice theirs (convoluted and specious arguments, or sound arguments for the unsound, or preoccupations with angels on the heads of pins).

Grice left us no more than a hint of how to establish a science of the unsaid; consequently, even among the Griceans there has been bickering ever since – are there really three maxims, or just two, or even only one? But there have also been strands of considered anti-Griceanism. The Cognitive Linguists think all meaning is undifferentiated psychology, lumping together levels of conceptualization, of semantics, and of pragmatics, so there is certainly no principled distinction between the said and the unsaid. The ethnographers of speaking take a look at how people use language in "their" society and report that Grice was only (at best) depicting language use at the high tables of Oxford: there's always an economy of information, so people don't tell the truth at all (Quality), certainly don't volunteer the whole of it (Quantity), don't always reply directly (Relevance) or find it appropriate to speak in unveiled ways (Manner). The conversational analysts think Grice's armchair ethnography is science fiction: people indulge in all manner of highly detailed practices which are much more revealing about the generation of the unsaid than Gricean principles. For example, I ask you "Why on earth did you do that?" and you say nothing, thereby signaling guilt – this works because the practice of asking a question assigns you a turn, and your withholding an answer indicates you do not have an adequate one.

But Grice's idea survives these radical doubts. If the Cognitive Linguists were right, there would be no exploitation of the unsaid – no rhetoric, no cross-cultural misunderstandings, no language of intimacy or politeness. If the ethnographers of speaking were right and no-one felt obliged to tell the truth, and there was no relation between what was said and how and when it was said (nothing governing Quantity, Relevance, and Manner), then not only could no child learn the language, but there would be no account of the special value of veiled speech, indirect reference, or how hints and allusions work (which is precisely what the ethnographers are interested in). As for the conversational analysts, they do indeed have a point: we won't have a science of the unsaid without doing the laborious archaeology of unearthing the common conversational practices we all employ but of which we are not conscious. But if Grice was even partly right, there are also special background assumptions that have an omnipresent relevance and whose very modulation constructs special contexts and signals social motivations (like politeness and deference) for deviating from them. Recent work in both linguistics and semiotics gets good mileage from such ideas applied cross-linguistically and cross-culturally.

There is a moral in Grice's maxims, principles that operate even when being flouted: there's a need throughout the social sciences for a new kind of explanatory principle, more flexible and semiotic than rule, norm, or custom. (Grice's maxim is clearer than Pierre Bourdieu's *habitus*, but a similar kind of beast.) It is presumptive heuristics that govern social life, constrain our behavior for fear of generating unwanted meanings, and allow us to generate the most subtle and extended meanings without ever having had to say them.

(See also *acquisition, act, competence, functions, intentionality, power, relativity, socialization, truth, turn*)

Bibliography

Bourdieu, Pierre
  1977   Outline of a Theory of Practice. Cambridge: Cambridge University Press.
Brown, Penelope, and Stephen Levinson
  1987   Politeness. Cambridge: Cambridge University Press.
Grice, H. Paul
  1989   Studies in the Way of Words. Cambridge, MA: Harvard University Press.
Horn, Laurence
  1984   Towards a New Taxonomy for Pragmatic Inference: Q-based and R-based Implicature. *In* Meaning, Form and Use in Context. Deborah Schiffrin, ed. Pp. 11–42. Washington, DC: Georgetown University Press.
Keenan, Elinor Ochs
  1976   The Universality of Conversational Implicature. Language in Society 5:67–80.
Leech, Geoffrey
  1983   Principles of Pragmatics. London: Longman.
Levinson, Stephen
  2000   Presumptive Meanings. Cambridge, MA: MIT Press.
Schegloff, Emanuel
  1984   On Some Questions and Ambiguities in Conversation. *In* Structures of Social Action: Studies in Conversation Analysis. Max Atkinson and John

Heritage, eds. Pp. 266–296. Cambridge: Cambridge University Press.
Sperber, Dan, and Deirdre Wilson
  1995   Relevance. 2nd ed. Oxford: Blackwell.
Strecker, Ivo
  1988   The Social Practice of Symbolization: An Anthropological Analysis. London: Athlone Press.

■ *Debra Spitulnik*

Media

T he term *media* is notoriously polyvalent. In the strict sense, *media* is the plural of medium, understood as a channel or conduit for the transmission of some kind of communication. Examples include print media, electronic media, televisual media, paint media, oral media, bodily media, and multimedia such as the simultaneous print-electronic-audio-visual media of computers.

Communication genres – culturally specific forms of communication such as songs, jokes, stories, and conversations – occur in media. Genre–media relations can be very tightly interlinked. For example, the genre of the "talk show" occurs almost exclusively in broadcast media. Genre–media relations can also be relatively looser. A narrative for example may occur in a hand-written letter, in a face-to-face encounter, in a book, or in a range of electronic media, including e-mail.

This definition of media differs from popular uses of the phrase *the media*, which denotes the dominant media and media professionals within a local, national, or international context. Correspondingly, *the media, mass media,* and *media* are often used as singular collective nouns – as in "the media glorifies violence" – highlighting a perception that they operate uniformly, with similar agendas and production values.

In media studies scholarship, the term is usually more far-reaching than in the above definitions. It encompasses communication channels, technologies, formats, genres, and products. At base, however, media in this sense is best defined by what it is not: face-to-face communication. There are several recognized sub-categories of media. Most familiar are the conventionally understood *mass media*, i.e., mainstream television, film, radio, newspapers, and magazines. Other mass-produced communications include novels, videos, comic books, and recorded music. *Alternative media* are antithetical to mainstream media, but they may use similar technologies. Pirate radio and independent newspapers are two common examples. *Small media* are a type of alternative media that individuals and small groups control and (re)produce. Examples include underground audiocassettes, leaflets, and graffiti. *New media* are new digital-based electronic media, such as e-mail, Internet listserves, faxes, and video games. *Indigenous media* are any of the above technologies used by Fourth World peoples.

From an ethnography of communication perspective, these media can be studied at the levels of production, circulation, reception, message form, message function, and message content. The theoretical and methodological concerns of linguistics are profoundly relevant for media studies at all of these levels. Crucially, investigating the linguistic dimensions of media should not be classified as an enterprise confined to sociolinguistics or linguistic anthropology. The cultural, social, psychological, and political functions of media all depend on the semiotic operations of language and discourse. In the following discussion I briefly outline four areas of greatest importance.

First, media are key agents in the political economy of language, as they give value and exposure to certain language codes, linguistic varieties, and discourse styles. Media are important sites for ethnolinguistic representation and the production of language ideologies. Utilizing certain linguistic varieties in national media can legitimate the social, economic, and political dominance of some social groups at the expense of others. It can have consequences for access to representation in the public sphere, and it may even contribute to language shift or the death of unrepresented linguistic varieties.

Second, and related to this, media can be important catalysts for language socialization and language change because of their high visibility and mass reach. They contribute to the circulation and valorization of standard phrases, key words, and ready-made formulations in public culture. Radio Zambia, for example, has inspired a range of linguistic innovations in popular speech. The name of the "Chongololo" radio program, a show about wildlife preservation, has become a derogatory term for Zambians who try to act like Europeans. Other program titles, such as "Over to You," are used in conversations to create a playful rapport. This is analogous to the way that media discourse such as the Star Trek phrase "beam me up" circulates in American culture.

The fact that media help to circulate and even canonize a basic repertoire of ways of speaking has implications not only for the social life of language, but for the production of culture, ideology, and identity. In a Foucauldian sense, media are part of discursive formations, understood as culturally specific and historically contingent domains of knowledge and practice that establish relations of power and truth. The modes of language use in media do not come out of thin air, and they are always inherently ideological. As media provide ways of talking about modernity, deviance, collective identity, economic value, otherness, or any other phenomenon that falls within the horizons of a social formation, they ultimately provide ways of thinking about, experiencing, and acting on these phenomena. Anthropological research needs to attend to the very expressions that are given prominence in media and to the way that they provide inhabitable discourses that form the substance of culture and experience.

Third, the ability of media to delineate social identities and to function as forums for collective participation is greatly dependent on language use. Specifically, in linguistic terms this involves the indexical signaling of participants in mediated communication. Social identities (e.g., class, gender, age, ethnicity) of both media producers and media audiences are constructed through the choice of topic, code, register, and style. In English language broadcasting, for example, using sociolinguistic variables such as regional dialects or verbal contractions affects the definition of the communication event itself and helps to define the type of social individuals that are targeted as audiences. Pronoun choices and other modes of address are also crucial. Finally, audiences are constructed and attracted through metapragmatic devices that frame mediated communication events. For example, in radio there are titles for distinct times of the day, and promotional slogans that exhort listeners and define moods.

A fourth area of emerging research focuses on the intertextual relations across different media and various forms of face-to-face communication. Topics include the influence of indigenous communication genres on media genres; the transformation of verbal art in electronic technologies; the instrumental role of media in the global dissemination of certain communication genres; and the transfer of older media conventions into new media genres such as Internet e-mail and chatroom communications.

In all of these domains, media's relevance for culture rests heavily on language's relevance in media. At the turn of the millennium this is a relatively unexplored territory that promises to be a rich research ground for scholars in all areas of anthropology and media studies.

(See also *genre, identity, ideology, indexicality, intentionality, power, register, socialization, style, truth*)

Bibliography

Bell, Allan, and Peter Garrett, eds.
    1998 Approaches to Media Discourse. Oxford: Blackwell.
Fairclough, Norman
    1995 Media Discourse. London: Edward Arnold.
Gal, Susan, and Kathryn A. Woolard, eds.
    1995 Constructing Languages and Publics. Pragmatics 5(2) (special issue).
Hall, Stuart
    1973 Encoding and Decoding in the Television Discourse. Stenciled Occasional Paper 7, Media Series. Birmingham, UK: Centre for Contemporary Cultural Studies, University of Birmingham.
Herring, Susan C., ed.
    1996 Computer-mediated Communication: Linguistic, Social and Cross-cultural Perspectives. Amsterdam: John Benjamins.
Scannell, Paddy, ed.
    1991 Broadcast Talk. London: Sage.
Spitulnik, Debra
    1993 Anthropology and Mass Media. Annual Review of Anthropology 22:293–315.

1996   The Social Circulation of Media Discourse and the Mediation of Communities. Journal of Linguistic Anthropology 6(2):161–187.

2001   Media Connections and Disconnections: Radio Culture and the Public Sphere in Zambia. Durham, NC: Duke University Press.

Tolson, Andrew

1996   Mediations: Text and Discourse in Media Studies. New York: St. Martin's.

■ *Dan Ben-Amos*

Metaphor

Over the years philosophy and linguistics, anthropology and psychology, folklore and literary theory and criticism have formulated theories of metaphor. At their root is the etymology of this compound word that derives from the Greek *meta* ("over") and *pherein* ("to carry") and the distinctions that Aristotle made. He considered four kinds of transference of meanings to be metaphorical: from the general (genus) to the particular (species), or the other way around; between two particular forms; or as a matter of analogy in which two things stand in the same relation to each other as two other things. Two other sub-forms of the metaphor are the synecdoche, from the Greek *synekdechesthai* ("to receive jointly"), in which meaning is transferred from the part to the whole, and metonymy, also derived from Greek, in which the transference of meaning occurs between two associated objects. Three basic ideas are implicit in metaphor and its theories: categories, transference of meanings, and the unity that language formulates in its consequence. Secondary issues, in order not in significance, concern the purpose and use of metaphor and its distribution among the modes of discourse and representation in society.

These sets of ideas as they motivate theories, or are inherent in metaphor, sustain the grip metaphors have on language and culture. They point to the semantic fields in language, which, in turn, correspond to cognitive categories of culture. By examining two types of aphasic disturbances, a selection deficiency and a contiguity disorder, and relating them to metaphor and metonym, respectively, Roman Jakobson and Morris Halle suggest the biological basis of metaphoric thought. Yet each community of speakers could construct its own systems of classification. Categories of thoughts and fields of meanings are implicit in the metaphors that connect them. At the same time, the metaphors used in a particular language follow rules of appropriateness for the transference of meanings. Claude Lévi-Strauss's famous dictum "animals are good to think with" established the distinction and potential analogy between humans and animals. Yet the use of animal metaphors for humans, as well the metaphoric attribution of human qualities to animals, is

147

subject to cultural rules. In several European languages the shift from a feline to a canine metaphor for the female of our species will transform terms of endearment to abuse.

Societies may have dominant semantic fields that generate their metaphors. The world of sport, for example, dominates the metaphor of American business and political discourse. The principle of seniority has such a rule over the language of religion and social order in many traditional societies. These may be "root" or "organizational" metaphors that help order reality.

Following appropriate transference rules, a metaphor brings to bear upon a particular situation, person, or action the combined load of two semantic fields, and thus increases the rhetorical impact of the phrase. Such a verbal intensity is more appropriate to poetic discourse in performance or ritual. Nevertheless, metaphors often occur in daily discourse, as they are rooted in the cultural categories within which speakers construct their conversations. The preponderance of metaphors in the context of poetic discourse, contiguously, has given room to the impression that they are a deviant form of language, contrasted with literal language. Indeed the relation between the two may be subject to social and religious history. The pressure on the chest that felt like a mare riding on top of a person generated the literal description of "nightmare" that went through a metaphoric stage before becoming a word for a bad dream. However, while literal language can become metaphoric, the literalization of a metaphor could easily end up in a joke. When Clever Hans, of the brothers Grimm fame, was told to cast an eye on a girl but instead threw at her the eyeball of an animal, he did not win her heart. It may be possible to explicate but not to undo metaphors because they are intrinsic to language. The formation of categories is necessary for thought, but the transference of meanings across them is in the nature of language.

(See also *category, genre, humor, iconicity, indexicality, meter, names, oratory, poetry, proverb, relativity, style, voice*)

Bibliography

Fernandez, James
    1986   Persuasions and Performances: The Play of Tropes in Culture. Bloomington: Indiana University Press.
Jakobson, Roman, and Morris Halle
    1971   Fundamentals of Language. 2nd rev. ed. The Hague: Mouton.
Kittay, Eva Feder
    1987   Metaphor: Its Cognitive Force and Linguistic Structure. Oxford: Clarendon Press.
Lakoff, George, and Mark Johnson
    1980   Metaphors We Live By. Chicago: University of Chicago Press.
Noppen, Jean Pierre van, et al.
    1985   Metaphor: A Bibliography of Post-1970 Publications. Amsterdam and Philadelphia: John Benjamins.

Noppen, Jean Pierre van, and Edith Hols

    1990 Metaphor II: A Classified Bibliography of Publication 1985. Amsterdam and Philadelphia: John Benjamins.

Ortony, Andrew, ed.

    1979 Metaphor and Thought. Cambridge: Cambridge University Press.

Ricoeur, Paul

    1977 The Rule of Metaphor: Multi-disciplinary Studies of the Creation of Meaning in Language. Robert Czerny with Kathleen McLaughlin and John Costello, Jr., trans. Toronto: University of Toronto Press.

Sapir, J. David, and J. Christopher Crocker, eds.

    1977 The Social Use of Metaphor: Essays on the Anthropology of Rhetorics. Philadelphia: University of Pennsylvania Press.

Shibles, Warren A.

    1971 Metaphor: An Annotated Bibliography and History. Whitewater, WI: Language Press.

White, Roger M.

    1996 The Structure of Metaphor: The Way the Language of Metaphor Works. Cambridge, MA: Blackwell.

■ *Giorgio Banti*

Meter

The formal features that typically mark poetic texts against ordinary discourse are called meter. This word may refer to recurring patterns of stress and other prosodic features or, in a wider sense, include also alliteration, rhyme, etc.

Meter is studied as an explicit system of rules in most literate societies where poetry is esteemed as a literary-aesthetic genre, even though elements of versification are learned explicitly as well in some non-literate communities such as the Dinka in southern Sudan, where young men are taught how to compose and perform different kinds of poems during the retirement that precedes initiation. However, the most frequent case is for meter to be absorbed unconsciously from exposure to performances of metrical texts, just as children learn how to form grammatical utterances through their exposure to surrounding speech. Epistemologically metrical patterns have thus some similarities to phonemes vis-à-vis the actual sounds uttered and heard in human speech. They can be viewed as sets of allowed variants, as psychological realities, or as abstract patterns whose relationship with the actual metrical texts is accounted for by means of derivational rules, etc. At any rate, three levels have to be distinguished ideally in a metrical text: (1) the metrical pattern, (2) the concrete text, as an abstract reality, and (3) the actual performance of the text. For instance, the text of a song conforms to a metrical pattern, but may be performed in many different ways. Written versions of it lie somewhere between (2) and (3) because they often represent features such as elisions, etc., that properly belong to its performance rather than to the form of its text required by meter.

The most general characterization of meter is as "recurring patterns in successive sections of the text," in Foley's words. In many traditions this involves phonological parallelism that consists segmentally in rhyme, alliteration, or assonance (respectively, similarity between final, initial, and internal sounds of words), with the addition of rarer types, such as the constraints on syllable-initial consonants in Moroccan Berber versification described by Jouad. Yet cultures differ in the role they assign to each of these three major kinds, and in how they are realized. For instance, they were optional in classical Greek versification, whereas rhyme is mandatory in most western European systems since the late Middle Ages. In the latter systems, alliteration and assonance are sometimes used in order to achieve special effects but are not constitutive of meter. In early Germanic and modern Somali, instead, alliteration is mandatory, while rhyme and assonance occur only occasionally. The alliterating sounds changed after each line in medieval Germanic poetry but are the same through all the lines of a poem in modern Somali. Prosodic parallelism usually also involves numerical regulation, as John Lotz pointed out. For instance, some systems require the lines in a text to have a specified number of syllables, as in classical Chinese or Japanese. In other systems heavy or light syllables have to occur in specific, numerically definable positions in a text section, with heaviness vs. lightness being realized as closed vs. open syllables, long vs. short, etc., according to the phonological makeup of the language, as in some Turkish systems and, respectively, Somali and Classical Greek. Still other systems (e.g., many western European ones) require stress to occur in certain positions or in certain numbers within a text's sections, or even rely on tones, as classical Chinese poetry does.

Other kinds of parallelism that play a constitutive role in some versification systems are grammatical and lexico-semantic parallelism. Grammatical parallelism may consist in recurring morphological patterns, as in some Uralic (e.g., Cheremis) and Native American systems, or in recurring syntactic patterns, as in poetry from the ancient Near East such as Biblical Hebrew or Ugaritic. For instance, Stanislav Segert points out that verses in Ugaritic poetry generally consisted of two cola (i.e., cohesive stretches), with the first colon "followed by a second colon exhibiting identical, similar or complementary syntactic structure but replacing some words." Lexico-semantic parallelism matches words or phrases in paired sets, so that one element is replaced with its pair in the following relevant text section. It is pervasive in many traditions, from Finnish to classical Chinese and Sumbanese in eastern Indonesia. In ancient Near Eastern poetry the paired terms were synonyms, opposites, complementary terms (e.g., "orphan" vs. "widow"), or expansions of each other (e.g., "wine" vs. "blood of vines").

Cultures differ in the genres for which they use metrical regulation. Even in some literate societies (e.g., in western Europe), meter does not characterize only literary poetry. Songs, nursery rhymes, and children's counts also conform to meter, and not infrequently also proverbs, charms, advertising jingles, and political slogans. Looking a little further away, one finds old Germanic law texts in meter to prevent alteration, eastern Indonesian ritual languages characterized by meter for political or marriage negotiations, historical narratives, communicating with spirits, divination. Among the Somali, meter also characterizes riddles, curses, and ritual praises; the Afar ginnili's prophecies are usually metrical.

Even though metrically regulated texts and everyday discourse are prototypically quite distinct, intermediate cases are also known. Among the most common ones are (1) genres with optional or partial metrical regulation and

(2) metrical prose. Examples of (1) are proverbs that in many cultures may optionally have partial or full metrical parallelism between their parts. For instance, while many English proverbs lack any metrical organization, the well-known "an apple a day keeps the doctor away" has two strong stresses preceded by one or two weak positions in each of its two halves (*an Apple a dAY / keeps the dOctor awAY*), alliteration (*day–doctor*), and rhyme (*day–away*). Examples of (2) can be found in classical Latin prose texts by Cicero and other authors, with metrical closes at the ends of sentences, or in the Arabic rhymed prose of the first and last suras of the Koran.

When metrically regulated texts are performed orally, the musical organization is quite often linked to the metrical pattern, as when musical ictuses coincide with strong stresses in accentual verse systems, or when the span of the melodic contour matches that of a line or group of lines.

Metrical systems change through time – for example, because a language has lost phonological oppositions relevant in its older metrical system, such as vowel length. Metrical systems may also be borrowed from one linguistic tradition to another, just as linguistic phenomena can be. It is important to point out, however, that the ensuing systems may be double-tiered, with the older metrical type surviving in some genres, and the new or borrowed type used in other ones. An instance of this is the survival of old Germanic alliterative strong-stress verse – with the addition of rhyme – in the above English proverb. Another one is Hungarian, in which the strictly syllabic verse of its older "national" system is used beside the Greco-Roman quantitative verse of its "higher" nineteenth-century poetry.

(See also *improvisation, music, oratory, poetry, prayer, repetition, style*)

Bibliography

Banti, Giorgio, and Francesco Giannattasio
   1996   Music and Metre in Somali Poetry. *In* Voice and Power: Essays in Honour of B. W. Andrzejewski. African Languages and Cultures, suppl. 3. R. J. Hayward and I. M. Lewis, eds. Pp. 83–127. London: School of Oriental and African Studies.
Foley, William A.
   1997   Anthropological Linguistics: An Introduction. Malden, MA, and Oxford: Blackwell Publishers.
Gasparov, Mikhail L., with Marina Tarlinskaja (trans.) and G. S. Smith (ed.)
   1996   A History of European Versification. Oxford: Clarendon Press.
Jouad, Hassan
   1995   Le calcul inconscient de l'improvisation. Poésie berbère – rhythme, nombre et sense. Paris-Louvain: Éditions Peeters.
Kiparsky, Paul, and Gilbert Youmans, eds.
   1989   Rhythm and Meter: Phonetics and Phonology. Vol. 1. San Diego, CA: Academic Press.

Lotz, John
  1960 Metric Typology. *In* Style in Language. Thomas A. Sebeok, ed. Pp. 135–148. Cambridge, MA, New York, and London: Technology Press of MIT and John Wiley & Sons.
Molino, Jean, and J. Gardes-Tamine
  1987–88 Introduction à l'analyse de la poésie, parts I and II. Paris: Presses Universitaires de France.
O'Connor, Michael
  1980 Hebrew Verse Structure. Winona Lake, IN: Eisenbrauns.
Segert, Stanislav
  1984 A Basic Grammar of the Ugaritic Language. Berkeley, Los Angeles, and London: University of California Press.
Wimsatt, William K., ed.
  1972 Versification: Major Language Types. New York: New York University Press.

■ *Steven Feld and Aaron Fox*

Music

The historically significant areas of the music/language encounter and their interdisciplinary dialogue can be separated into four arenas: (1) considerations of music as a language and of linguistic models of music; (2) considerations of music in language and of language in music, that is, of the centrality of vocal sound to verbal significance and of sung, texted vocalization; (3) considerations of music about language, that is, of speech surrogates; and (4) considerations of language about music, that is, the intertwining of verbal and musical discourse. After sketching the research issues broadly associated with each of these four arenas, we will suggest the importance of the most recent site of music/language dialogue, the voice.

Within Western academic histories, language and music share a heritage of formal, mathematical, and logical analysis. Considered as a semiotic system, music is, typically, syntactically far more redundant and overdetermined yet semantically far more diffuse and underdetermined than language. Nonetheless, there has been a long history of, and fascination with, the application of language models to musical analysis. Such application has been made by musical analogy to phonological and syntactic structures, analyzing both Western and non-Western musical (instrumental and vocal) forms. These models range from analogies between the distributional character of pitch systems and phonetic inventories, to analogies between syntactic structure and the harmonic, metrical, and motival organization of musical pieces.

Paralleling a broad trend in the human sciences, research that began in linguistic modeling has increasingly been developed, refined, and pursued within an integrated cognitive science approach linking psychology with music theory. Some cognitive approaches have been greeted by criticism of their cross-cultural limitations and of their seeming hostility to social agency. At the same time, the cognitive psychology of music has undoubtedly contributed to our understanding of the ineffability of musical experience.

A more empirical orientation has focused on the common ground music and language share in poetics and performance. Here language and music meet in voice, phenomenologically intertwined as a play of sound and sense, i.e., the play of sensuality and the signifying properties of vocal sound. Language's musicality – its tonal, timbral, prosodic, and gradient dynamic qualities – highlights the role of vocal performance for linguistic meaning. Music's language – the texted dimensions of songs and other sung poetic genres – highlights verbal art as vocal art. It is in this interface – vocal performance and song texts – that linguistic and musical anthropology have historically found their most productive ethnographic dialogue.

Earlier work on music in language and language in music was more concerned with charting comparative continua, boundaries, and distinctions between speech and song. More recent work brings ethnographic sophistication to the description both to the interplay of verbal and vocal art, and to forms intermediate to speech and song (e.g., chant, recitative, intoned oratory), and genres that distinctively cross between them (e.g., verbal dueling, preaching, lamenting). Ethnographic attention to contextual and performative aspects of language has resulted in more sophisticated translations of poetic song texts, analyses of the coincident parallelism of textual and melodic stanzas, and approaches to interactions between tonal language and musical pitch contour.

Speech surrogates constitute another semiotic for musicking language, involving the transposition of linguistic tonal and temporal contours to surrogate articulatory modes and media. These can be vocal – for example, humming and whistling – or instrumental – for example, flutes or "talking drums." Surrogate systems are typically divided between those systems based on abridgement, where a limited number of phonemic elements is imitated by the surrogate, and those based on logographic or ideographic structure, where the surrogate sounds symbolize concepts without an intermediary connection to the phonemic structure of the base language. Speech surrogates participate in a wide variety of communicative practices, ranging across signal and aesthetic functions, referential to ambiguous messages, and stereotypic phrases to dialogic production of novel utterances.

The foundations of music as a mental construct and a performative practice obscure one of its most significant social facts – namely, that music is a ubiquitous topic for discourse. Musicians and listeners everywhere spend much productive social energy talking about music, and from that simple observation three important domains for social analysis have unfolded. First, stimulated by work in lexical semantics, research has developed on the relations between musical terminology, ethnotheories of music, and the metaphoric basis of language about music. Second, stimulated by work on dialogism, researchers have studied the intertwining of speaking and musicking as a site of social interaction among musicians. Finally, engaging debates originating in the philosophy of musical aesthetics, research linking language and music has investigated the social location of evaluative, critical, and interpretive musical discourse.

Voice is the embodied locus of spoken and sung performance, the site where language and music have received closest ethnographic scrutiny. But voice has a more familiar articulation in contemporary anthropology, having also become a metaphor for difference, a key representational trope for identity, power, conflict, social position, and agency. The connection between these empirical and metaphorical invocations of voice indexes a broader anthropological project, one that means to link embodied expression with social agency. This connection explores how vocality is a social practice that is locally understood as a conventional index of authority, evidence, and experiential truth. As such, voice and vocality is a particularly significant site for the articulation of opposition and difference. This is no doubt why phrases like "giving voice," "taking voice," "having voice" are so linked to the politics of identity, to the ability of the subaltern to speak, to the ability of indigeneity movements to "talk back" and class, gender, and race politics to "back talk" the dominant. Linking the histories of vox populi to "lift every voice and sing," vocality has become the site where linguistic and musical anthropology most strikingly conjoin a poetics and politics of culture.

In conclusion, music and language are fundamentally interrelated domains of expressive culture and human behavior and experience. Although music and language have been treated as distinct objects of inquiry within specific disciplines, their relationship has periodically been an object of focused attention within dialogues between linguistics, anthropology, ethnomusicology, music theory, philosophy, and cognitive science. In the past, such work has often focused on formal musical "grammars," on semiotic differences between musical and linguistic modes of signification, and on the intertwining of musical and linguistic expression in musical speech surrogates, paralinguistic and non-segmental dimensions of language, and in texted song. More recently, ethnographic and theoretical interest has focused on evaluative and theoretical verbal discourses about music and musical meaning, and on a metaphorical and empirical interest in the voice as the embodied site of both musical and linguistic expressivity, and of social distinction. Ethnographic description of the micro-politics of emplaced, embodied, and voiced identity in particular local lifeworlds has developed across linguistic and musical anthropology in recent years. This signals renewed attention to the materiality and social intimacy of vocality, and its significance for understanding how social identities are indexed and expressed in musical and verbal practices.

(See also *body, expert, identity, meter, performativity, poetry, power, truth, voice*)

Bibliography

Feld, Steven, and Aaron Fox
    1994 Music and Language. Annual Review of Anthropology 23:25–53.
Herzog, George
    1950 Song. *In* Funk and Wagnall's Dictionary of Folklore, Mythology and Legend. Vol. 2. Maria Leach, ed. Pp. 1032–1050. New York: Funk and Wagnall's.
Hinton, LeAnn
    1984 Havasupai Songs: A Linguistic Perspective. Tübingen: Gunter Narr Verlag.

Jakobson, Roman
  1987 Musicology and Linguistics. *In* Language and Literature. K. Pomorska and
    S. Rudy, eds. Pp. 455–457. Cambridge, MA: Belknap.
Keil, Charles, and Steven Feld
  1994 Music Grooves. Chicago: University of Chicago Press.
Lerdahl, Fred, and Ray Jackendoff
  1983 A Generative Theory of Tonal Music. Cambridge, MA: MIT Press.
List, George
  1963 The Boundaries of Speech and Song. Ethnomusicology 7(1):1–16.
Nattiez, Jean-Jacques
  1990 Music and Discourse: Toward a Semiology of Music. Princeton, NJ:
    Princeton University Press.
Titon, Jeff Todd
  1988 Powerhouse for God: Speech, Chant and Song in an Appalachian Baptist
    Church. Austin: University of Texas Press.
Urban, Greg
  1988 Ritual Wailing in Amerindian Brazil. American Anthropologist 90: 385–
    400.

■ *Betsy Rymes*

Names

Proper names are often viewed as arbitrary labels to refer to individuals or locations. From an anthropological perspective, however, proper names and their meanings are inseparable from social and historical context. Linguistic anthropologists look at the context-bound nature of language in general and, when it comes to names, investigate questions about their function in different societies. From an anthropological perspective, names are not simply arbitrary labels. How we get them, who says them, how they are used, and in what context they are spoken are inseparable from a human being's social identity.

One reason that proper names can be powerful markers of social identity is that names depend on a social history for their legitimacy. The most typical way names can be connected to a particular social history is through the event of naming. Philosophers of language have discussed such "baptismal events" as the links that attach a label arbitrarily to an individual. At one level, this is a simple pragmatic phenomenon of reference fixing. At another level, however, there are the institutional and social conditions that legitimate such an event. The baptismal event, the act of naming, is only valid within certain contexts. Like marriage vows, which may be honored only by those who respect the ceremony, certain names may only be legitimate to those who respect the particular naming, or "baptismal" event. These baptisms come in all forms, not just the familiar religious sprinkling or dunking event. Youth gang members in Los Angeles, for example, earn their nicknames through a "jumping in" ceremony, in which they are severely beaten by their new "family." The name is not considered legitimate until one takes part in this ceremony, and any attempt to use this name without such a ceremony would be ineffectual or even worthy of punishment, at least in the context of the gang. Having been through the jumping in confirms a gang member's tenacity, ability to stand up to physical pain – his or her worthiness of the new gang name. Thus the baptismal event not only fixes the referent of a name, it also reflects certain beliefs and values.

Names also come with a social history earned prior to any baptismal event.

158

This prior association may highlight, among other things, connections to family members or, in the case of Muslim names, God or his qualities. Like a baptismal ceremony, the name's history highlights values of the community. Traditionally, African Muslim names like Abdallah (Servant of God) are constructed so that they always mention some aspect of or signify devotion to God. This prevalence of God in the names of Muslims reflects their beliefs about the importance of God in everyday interaction. In the United States, African Muslim names take on another role in the creation of social identity when people take these names to draw attention to their African roots. Malcolm Little became Malcolm X, then Malcolm X Shabazz, and finally, after a pilgrimage to Africa, El-Hajj Malik El-Shabazz. All these name changes would seem unnecessary were names merely pragmatic signifying labels, but to the named such changes carry important messages about religious and cultural identity. Far from being arbitrary labels, the meaning behind these names depends on the community (including that community's shared knowledge and beliefs) that does the naming.

Despite the reference-fixing function of a baptismal event, a name does not indelibly affix an identity to an individual. Like Malcolm X, people usually have several names throughout a lifetime. People also may use different names for different situations. The proliferation of proper names for one person reflects the multiplicity of selves within an "individual," and each of these facets might be highlighted in certain contexts. Name changes facilitate and even create different identities through time and across contexts. Clifford Geertz describes the use of contextually variable *nisbas*, names used in Moroccan society. These names identify the country, town, or family (among other things) of the named individual, but change according to which trait is most useful or relevant in a particular situation. If an individual is in one's hometown, for example, one might not use the name that identifies this, but instead one more specific. The ethnicity-identifying nisba, then, changes according to context and makes relevant a certain generic aspect of a Moroccan's identity. In turn, individuals can control which facet of their identity shines by referring to themselves by a certain name. Choosing a certain nisba can also function to create context by narrowing or broadening the relevant frame of reference.

Because names can create both identity and context, using someone's proper name is a potentially powerful act. Americans recognize the stereotype of the pushy salesman who inserts a customer's first name after each sentence of his pitch. This salesman is aware of the power of names to create a context of familiarity; however, he attempts to use the power of naming not to establish genuine closeness, but to accomplish his own, individual ends (make a sale). The Apache's portrayal of "the white man" is marked by, among other things, the frequent use of proper names, reminiscent of the pushy salesman. For the Apache, this portrayal communicates the irreverence of the white man for the personal power behind names and the connections name use invokes. The Malagasy of Madagascar also recognize the power of individuals' names and use them scrupulously, preferring to avoid using birth names at all. The Malagasy rename infants immediately after giving them their birth name, for they believe that ancestral spirits of ill will could otherwise easily overhear an individual's name and use it to take the child's life. Their beliefs regarding the use of names by ancestral forces led the Malagasy to change their names so many times that names' pragmatic referential purpose was being subverted and a national law (limiting the number of name changes to seven) was put into effect to curb the confusion.

Beliefs about the power of names clearly vary across communities, and the power of names to define individuals and context changes over time and is negotiated in each instance of naming. The power of a name to hurt or harm someone also arises from pre-existing power structures. To return to the example of gang nicknames, a student's gang nickname, when used in place of his birth name and penned on a piece of paper, can have varying effects on the individual, depending on where and with whom he uses that name. It can be seen by a teacher as an act of defiance and used to expel a student from school. That same writing can be seen by a police officer as grounds for arrest. But peers may see this name as an act of loyalty, a link between his peers, and even between generations who have shared that name. Between gang members, use of a certain name can either deter or incite violence. Which meaning for a name is legitimate? Who can legitimately use that name? What are the results of the naming? The answers to these questions are partially determined by power relations. The meaning powerful others give to an individual's name can determine, for example, whether a gangster in Los Angeles is viewed as a loyal peer, expelled from school, or sent to jail.

Names, then, while associated with an individual, are laden with social history and power, and they are easily manipulated in the hands of others. Across societies, people carefully control the way names are used, who uses them, and in what context. A proper name, then, is not simply a useful label, but a repository of accumulated meanings, practices, and beliefs, a powerful linguistic means of asserting identity (or defining someone else) and inhabiting a social world.

(See also *identity, individual, narrative, power, prayer, relativity, space*)

Bibliography

Basso, Keith H.
> 1979   Portraits of "the Whiteman": Linguistic Play and Cultural Symbols among the Western Apache. Cambridge and New York: Cambridge University Press.

Geertz, Clifford
> 1983   Local Knowledge: Further Essays in Interpretive Anthropology. New York: Basic Books.

Keenan, Elinor Ochs
> 1976   The Universality of Conversational Postulates. Language in Society 5:67–80.

Kripke, Saul
   1977   Speaker Reference and Semantic Reference. *In* The Philosophy of Language. A. P. Martinich, ed. Pp. 248–266. New York: Oxford University Press.
Putnam, Hilary
   1989   Representation and Reality. Cambridge, MA: MIT Press.
Rymes, Betsy
   1996   Naming as Social Practice: The Case of Little Creeper from Diamond Street. Language in Society 25:237–260.
Searle, John R.
   1958   Proper Names. Mind 67:166–173.
Zawawi, Sharifa M.
   1998   African Muslim Names: Images and Identities. Trenton, NJ: Africa World Press, Inc.

■ *Harriet E. Manelis Klein*

Narrative

T he key term *narrative* has appeared in analyses of myths, legends, life histories, conversational analysis, as an exemplar of discourse, as a pragmatic entity, and as a tool of political rhetoric. For anthropologists, and linguistic anthropologists in particular, narrative has often meant a form of oral literature, but its contemporary use has included a written form, divulged by speakers who provide tokens of their culture through speech and by interpreters of those tokens.

In its most basic usage, narrative is a genre that can be created or elicited. The type of narrative is defined by the roles of the narrators and listeners. Narratives can be personal: they can be autobiographical. Narratives can be fictional or non-fictional. They can be traditional folktales that include mythic or fantastic elements, as well as other types of traditional tales that include "real" elements. Depending on the narrator's interpretation of the genre, one can find, for example, disembodied narratives, first-person narratives, contextualized narratives, and romantic and particularistic narratives. Narratives depend on an audience and, for an appropriate response, require a variety of techniques that at times indicate implicit or explicit evidence of the narrator's preconceptions and aims. They also represent some kind of interaction, which results in the concomitant use of a variety of verbal and nonverbal communicative modes. Themes for these narratives are culturally determined.

Different types of narratives may display different types of phonology, morphology, syntax, and lexical properties. Linguistic repertoires utilize different combinations of these grammatical properties to suit the function of the narratives.

There may be specific linguistic forms that transform simple narratives into more elaborate ones, and the retellings result in a revelation of what are obligatory and optional narrative elements.

Narratives tend to have core structural features such as an introduction or preamble, permission to speak, overview, main body of narration, including divisions into episodes, conclusions, and codas. And although there may be distinctions in the structure deriving from the skill of the narrator, the distribution of rhetorical devices, or grammatical resources, we may say that these are part of the universal characterization of narratives.

In much contemporary anthropological writing, narrative involves ethnography and the latter's definition. The greatest conflict in the use of the appropriated term *narrative* occurs in ethnography because postmodern literary critics judge ethnographic writing as lacking analysis. These critics have trouble seeing how the recounting of the story that is central to the ethnography is simultaneously the anthropological product and project. For them, narrative must have an analytic point. It must be self-reflexive.

So how can we explain the link between the use of narrative by anthropologists as well as by practitioners of other disciplines? One way is by acknowledging the issue of the ownership of the narrative, thereby offering a way of dealing with the appropriations of the term *narrative* by literature and by anthropology.

For any given "narrative" or "well-known story," different versions may exist, some of which may be more valued. In the telling and retelling of narratives, the narrator claims his or her distinctive style of narrative authority as well as the strategy for narration. Counter-narratives are created. That narratives have a life and/or function beyond their simple essence or creation has led to further discussion of narratives as tokens of the discourse of the dominated, discourses that are often in narrative form and that are an aspect of contemporary ethnographic narrative.

In response to the general loss of confidence in the truth-value of representations by social scientists, anthropologists have increasingly turned to narrative analysis. By making stories out of fieldwork data, anthropologists avail themselves of a unique way of making the facts comprehensible. Narrative order links anthropological and literary narratives. And it is precisely the order and style of their narratives and texts that suggest a narrative future. This projected future is articulated in their narratives in the retelling of past stories and the creation of the narrative present. But it is also structurally suggested in the overt temporal dimension that the narrative imposes on its narrator, its listeners (and implied audience), its stories. For if narration is the linking of events and elements in a construction of meaning, that linking is equally a spatial and temporal ordering of those elements or events. The narrative designates and systematizes.

Furthermore, narratives do not contain within them a measure for their truth-value. A narrative gets truth-value from being conscious of the conditions of its production, and being cognizant of, and able to learn something from, its own evolution.

Narrative remains deeply problematic, and different disciplines continue to argue its meaning at the same time as they utilize the term. Historians over the last twenty years have debated the value of narrative historiography over non-narrative approaches. Ethnographers are now confronted with similar value judgments between narrative and non-narrative approaches to writing about the individuals, societies, or cultures they study. And literary critics have developed a rather sophisticated understanding of how data – utterances, actions, events, and happenings – are incorporated into structures of meaning and are then transformed into narrative form.

(See also *genre, grammar, poetry, prayer, style, truth, voice*)

Bibliography

Brenneis, Donald
   1996   Telling Troubles: Narrative, Conflict, and Experience. *In* Disorderly Discourse: Narrative, Conflict, and Inequality. Charles L. Briggs, ed. Pp. 41–52. Oxford: Oxford University Press.
Hofling, Charles Andrew
   1993   Marking Space and Time in Itza Maya Narrative. Journal of Linguistic Anthropology 3(2):154–184.
Kernan, Keith, Sharon Sabsay, and Phyllis Schneider
   1991   Structure and Repair in Narratives of Mentally Retarded Adults. Journal of Linguistic Anthropology 1(2):143–164.
Mannheim, Bruce, and Krista Van Vleet
   1998   The Dialogics of Southern Quechua Narrative. American Anthropologist 100(2):326–346.
Martin, Laura
   1994   Discourse Structure and Rhetorical Elaboration in Mocho Personal Narrative. Journal of Linguistic Anthropology 4(2):131–152.
Ochs, Elinor, and Lisa Capps
   1996   Narrating the Self. Annual Review of Anthropology 25:19–43.
Patrick, Peter L., and Arvilla Payne-Jackson
   1996   Functions of Rasta Talk in a Jamaican Creole Healing Narrative: "A Bigfoot Dem Gi' Mi." Journal of Linguistic Anthropology 6(1):47–84.
Rose, Dan
   1996   Narrative Ethnography, Elite Culture, and the Language of the Market. *In* Culture/Contexture: Explorations in Anthropology and Literary Studies. E. Valentine Daniel and Jeffrey M. Peck, eds. Pp. 105–131. Berkeley: University of California Press.
Silverstein, Michael, and Greg Urban, eds.
   1996   Natural Histories of Discourse. Chicago: University of Chicago Press.
Thornton, Robert J.
   1983   Narrative Ethnography in Africa, 1850–1920: The Creation and Capture of an Appropriate Domain for Anthropology. Man 18(3): 502–520.

■ *Alan Rumsey*

Orality

L ike most technical terms, *orality* has taken on a specific sense in linguistic anthropology through the way it is contrasted with something
else – in this case with literacy. Structural linguistics asserts the primacy of spoken language over written, and has often treated the latter as
merely parasitic on the former. This view has a certain plausibility with respect to alphabetic or syllabic writing, where we can regard each letter or
character as the (more-or-less accurate) representation of a given sound. It is
less plausible with respect to ideographic scripts such as the Chinese, and
even less so with respect to gestural systems such as American Sign Language. For these do not simply transpose spoken language into a different
medium, but instead take advantage of their realization in three-dimensional
space, allowing for the building up in signed discourse of a kind of "random
access memory" whereby the characters or objects referred to in an ongoing
narrative can be literally "placed" at various points within the signer's hand-
reach, momentarily left aside as she introduces new ones with different placement, and then taken up again by redirecting her gaze and/or hands toward
the place associated with the earlier referent. This is functionally analogous
to the anaphoric or "reference tracking" systems of spoken language, but by
no means a mere transposition of any of them.

This example shows how the physical properties of a communicative medium figure crucially in establishing potentials and limits on what can be
done with it. This has long been understood to be true of alphabetic writing,
but it wasn't until more recently that the oral–aural (mouth-to-ear) channel
came to be thought about as a medium in its own right, with equally fateful
consequences for the peoples and cultures that were identified with it. This
was done by various theorists more or less independently in several branches
of the human sciences, but for linguistic anthropology one of the most important has been Milman Parry, who in the 1930s argued that the *Iliad* and
the *Odyssey* of Homer were orally composed. Drawing upon their study of
these and formally similar epics still being performed by bards in Yugoslavia,
Parry and Lord showed how the process of oral composition was facilitated

by the use of regular metrical lines and what they called formulae – fixed wordings each of which was regularly employed under the same metrical conditions.

Cross-cultural studies of verbal art have been strongly influenced by this work, which treats the form of Homeric and south-Slavic texts as exemplary of oral epic or even oral poetry in general, and oral composition as a special process that eventuates in formally similar textual products wherever it is used. Theorists such as Eric Havelock, Marshall McLuhan, and Walter Ong took this even further. For example, Ong posits a universal category of "primary orality," which he characterizes as additive rather than subordinative, aggregative rather than analytic, redundant or copious, agonistically toned, and empathetic and participatory rather than objectively distanced. Drawing on the psychological studies of Alexander Luria and Lev Vygotsky, Ong sees these characteristics not just as features of language or language use, but as aspects of a distinct mode of consciousness shared by "oral" peoples everywhere. In a somewhat more tempered, but equally dichotomizing, vein, anthropologist Jack Goody has argued that the differences between forms of thought that Claude Lévi-Strauss had attributed to "hot" vs. "cold" societies can be better understood as consequences of literacy vs. orality, respectively.

More recently there have been a number of case studies by anthropologists who have argued that the introduction of literacy does not have a single, cross-culturally uniform set of consequences, but that these depend very much upon the nature of the sociocultural setting into which it is introduced. A project for linguistic anthropologists in the new millennium is a parallel critique of the dichotomously related notion of orality as a cross-culturally uniform phenomenon. My sign language example already shows that the orality–literacy dichotomy is not exhaustive; other modes of inscription are possible. And, as shown in different ways by both Jacques Derrida and Mikhail Bakhtin, many of the features that we associate most closely with writing – its iterability, detachability from its source, etc. – pertain to speech as well. Furthermore, in their actual contexts of use, no single channel of communication or mode of inscription is ever self-sufficient. Each is deployed within an overall economy of inscriptive and interpretive practices that are shared within a given social field. Thus, for example, even in the most "literate" of societies, no book is ever written or read except in relation to an extended series of oral speech acts: those through which literacy is taught, authors socialized, readers' ears attuned, books bought and sold, etc. And even in supposedly "oral" societies, the oral–aural channel is never the only one used. Among central Australian Aborigines for example, widows were prohibited from speaking for many years after their husband's death and instead used a highly developed form of sign language. And in the same communities, the most highly valued narratives, those that tell of the creation of the world by ancestral beings, are, *pace* Ong, neither formulaic nor copious, but prosaic and extremely condensed in the telling. This can be related to the fact that the main form in which the creation stories are thought to be preserved is not human speech, but *the landscape itself* ("There," people say, pointing to a rock formation, *"That's* the story"). Of course this topographic form of inscription could not be read without the support of speech, any more than could the book in my previous example. But the role of speech here is avowedly exegetical rather than self-sufficient: the landscape is read primarily by *walking over it,* "following up" the actions of the creator figures.

From such examples we can see that it is misleading to use the term *orality* in reference to an entire society, culture, or communicative regime. This is not to deny the importance of differences among the various media used in such a regime. Rather, the point of my recommended project (already begun by Ruth Finnegan) is to elucidate the wide range of ways in which the various media are brought into interaction with each other in locally specific constellations of communicative practices.

(See also *deaf, gesture, iconicity, improvisation, indexicality, literacy, meter, narrative, oratory, signing, voice, writing*)

Bibliography

Bakhtin, Mikhail
   1986   Speech Genres and Other Late Essays. Austin: University of Texas Press.
Derrida, Jacques
   1976   Of Grammatology. Baltimore: Johns Hopkins University Press.
Finnegan, Ruth
   1988   Literacy and Orality: Studies in the Technology of Communication. Oxford: Basil Blackwell.
   1992[1977]   Oral Poetry: Its Nature, Significance and Social Context. Bloomington: Indiana University Press.
Goody, Jack
   1977   The Domestication of the Savage Mind. Cambridge: Cambridge University Press.
   1987   The Interface between the Written and the Oral. Cambridge: Cambridge University Press.
Lord, Albert
   1960   The Singer of Tales. Cambridge, MA: Harvard University Press.
Ong, Walter
   1982   Orality and Literacy: The Technologizing of the Word. London: Methuen.
Rumsey, Alan
   1994   The Dreaming, Human Agency and Inscriptive Practice. Oceania 65: 116–130.
Tedlock, Dennis
   1983   The Spoken Word and the Work of Interpretation. Philadelphia: University of Pennsylvania Press.

■ *Joel Kuipers*

Oratory

As an analytical term for linguistic anthropologists, *oratory* harbors rich associations with classical rhetoric. For Aristotle, oratory referred primarily to the art, rather than the act, of effective public speaking: the skills, competencies, and tactics of persuasive talkers rather than the actual events, practices, and performances that frame and define such displays of verbal ability. As in much of linguistic anthropology, the analytical tension between the art and the act creates opportunities for research and reflection.

Some of the classical connotations of oratory give reason for caution when applying it comparatively. In its focus on effective speech, oratory implies a contrast between instrumental, practical action, and more literary, poetic, and entertaining discourse. Yet studies of public discourse in Polynesia, Southeast Asia, Africa, and Native America reveal a very complex relation between stylistic form and expected outcomes. In some communities, a performance of highly structured, elaborate speech may be linked with not only secular results for social action, but sacred, aesthetic, and emotional effects that are not as easily observable. In some speech communities, such as the Wolof of Senegal, a griot's song might function as an effective and persuasive vehicle of public communication. As argued by Marshall Sahlins, culture and "practical reason" are deeply intertwined.

Local beliefs about language and its structures – or "language ideology" – also contribute to the meaning of oratory and its effectiveness. In some communities such as Weyewa of Indonesia or Merina of Madagascar, the more highly structured the speech code, the greater the general confidence people have in its effectiveness; among other groups, such as the seventeenth-century Quakers described by Richard Bauman or, indeed, late-twentieth-century Americans, elaborate formal code structuring in public verbal displays may be regarded as the antithesis of effective speech. The extent to which discourse is effective is associated with its simplicity. Some politicians are thought to be "great communicators" to the extent that they can express complex ideas simply with a minimum of artifice.

For anthropologists, oratory exhibits a problematic relation to the concept of "public." This notion also raises important questions (and analytical opportunities) when thinking about oratory comparatively. In general terms, oratory both constitutes and is constituted by an ideal of performance in relation to a larger community. In classical antiquity, however, oratory implied a performance in a non-domestic, collective space directed to an audience of non-kin. This definition effectively rules out the existence of oratory in small scale, kin-oriented communities such as "tribal" societies.

Oratory has generally been regarded as a predominantly male activity. Women are occasionally orators, but they are often portrayed as unusual, or as acting in a "deputy" capacity for a male. Important questions arise, however, as to whether there are women's forms of oratory that have been overlooked (perhaps because most anthropologists have been male). Furthermore, does oratory help constitute males as political creatures and reciprocally, women as domestic ones? Among the Weyewa in eastern Indonesia, both men and women perform in public speaking events, but their contributions are construed as complementary rather than competitive.

Oratory is a linguistically self-conscious form of speaking, rich in devices that frame and re-frame its use and contexts of interpretation. Many formal devices – including rhythm, pitch, pauses, even musical conventions – play a key role in the effectiveness of oratory. Some scholars, such as Maurice Bloch, have argued that the rules governing the structure of the verbal code so dominate the performance frame that other features of the performance – role definition, situational focus, and rules of alternation among styles – are guided by the features of the code structure. Others, such as Judith Irvine, have argued that the formal structure of roles, situational focus, style switching rules and code structure are all more or less independent features of oratory that can vary in their importance depending on the cultural context.

There is often no way to know in advance which features of oratory will be important in a given performance, because orators and audiences often use the context of performance to define the oratorical features that are relevant for the interpretation. Malagasy orators, for example, often deny they are even "truly" orating, pointing variously to features of the participants, setting, and code use to suggest that the performance is not yet quite authentic. As these features are addressed in turn, the performance takes shape as a process of contextualization.

The methodological and linguistic obstacles to studying oratory in depth can be daunting. Although the comparative analysis of politics, for example, often depends on data derived from public performances involving oratory, few anthropologists carefully study acts of oratory in context. This is partly because the language used in these events is often distinct from the everyday language and poses additional linguistic burdens and challenges on the visiting anthropologist. However, as volumes such as Donald Brenneis and Fred Myers's *Dangerous Words* and Bloch's *Political Language and Oratory in Traditional Society* have shown, careful study of oratory repays the linguistic investments because it not only reveals important insights about the nature of discourse, but also about politics.

Relatively little is known about how oratory changes, raising important questions for future research. While it seems clear that changes in oratory are linked to the sociopolitical circumstances that define the contexts of its use, the nature of those links are subtle and complex. Changing conceptions of the nature of the "public sphere" in many developing countries, for example, are accompanied by dynamic new patterns of oratory. In most cases, however, the relationship between sociopolitical structures and sociolinguistic practice is not simple, direct, or one-way. In Indonesia in 1998, for example, student demands for increased democratization were dramatically accompanied by the use of the relatively novel practice of *interupsi*, "interruptions" of the oratory of the political establishment. This shocking violation of Indonesian norms of verbal conduct highlighted the need for new patterns of political participation in ways that more standard political practices had not. These sociopolitical changes, in turn, then may give rise to further sociolinguistic shifts in sentence length, clause structure, and vocabulary, which in turn further affect changes in the political sphere.

Another important issue is the impact that mass media (television, radio, Internet) have had on the contexts and definition of oratory as public speaking. For example, it seems clear that oratory on television cannot be interpreted in the same terms as its more face-to-face relative. There is evidence to suggest that television-mediated oratory results in simplification, compartmentalization and even trivialization, isolating sources of meaning from audiences. On the other hand, in some cases, new cultures of spectatorship have emerged that themselves require oratorical response. As processes of globalization continue to transform both the concept of "the public" and "communication" in the new millennium, oratory poses intellectual and methodological challenges to linguistic anthropology. How the field responds to that challenge will speak eloquently about the shape of the discipline itself.

(See also *codes, gender, genre, ideology, media, music, orality, poetry, power, prayer, style*)

Bibliography

Bauman, Richard
    1983 Let Your Words Be Few: Symbolism of Speaking and Silence among 17th
        Century Quakers. Cambridge and New York: Cambridge University Press.
Bloch, Maurice, ed.
    1975 Political Language and Oratory in Traditional Society. London: Academic
        Press.
Brenneis, Donald, and Fred Myers, eds.
    1984 Dangerous Words: Language and Politics in the Pacific. New York: New
        York University Press.

Duranti, Alessandro
  1997 Oratory. *In* Folklore, Cultural Performances, and Popular Entertainments: A Communications-Centered Handbook. Richard Bauman, ed. Pp. 154–158. Oxford: Oxford University Press.
Irvine, Judith
  1979 Formality and Informality in Communicative Events. American Anthropologist 81(4):773–790.
Keenan, Elinor Ochs
  1973 A Sliding Sense of Obligatoriness: The Poly-Structure of Malagasy Oratory. Language in Society 2:225–243.
Kuipers, Joel
  1990a Power in Performance: The Creation of Textual Authority in Weyewa Ritual Speech. Philadelphia: University of Pennsylvania Press.
  1990b Talking about Troubles: Gender Differences in Weyewa Ritual Speech Use. *In* Power and Difference: Essays on Gender in Island Southeast Asia. Jane Atkinson and Shelly Errington, eds. Pp. 153–175. Stanford, CA: Stanford University Press.
Ryan, Mary
  1990 Women in Public: Between Banners and Ballots, 1825–1880. Baltimore: Johns Hopkins University Press.
Sahlins, Marshall
  1976 Culture and Practical Reason. Chicago: University of Chicago Press.

■ *Marjorie H. Goodwin*

Participation

In order for human beings to coordinate their behavior with that of their coparticipants, in the midst of talk participants must display to one another what they are doing and how they expect others to align themselves toward the activity of the moment. Language and embodied action provide crucial resources for the achievement of such social order. The term *participation* refers to actions demonstrating forms of involvement performed by parties within evolving structures of talk. Within the scope of this essay the term is not being used to refer to more general membership in social groups or ritual activities.

When we foreground participation as an analytic concept we focus on the interactive work that *hearers* as well as speakers engage in. Speakers attend to hearers as active coparticipants and systematically modify their talk as it is emerging so as to take into account what their hearers are doing. Within the scope of a single utterance, speakers can adapt to the kind of engagement or disengagement their hearers display through constant adjustments of their bodies and talk. This is accomplished by speakers through such things as adding new segments to their emerging speech, escalating the pitch of their voices or the size of their gestures, changing their facing formations, or possibly abandoning their talk.

In his early statement concerning the components of speech acts, Dell Hymes argued that "participant" was perhaps the most critical dimension necessary for an adequate descriptive theory of ways of speaking; a focus on the individual speaker or at best a speaker–hearer dyad (as elaborated in information theory, linguistics, semiotics, literary criticism, and sociology), he argued, was inadequate. Notions of the inadequacy of traditional models of speaker–hearer role structure were further elaborated in Erving Goffman's essay on "footing." Goffman argued that in addition to the concepts of ratified or unratified participants (overhearers), we need to consider forms of "subordinate communication" across the principal talk on the floor – byplay, crossplay, and sideplay. The concept of "participation framework" he proposed embraces the relationship, positioning, or total configuration of all participants to a gathering relative to a present speaker's talk.

Goffman treated participation (hearers' involvement) and speaker's "production" aspects of talk as separable features of conversational interaction. In critiquing traditional ways of considering speaker roles he argued that speakers not only portray events, but also animate characters and provide indications of their own alignment toward the events being recounted. Goffman's major concern was with the array of roles available to a *speaker* as *producer* of an utterance – animator, author, and principal for example. He was less engaged in providing descriptions of how hearers actively engage themselves as coparticipants in ongoing talk. Work on mutual monitoring describes the ways participants attend to talk through various sorts of assessments and non-vocal displays (headshakes that express awe at what the speaker is saying, nods that enthusiastically endorse the speaker's talk). Alternatively, hearers can also choose to distance themselves from the speaker's talk through displays of disattention, byplay, or heckling. Rather than constituting an internal, psychological process, evaluation and assessment are embedded within the kinds of participation that hearers and speakers engage in. The public, interactive dimension of this process is important for issues posed in the analysis of culture; by focusing on participation we can begin to investigate the interactive processes through which members of a social group come to view the world through a similar lens.

The concept of participation shifts the focus from the *structure* of speech activities to forms of *social organization* made possible through talk. Stories are often treated as artifacts that can be abstracted from their local circumstances and examined in terms of their internal features. By examining instead the participation structure within stories, I have analyzed how in the midst of disputes children can strategically invoke stories to rearrange their social organization. Disputes frequently take the form of reciprocal counters that restrict participation to two focal parties; each subsequent challenge selects prior speaker as next speaker and restricts participation to a dyad.

However, in the midst of a dispute by introducing a story, a participant can invoke a new multi-party participation framework that provides positions within it for all those present; differentiated forms of hearers can provide their own evaluation of the events being related. A protagonist can create a visible multi-party consensus against his opponent as hearers use the participation displays available to the audience of a story to affiliate to his position.

The analysis of participation within activities makes it possible to view actors as not simply embedded within context, but as actively involved in the process of building context. Among the African American girls with whom I did fieldwork in Philadelphia, stories about the past, present, and hypothetical future are crucial tools for bringing about engagement in an elaborate political event involving the entire neighborhood – a gossip dispute that the girls in the group call "he-said-she-said." In constructing a story, a teller crafts her narrative in light of the current hearers and the alignment of the audience members to figures in the story. Listener response to stories is critical to the ongoing development of the event.

Goffman's insights regarding participation have been useful for linguistic anthropologists – for example, in understanding inter-relationships of participation frames and genres within Mayan shaman ritual performances (described by William Hanks) and participant roles and textuality in Wolof insult poem performances (described by Judith Irvine) – as well as for considering variation in communicative norms cross-culturally. Susan Philips's early study of "participant structures" in American Indian classrooms in Warm Springs examined how ways of orchestrating student–teacher interaction, allocating turns at talk, and structuring student attention vary across different activities in the classroom. Philips analyzed the mismatch between contexts for learning at home and at school in Warm Springs, which lead to poor school performance. Similarly, Frederick Erickson's studies of black–white interaction during interviews show how different norms for interpreting "listening responses" (involving gaze and back channel cues) can lead to interactional "trouble." A focus on participation provides the anthropologist an opportunity to study from an integrated perspective how members of discourse communities use language and embodied action to constitute their social worlds.

(See also *body, community, competence, gesture, identity, improvisation, indexicality, oratory, power, theater, turn, vision, voice*)

Bibliography

Erickson, Frederick
  1979 Talking Down: Some Cultural Sources of Miscommunication in Interracial Interviews. *In* Nonverbal Communication: Applications and Cultural Implications. A. Wolfgang, ed. Pp. 99–126. New York: Academic Press.
Goffman, Erving
  1981 Footing. *In* Forms of Talk. Pp. 124–159. Philadelphia: University of Pennsylvania Press.
Goodwin, Charles
  1981 Conversational Organization: Interaction between Speakers and Hearers. New York: Academic Press.
Goodwin, Marjorie H.
  1980 Processes of Mutual Monitoring Implicated in the Production of Description Sequences. Sociological Inquiry 50:303–317.
  1990 He-Said-She-Said: Talk as Social Organization among Black Children. Bloomington: Indiana University Press.
  1997 By-Play: Negotiating Evaluation in Story-telling. *In* Towards a Social Science of Language: Papers in Honor of William Labov. Vol. 2: Social Interaction and Discourse Structures. G. R. Guy, C. Feagin, D. Schiffrin, and J. Baugh, eds. Pp. 77–102. Amsterdam and Philadelphia: John Benjamins.
Hanks, William F.
  1996 Exorcism and the Description of Participant Roles. *In* Natural Histories of

Discourse. M. Silverstein and G. Urban, eds. Pp. 160–202. Chicago: University of Chicago Press.

Hymes, Dell
    1972 Models of the Interaction of Language and Social Life. *In* Directions in Sociolinguistics: The Ethnography of Communication. J. J. Gumperz and D. Hymes, eds. Pp. 35–71. New York: Holt, Rinehart and Winston.

Irvine, Judith T.
    1990 Registering Affect: Heteroglossia in the Linguistic Expression of Emotion. *In* Language and the Politics of Emotion. C. A. and L. A.-L. Lutz, eds. Pp. 126–185. New York: Cambridge University Press.

Levinson, Stephen C.
    1987 Putting Linguistics on a Proper Footing: Explorations in Goffman's Concepts of Participation. *In* Goffman: An Interdisciplinary Appreciation. Paul Drew and Anthony J. Wootton, eds. Pp. 161–227. Oxford: Polity Press.

Philips, Susan U.
    1972 Participant Structures and Communicative Competence: Warm Springs Children in Community and Classroom. *In* Functions of Language in the Classroom. C. B. Cazden, V. P. John, and D. Hymes, eds. Pp. 370–394. New York: Columbia Teachers Press.

■ *Haruko M. Cook*

Particles

P articles are short, usually uninflected and invariable words, covering a wide range of grammatical functions. For example, in English, adverbs such as *on*, *up*, and *off* are called particles when they are the second element of a phrasal verb such as *put on*, *give up*, and *take off*. The prepositions and postpositions that mark grammatical relations are also referred to as *case particles*. For example, the preposition *e* in Samoan is a particle that marks ergative case, and the Japanese postposition *ga* is a particle that marks nominative case. The particles that are the most interesting from the point of view of the study of culture are pragmatic particles, i.e., particles that evoke or help constitute particular types of context.

Perhaps because these are the most elusive, the hardest to describe, and often beyond the bounds of syntactic analysis, they have attracted the attention of discourse analysts and other scholars interested in the use of language in social interaction.

Pragmatic particles are also called *discourse* particles, and in the German linguistic circle in particular they are known as *modal* particles. Pragmatic particles that occur in sentence-final position (and sometimes sentence-medial position) are called sentence particles or sentence-final particles. A number of particles in diverse languages are of this type: *ne, yo, sa, wa, ka, ze*, and *zo* in Japanese, *eh* in New Zealand English, *ba, a/ya*, and *ne* in Chinese, and *na* and *nia* in Thai, among others.

Since particles in general are not used as content words, they do not carry referential meaning. Pragmatic particles typically occur in face-to-face interaction and signal the speaker's epistemic and/or affective stance toward the addressee(s), the content of talk, or other aspects of the speech context. Diverse epistemic stances are marked by pragmatic particles. For example, both the German particle *ja* and the Japanese particle *yo* point to some aspect of the speech context that has just become apparent and make the hearer aware of it. This aspect of the context can be background knowledge that the speaker and the hearer share or the firsthand evidence found in the speech context. The particle *nâ* in Thai signals that the aspect of context in question is a matter of minor importance. The Japanese particle *no* indexes information that is accessible to the participants, including information that is supposedly known to the members of society. The Japanese particle *ne*, on the other hand, is primarily a marker of the speaker's affective stance. The speaker uses *ne* to indicate affective common ground (i.e., we feel the same way). In this sense, pragmatic particles provide metapragmatic instructions as to how the referential message is to be interpreted in speech context. In this way they are similar to suprasegmentals (stress, pitch, and intonation). In fact, they often combine with suprasegmentals and thereby give rise to more specific social meaning. For example, the Japanese particle *ne*, when it co-occurs with a rising intonation, indicates a request for confirmation.

Since pragmatic particles index the speaker's epistemic and/or affective stances, they can mitigate face-threatening acts. In this sense they are often associated with politeness phenomena. In Penelope Brown and Stephen Levinson's theory of politeness, hesitation, uncertainty, and indirectness are negative politeness strategies. The use of a pragmatic particle that marks knowledge acquired in an indirect fashion or belonging to the third party, for example, can be interpreted as a negatively polite act. In contrast, the use of a particle that indexes shared knowledge or feelings is a positive politeness strategy. For example, the Chinese particles *ba* and *ne* index probability or uncertainty, and thus tone down the illocutionary force of request. The Japanese particle *no*, which indexes knowledge shared by the speaker and the addressee or the third party, can function as a positive politeness marker. Thus it is often used when the speaker performs a face-threatening act such as persuading or explaining. The particle *no* in these instances points to the shared assumption and makes it harder for the addressee to reject the speaker's proposition.

A pragmatic particle is a typical example of what Michael Silverstein calls a "creative index," in the sense that it makes particular aspects of context happen in an immediate speech context. The meaning of a particle at least in part emerges from the immediate speech context, so it differs from context to context. For this reason, the social meanings of a pragmatic particle are beyond the limits of the native speakers' conscious awareness. Pragmatic particles used in various social contexts can constitute speech acts and social identities including gender identity. For example, because they foreground an aspect of context and make the addressee aware of it, particles such as the German particle *ja* and the Japanese particle *yo* can be assigned the speech act of reminding when the speaker wants the addressee to perform some act. The same particles can be used to convey the speech act of asserting when the speaker wants to convince the addressee of his or her opinion. They can constitute the social identity of an expert when the speaker is more knowledgeable than the addressee about the topic of conversation and uses the particle to mark such knowledge. Pragmatic particles such as the Japanese particle *wa* that index softness or hesitant attitude can index the speaker's female gender. Because softness and hesitant attitude evoke the Japanese ideal image of a woman, *wa* can constitute the gender identity of a woman.

Pragmatic particles can function as solidarity markers as well. When a particle is used with a high frequency by a certain group of people, it becomes an in-group marker, which indexes solidarity among the group members. In New Zealand English, the pragmatic particle *eh*, which is used as a tag in casual speech, is noticeably more frequently used by Maori men than by Maori women or British/European New Zealanders and functions as an in-group marker of ethnic identity for Maori men.

Pragmatic particles play an important role in allowing language to be a resource for creating and maintaining social worlds. They indicate, among other things, the assumptions that the speaker and addressee share, the aspect of context the addressee should pay attention to, the speaker's feelings toward the addressee or the topic of talk, and the identity of the speaker. The existence of pragmatic particles in language is true evidence that language is social activity.

(See also *functions, gender, indexicality, maxim, reflexivity*)

Bibliography

Abraham, Werner, ed.
   1991a   Discourse Particles. Amsterdam: John Benjamins.
   1991b   Discourse Particles across Languages. Multilingua 10(1/2) (special issue).
Brown, Penelope, and Stephen C. Levinson
   1987   Politeness: Some Universals in Language Usage. Cambridge: Cambridge University Press.
Cook, Haruko M.
   1990   An Indexical Account of the Japanese Sentence-final Particle *No*. Discourse Processes 13:401–439.
   1992   Meanings of Non-referential Indexes: A Case of the Japanese Particle *Ne*. Text 12:507–539.
Horie, Preeya I., and Shoichi Iwasaki
   1996   Register and Pragmatic Particles in Thai Conversation. Paper presented at the Proceedings of the Fourth International Symposium on Languages and Linguistics, Institute of Language and Culture for Rural Development, Mahidon University at Salaya, Thailand.
Lee-Wong, Song Mei
   1998   Face Support – Chinese Particles as Mitigators: A Study of *Ba, A/Ya* and *Ne*. Pragmatics 8:387–404.
Meyerhoff, Miriam
   1994   Sounds Pretty Ethnic, Eh? A Pragmatic Particle in New Zealand English. Language in Society 23:367–388.
Okamoto, Shigeko
   1995   Pragmaticization of Meaning in Some Sentence-final Particles in Japanese. *In* Essays in Semantics and Pragmatics: In Honor of Charles J. Fillmore. M. Shibatani and S. Thompson, eds. Pp. 219–246. Amsterdam and Philadelphia: John Benjamins.

Silverstein, Michael
  1976 Shifters, Linguistic Categories, and Cultural Description. *In* Meaning in Anthropology. K. H. Basso and H. A. Selby, eds. Pp. 11–55. Albuquerque: University of New Mexico Press.
Squires, Todd
  1994 A Discourse Analysis of the Japanese Particle *Sa*. Pragmatics 4:1–29.
Suzuki, Ryoko
  1990 The Role of Particles in Japanese Gossip. Berkeley Linguistic Society 16: 315–324.

■ *Kira Hall*

Performativity

The concept of the performative utterance, born within J. L. Austin's
ordinary language philosophy, has influenced the trajectory of linguistic anthropology in ways that I can only hint at here, capturing the
attention of scholars working within areas as diverse as ethnography of speaking, language socialization, pragmatics, discourse analysis, and more recently,
gender and language. The origin of the term *performative* can be traced back
to Austin's posthumous *How To Do Things with Words*. Austin, objecting to
the logical positivists' focus on the verifiability of statements, introduced the
performative as a new category of utterance that has no truth value since it
does not describe the world, but acts upon it – a way of "doing things with
words." The classic constative "snow is white" is descriptively true or false,
but statements such as "I now pronounce you husband and wife" are something different, their successful outcome depending on a number of conditions (i.e., "felicity conditions") that cannot be evaluated in terms of truth.
Such declarations are performative, not constative, because it is by the utterance of the words that the act is performed. By the end of his book, Austin
cleverly argues that all utterances are performative, even those that appear
merely to describe a state of affairs, since such utterances do the act of informing. This is a revolutionary conclusion, for all utterances must then be
viewed as actions, an equation which linguistic anthropologists have of course
embraced with fervor.

With Austin's exposition, the broader area of speech act theory emerged.
Within anthropology, Austin's work had its most immediate impact on the
paradigm of ethnography of speaking, and in particular on the study of ritual
and performance, when ethnographers took to the field to see if theory could
inform practice. The answer coming out of early texts such as Ruth Finnegan's
discussion of performative utterances among the Limba, Michael Foster's
study of Iroquois longhouse speech events, and Michelle Rosaldo's analysis
of Ilongot speech acts is that language philosophers must pay more attention
to the localized ideologies that govern language use before making sweep-
ing generalizations about how language operates in culture. Most telling in

this respect is Rosaldo's rejection of Austin's and Searle's five-part taxonomy of speech acts. She argues that intention and sincerity, both of which are granted esteemed positions in these discussions, are irrelevant to the success of speech acts in Ilongot culture. The philosophical emphasis on the speaker's psychological state does not underlie a universal theory of speech acts, but rather an "ethnography of contemporary [Western] views of human personhood and action."

These early critiques of speech act theory resulted in more nuanced ethnographic accounts of performance and ritual in linguistic anthropology, ultimately giving new life to Austin's performative. Many of the subsequent studies on ritual could be viewed as ethnographic extensions of the "dual-direction-of-fit" that John Searle identifies for the classic performative. While the words of a performative do in some sense "fit" the world, conforming to the conventions that govern their success, they also constitute it, so that by their very utterance the world is also made to fit the words. The same duality could be said to be true of ritualized performance (as Tambiah suggests in a direct application of Austin's felicity conditions to ritual in the late 1970s), prompting anthropologists to demand more discussion of the creative qualities of ritual alongside the constraining ones. Hymes' repeated call to "understand structure as emergent in action" is critical here, as he and other scholars of performance, most notably Briggs and Bauman, led us away from the analysis of ritual as mere reiteration. Their work has encouraged a new line of thinking in the last two decades of cultural anthropology as well, exemplified by Turner's work on liminality and creativity and by recent feminist work on the gendered aspects of ritual.

No discussion of performativity would be complete without reference to its uptake in literary criticism, particularly as Austin's performative, reworked by poststructuralist patriarch Derrida, instigated something akin to a revolution in literary theory. Paralleling early ethnographers of speaking, Derrida criticized speech act theory for its focus on intentionality, albeit from a markedly different perspective. While linguistic anthropologists looked to culture for their criticisms, Derrida looked to literature, arguing in a deconstructive vein that because the text can always be detached from the context in which it is written, the intentionality of its author is irrelevant. For Derrida, context can never be identified, since speech acts work through a potential of never-ending citationality; for linguistic anthropologists, context must be identified, since speech acts are realized only through the cultural conventions that govern their use. It is this differing understanding of context that continues to prohibit dialogue between these two uptakes. The buzzword in poststructuralist literary theory becomes "iterability," the endless repetition of speech acts within a discursive history that has lost its original context. Our anthropological buzzword, in contrast, becomes "the total speech act," as ethnographers attempt to define the cultural conventions that make performance, ritual, and even everyday conversation felicitous, while at the same time acknowledging the emergent and creative aspects of any speech event.

We are now entering what might be called the second generation of the performative in linguistic anthropology, one that promises to mimic its earlier uptake, as language and gender scholars, inspired by gender theorist Judith Butler's notion of "performativity," seek to ground her philosophical claims in more localized, ethnographic accounts of diverse communities of practice. Butler's argument that gender works as a performative, constituting the very act that it performs, is, as linguists such as Anna Livia, Deborah Cameron, Mary Bucholtz, and myself have pointed out, a promising idea for discourse analysis, as it leads us away from sociolinguistic approaches to identity that view the way we talk as directly indexing a prediscursive self. To a poststructuralist like Butler, there is no prediscursive identity, as even our understanding of biological sex is discursively produced. This perspective puts more weight on the speech event itself, requiring us to examine how speakers manipulate ideologies of feminine and masculine speech in the ongoing production of gendered selves. Still, it must be stated that Butler, like her poststructuralist predecessors, largely discounts the emergent properties of gendered acts and the agency of the subjects that perform them, focusing primarily on the repetitive nature of gender. For Butler, there is no agency in the sense of a voluntarist subject, as actors are little more than ventriloquists, iterating the gendered acts that have come before them. The only way out of this performative trap is resignification, which if done appropriately (and Butler points to the recent in-group reclaiming of the word "queer" here as well as drag performance) can turn this iterability on its ugly head and betray its constructed nature. It remains to be seen how linguistic anthropologists will reconcile Butler's theory with an ethnographic understanding of context and the diverse conceptualization of agency that comes with it, but we can be certain that Austin's performative will continue to enliven our field in unexpected ways well into the new century.

(See also *act, agency, functions, gender, healing, humor, music, names, narrative, orality, oratory, power, theater*)

Bibliography

Austin, John L.
   1962   How To Do Things with Words. Cambridge, MA: Harvard University
      Press.
Bauman, Richard, and Charles L. Briggs
   1990   Poetics and Performance as Critical Perspectives on Language and Social
      Life. Annual Review of Anthropology 19:59–88.
Butler, Judith
   1990   Gender Trouble: Feminism and the Subversion of Identity. New York:
      Routledge.
Cameron, Deborah
   1997   The Language-Gender Interface: Challenging Co-optation. *In* Rethinking
      Language and Gender Research: Theory and Practice. Victoria L. Bergvall,
      Janet M. Bing, and Alice F. Freed, eds. Pp. 31–49. London: Longman.

Finnegan, Ruth
  1969   How To Do Things with Words: Performative Utterances among the Limba
    of Sierra Leone. Man 4:537–552.
Foster, Michael
  1989[1974]   When Words Become Deeds: An Analysis of Three Iroquois
    Longhouse Speech Events. *In* Explorations in the Ethnography of Speaking.
    2nd ed. Richard Bauman and Joel Sherzer, eds. Pp. 354–367. Cambridge: Cam-
    bridge University Press.
Hymes, Dell
  1975   Breakthrough into Performance. *In* Folklore: Performance and Com-
    munication. D. Ben-Amos and K. S. Goldstein, eds. Pp. 11–74. The Hague:
    Mouton.
Livia, Anna, and Kira Hall
  1997   "It's a Girl!" Bringing Performativity back to Linguistics. *In* Queerly
    Phrased: Language, Gender, and Sexuality. Anna Livia and Kira Hall, eds.
    Pp. 3–18. New York: Oxford University Press.
Rosaldo, Michelle Z.
  1982   The Things We Do with Words: Ilongot Speech Acts and Speech Act Theory
    in Philosophy. Language in Society 11:203–235.
Searle, John
  1976   The Classification of Illocutionary Acts. Language in Society 5(1): 1–23.
Tambiah, S. J.
  1979   A Performative Approach to Ritual. Proceedings of the British Academy
    65. London: Oxford University Press.
Turner, Victor
  1984   Liminality and Performative Genres. *In* Rite, Drama, Festival, Spectacle:
    Rehearsals toward a Theory of Cultural Performance. J. J. MacAloon, ed. Pp.
    19–41. Philadelphia: Institute for the Study of Human Issues.

■ *Ron Scollon*

Plagiarism

P lagiarism is not so much a linguistic category as a social issue to which linguists and anthropologists have sometimes directed attention. As a social issue, the term indexes a range of moral, ethical, legal, and positioning issues that have importance for research in linguistics and in anthropology. As a theoretical issue, plagiarism is a subset of a wide variety of questions that are suggested by terms such as *intertextuality* and *interdiscursivity*, *reported speech*, *constructed dialogue*, *discourse representation*, and *dialogicality* and *polyvocality*. What is at stake, whether we view plagiarism as a social issue or a theoretical one, is the analytical and responsible position taken in respect to the appropriation of text from one discourse which is then recontextualized (entextualized, embedded) within another subsequent text.

In much contemporary linguistic analysis it is taken as axiomatic that all text is constituted to a considerable extent by combining prior texts, from words and utterances to full literal texts, and that much of what gives any particular text its generic characteristics as well as what gives the author—a highly problematic consideration in this view—originality derives from the particular mixes, combinations, and hybridities that result. In this view a text with no history in prior utterance would be a theoretical impossibility. Thus what emerge as the central questions are the questions of accuracy of citation, of clarity of attribution to prior sources, of legal ownership of texts that are transformed in new encontextualizations, and of the moral, ethical, and power relationships among those who have been responsible for prior utterances and those who are engaged in recontextualizations.

The wide range of recontextualizations that have been studied make it clear that we cannot easily take direct quotation as the prototype of entextualization. Attention must be equally given to indirect quotation, paraphrase, presupposition, negation, staged enactments, and hidden dialogicalities where the other voice is only represented through responses to it and a host of other modes of intertextuality. In this sense the poetic discourses of poetry and song, advertising, and mythology come closer to representing the full complexity of the nature of discourse than the direct citations with clear attributions set up as norms in academic discourse.

Accusations of plagiarism within an understanding of the hybrid nature of all discourse, then, can be viewed as hegemonic and derogatory positioning. Practices of entextualization, which are the norms in advertising and journalism, are viewed as plagiarism in academic discourses. In making assertions about plagiarism, broader social issues of personal character, social networking, in-group and out-group membership, and the power to (mis)-appropriate are inevitably indexed.

Plagiarism in the form of copyright and patent infringement indexes a subset of intellectual property issues in which the power of the nation-state through the legal discourses it authorizes intervenes in the common discourses of daily life. Among intellectual properties are the commodity/signs of brand names, logos, trademarks, and product and brand slogans. These commodity/signs, which are protected against unauthorized uses, bring into common discourse injunctions based in corporate ownership. To the felicity conditions on speech acts of pragmatics have now been added conditions of fear of infringement. An unauthorized use of a brand name on a television talk show, for example, or in a newspaper story will bring a letter of injunction or a legal action to produce legal remedies for damages to the product or the corporate owners. The discursive consequence is that a form of hidden dialogicality or indirectness in discourse may arise in which common brand names, logos, and trademarks are only present by their studied absence in discourse. One uses a facial tissue rather than a Kleenex® and makes a photocopy rather than a Xerox®.

Plagiarism has been discussed as an issue in mentoring, particularly in reference to "international" students, "international" colleagues, or other "latecomers" to academic discourses. Couched in the most positive terms, the problem is seen as one of analyzing academic discourses to produce clear descriptions of practice to enable entrance into these discourses. Couched in more critical terms, the problem is seen as the assertion of the practices of an "inner circle" of academics as a hegemonic move to maintain exclusion. This latter argument is strengthened by research suggesting that academic practice is far from universal even within the "inner circle" and that "international" practice more resembles the "inner circle's" discourses of journalism and advertising, of art and literature.

Plagiarism as the violation of secret or privileged knowledge had been rarely scrutinized by linguists and anthropologists, but in recent years studies of this kind are increasing. As the inverse of the "mentoring problem," the texts that linguists and anthropologists produce in the field are normally recontextualizations or entextualizations of privileged and ritually controlled discourses. There is a growing concern with the study of the relative positionings of linguists-anthropologists and the authors or ritual owners of the texts upon which our research crucially rests. In the best cases this has led to an understanding of the processes of co-construction and co-production of linguistic descriptions and ethnographic analyses and to an appreciation of the intertextual and interdiscursive constitution of all of our discourses whether descriptive or analytic, whether produced in the field or presented in academic publication.

(See also *genre, heteroglossia, improvisation, media, reflexivity, relativity, truth, voice*)

Bibliography

Bakhtin, Mikhail M.
  1981[1934–35]   The Dialogic Imagination: Four Essays. Ed. by M. Holquist, translated by C. Emerson and M. Holquist. Austin: University of Texas Press.
Coombe, Rosemary J.
  1998   The Cultural Life of Intellectual Properties: Authorship, Appropriation, and the Law. Durham, NC, and London: Duke University Press.
Duranti, Alessandro
  1993   Beyond Bakhtin, or the Dialogic Imagination in Academia. Pragmatics 3(3):333–340.
Fairclough, Norman
  1992   Discourse and Social Change. Cambridge: Polity Press.
Pennycook, Alastair
  1996   Borrowing Others' Words: Text, Ownership, Memory, and Plagiarism. TESOL Quarterly 30(2):201–230.
Scollon, Ron
  1995   Plagiarism and Ideology: Identity in Intercultural Discourse. Language in Society 24(1):1–28.
Silverstein, Michael, and Greg Urban
  1996   Natural Histories of Discourse. Chicago: University of Chicago Press.

Poetry

T he terms *poetry* and *poetics* have ranges of use beyond language. Poetry can express aesthetic pleasure in almost any sphere ("sheer poetry," "poetry in motion"). Poetics can apply the sense of "making" of the classical Greek verb *poein* to shaping in any or all aspects of cultural life. Here I will consider only shaping of language.

One kind of shaping of language has to do with "fashions of speaking." Characteristic ways of naming, predicating and interacting in one language may differ from those in another, and suggest differences in the ways users of the languages interpret aspects of their worlds. When users of Wasco encountered windows, someone coined a nominalized verb theme that is literally "they-two-see-each-other-through-it," a choice ratified by others.

Such a coinage fits other features of the language, including its system of tenses. The directional marker preceding transitive verb stems is not simply either "to" or "from," but "from this point to that" or "from that point to this." Recent elaboration of the tense system to distinguish near and distant in the future and remote past cannot be explained without recognizing analogy from this bipolar orientation.

Such "cognitive styles" can sometimes be traced not only within a language but also in its use. For speakers of Wasco-Wishram Chinook, unqualified use of the future tense has depended upon certainty that something will happen, and so do certain events of disclosure (of a guardian spirit experience, of a personal name, of myths).

Interest in such matters has focused on features of languages as determinants of perception, cognition, conduct, and behavior. Their effect of course depends partly on situational factors. Still the existence of cognitive styles is itself evidence of a shaping relation between a language and its users. Users of the language have put them there.

Those skeptical of language as a constraint on thought and behavior still may accept it as a constraint on poetry. But what is poetry? A definition that fits its diversity is organization in terms of relations within and among lines. What can count as a line depends in part on the makeup of the language.

In many traditions lines are in some sense metrical, defined by internal count. What is counted may be syllables (as in haiku, and the poetry of Marianne Moore and Elizabeth Daryush), or alliterating syllables (Old and some Middle English), or types of feet as short and long (Classical Greek, Latin), or one type (six iambic feet make an alexandrine), or tone sequences of certain kinds (Classical Chinese). Of course relations among lines may play a part, through rhyme (sonnets, triolets) and changes of length (as in ballads, the poetry of Ogden Nash).

Here languages differ as to material base. True, it is difficult to say what a language cannot be made to do. But if it has no tones, tone is out. Recurrence of a vowel is so common in Japanese as to be said to preclude rhyme. Still, there are forms in some languages in which every line rhymes, including a genre (*hitat baladi*) that is part of epic narratives in Egyptian Arabic.

Not all lines are metrical, of course. Recent decades have seen proliferation of free verse (sometimes called so only from failure to recognize its character), expressive use of space in placing lines and words on the page, varieties of prose poem, and new attention to forms combining verse and prose.

Spoken and written remain shibboleths, some valuing the oral as original, authentic, arising in performance, others drawn to meanings that external silence permits to emerge. (Some, of course, do not choose.) The work of Milman Parry and Albert Lord with Serbo-Croatian singers of epic is a reference point for this. They gave reason to believe that formulae in these epics and those of Homer ("rosy-fingered dawn") arose to make it possible to compose while performing. Stock formulae fitting metrical requirements at the ends of lines (dactylic hexameter in Homer) allowed a singer to improvise elsewhere with assurance of coming out right.

Some take formulae as defining all oral poetry. Others point out their limitations (not necessarily stock – epithets for Achilles may each have a point where they occur; not necessarily oral – consider Pope's command of phrases to fill thousands of heroic couplets). Still, oral epic has been central to societies across large stretches of Europe, Africa, and Asia, and its interpretation remains important.

For the most part, anthropologists have found poetry in songs. Obviously, songs have lines. Narratives presumably are prose, hence paragraphs. It now appears that oral narratives organize lines, and are poetry as well. When heard, final sentence contours distinguish verses (a verse may have more than one line). Verses form stanzas; stanzas, scenes.

Many narratives transcribed by anthropologists exist now only on the page. Still, their form is recoverable. Time expressions, initial particles, turns at talk, and other features show relations, not within lines (meter), but among lines (measured verse) – what Roman Jakobson called "equivalence." Freed from arbitrary paragraphs, stories take on life. Lines, verses, and stanzas cohere in what Kenneth Burke called "arousal and satisfaction of expectation." Analysis as lines reveals imagination and power. This can serve those whose heritage the stories are, and be a kind of repatriation.

Probably there have always been anthropologists who wrote poetry. Today poetry has increasingly become a public way to convey ethnographic experience. Do some aspects of experience find expression only or mainly in poetry? That would be a part of ethnography of ourselves, past and present – of our shaping and being shaped by language.

(See also *iconicity, ideophone, indexicality, literacy, meter, music, narrative, orality, oratory, particles, performativity, proverb, repetition, style, translation, voice*)

Bibliography

Burke, Kenneth
   1925   Psychology and Form. The Dial 79(1):340–346.
Foley, John Miles
   1995   The Singer of Tales in Performance. Bloomington: Indiana University Press.
Harris, Joseph, and Karl Reichl, eds.
   1997   Prosimetrum. Crosscultural Perspectives on Narrative in Prose and Verse. Cambridge: D. S. Brewer.
Hymes, Dell
   1996   Ethnography, Linguistics, Narrative Inequality: Toward an Understanding of Voice. London: Taylor and Francis.
   1998   When Is Oral Narrative Poetry? Generative Form and Its Pragmatic Conditions. Pragmatics 8(4):475–500.
Jakobson, Roman
   1960   Concluding Statement: Linguistics and Poetics. *In* Style and Language. T. A. Sebeok, ed. Pp. 350–377. Cambridge, MA: MIT Press.
Meschonnic, Henri
   1982   Critique du rythme. Anthropologie historique du langage. Lagrasse, France: Editions Verdier.
Reynolds, Dwight
   1995   Heroic Poets, Poetic Heroes: The Ethnography of Performance in an Arabic Oral Epic Tradition. Ithaca, NY: Cornell University Press.
Sapir, Edward
   1921   Language and Literature. *In* Language. Pp. 221–231. New York: Harcourt Brace.
Stolz, Benjamin, and Richard S. Shannon, eds.
   1976   Oral Literature and the Formula. Ann Arbor: Center for the Coordination of Ancient and Modern Studies, University of Michigan.

■ *Susan U. Philips*

Power

In anthropology today, the constitution of social reality is itself considered a central form of power. Within this view, the power of language lies in its reality-creating capacity. In linguistic anthropology, three different ways of conceptualizing the site of this reality-creating emerged during the twentieth century. All of these are still with us, and I will deal with each of them in turn. I suggest that all three are needed for a complete anthropological understanding of the relationship between language and power.

The *first* and oldest view is that the reality-constituting capacity of language is located in the *structure of the language* itself, most specifically in the lexical and morphological semantic structures of all languages. The idea that the language a group speaks entails a culturally distinctive worldview came into the United States from Germany with Franz Boas in the late nineteenth century. It has been developed through the work of Edward Sapir, Benjamin Lee Whorf, Ward Goodenough, and others still working on the relation between language and cognition. However, it is important to note that while the reality-constituting role of language structure has been clearly articulated, that reality-creating capacity has not been represented as a form or expression of power in this tradition.

The *second* vision of language as fundamental to the creation of social realities, which emerged in the 1960s, located this creation in the process of *discourse* in face-to-face interaction, in the speech of human actors. Different versions of this vision, each of which entails a somewhat different theory of the power of language, have been articulated over the past thirty years.

In the earliest politicized work focusing on discourse, power was understood as something that some people have more of than others. So some people have more control over and determination of the nature of social realities that get constituted through face-to-face interaction than others do, primarily by virtue of being able to exert control over the production of discourse. Thus teachers, doctors, and lawyers have more reality-defining power than students, patients, and witnesses, by virtue of their control over turn allocation in classrooms, examination rooms, and courtrooms. To the degree that members of the dominant white culture in the United States occupied bureaucratic positions associated with control over turns at talk more than ethnic minorities, white people are able to define the social realities of blacks, Indians, Hawaiians, and Mexican Americans in situations where they co-interact. Men have more power than women in defining social realities by virtue of their control over turns at talk, topics, and their deployment of linguistic devices that direct attention to the certainty and reliability of their assertions.

More recently, primarily in the 1990s, other ideas have emerged that still envision reality-creating in discourse as a form of power yet do not focus attention on the haves and the have-nots of power. One idea is that reality-creating power lies in discourse itself, so that all of us are dominated by discourse and subordinated to it, and individual human agency is relatively inconsequential in the face of this power. Michel Foucault bears significant responsibility for this vision, which has deeply penetrated cultural and linguistic anthropology. However, the linguistic anthropological concept of entextualization can be seen as a variant of this view. Entextualization refers to the process through which the content and form of particular texts become fixed in varying degrees in performance. Fixed texts entail more power than context-dependent texts because of the way in which they culturally and ideologically reproduce the same ideas over and over.

Another idea of reality-creating in discourse emerged in the 1990s, which envisions ALL interactants as having the power to shape a continually emerging reality through the process of taking turns at talk in conversation. Both the so-called powerful and the powerless, the dominated and the subordinated, the high status and the low have this power merely by virtue of their involvement in the communicative process. And they have it whether they are participating in relatively entextualized or scripted kinds of discourse, or in relatively open-ended kinds of inter-actions. This model of how the power of language works offers us a way to recognize and conceptualize agency at the level of individual actions, and to sort out one individual's agency from that of another by conceptualizing their agentive contributions as turns at talk. Those espousing this view have clearly been influenced by conversation analysis, and particularly Harvey Sacks's early contributions to it, notably his emphasis on the way in which every single turn at talk transforms the meaning of all that has gone before it. But conversation analysis, like the theories of the worldview or cognitive structure to be found in the structure of language, lacks an explicit theory of power. It has been left to others to conceptualize the emergent meaning in talk as a form of power.

So far I have considered the reality-creating power of language as cited in language structure and in discourse. The *third* current theoretical locus for the reality-creating power of language is in very large-scale, power-laden *social historical processes* that both shape and are shaped by the power of language. In this framework, the reality-creating role of language is theoretically conceptualized as serving the production of relatively abstract relations of domination and subordination. These abstract power relations include those of a global political economy, the historical processes of European colonialism, and the emergence of nation-states. In this framework, talk about talk, or language ideologies, are shown to play an important role in the European colonial defining and management of colonized populations and in the maintenance of state hegemony through ideologically diverse discourses of state institutional complexes engaged in the production of nationalist ideologies.

In anthropological theory about the relation between language and power, then, the creation of social realities through the deployment of language structures in discourse is the process through which broader socio-historical power relations are sustained and transformed through time.

(See also *agency, conflict, control, conversation, functions, gender, ideology, indexicality, participation, poetry, relativity, space, turn, vision, voice*)

Bibliography

Bauman, Richard, and Charles L. Briggs
    1990   Poetics and Performance as Critical Perspectives on Language and Social Life. Annual Review of Anthropology 19:59–88.
Bloch, Maurice, ed.
    1975   Political Language and Oratory in Traditional Society. New York: Academic Press.
Bourdieu, Pierre
    1991   Language and Symbolic Power. Cambridge, MA: Harvard University Press.
Danet, Brenda
    1980   "Baby" or "Fetus"? Language and the Construction of Reality in a Manslaughter Trial. Semiotica 32(3/4):187–219.
Duranti, Alessandro
    1994   From Grammar to Politics: Linguistic Anthropology in a Western Samoan Village. Berkeley: University of California Press.
Erickson, Frederick, and Jeffrey Schultz
    1982   The Counselor as Gatekeeper. New York: Academic Press.
Foucault, Michel
    1980   The History of Sexuality. Vol. 1: An Introduction. New York: Vintage Books.
Hymes, Dell
    1973   Speech and Language: On the Origins and Foundations of Inequality among Speakers. Daedalus 102(3):59–80.
Keating, Elizabeth
    1998   Power Sharing: Language, Rank, Gender, and Social Space in Pohnpei, Micronesia. New York: Oxford University Press.
Schieffelin, Bambi B., Kathryn A. Woolard, and Paul V. Kroskrity, eds.
    1998   Language Ideologies: Practice and Theory. New York: Oxford University Press.

■ *Patricia Baquedano-López*

Prayer

Despite the importance of religion and ritual in anthropology, prayer, a key component of religious practices and institutions, has received very little empirical attention. In its broadest sense, prayer is a discursive act that bridges human limitation and the spiritual realm. To pray is to be conscious of mortal existence. Perhaps there is no other single speech event that engages people at the critical points of the life cycle more than prayer. In Western traditions, people celebrate transitions in social life with prayer, bury the dead with both eulogy and prayer, and remember the dead in moments of silent prayer. This celebratory essence of prayer has been shared across time and cultural groups. Indeed, archaeological work has confirmed this link. Symbols and objects related to prayer have been uncovered as silent testimonials of ancient traditions and communities with a profound preoccupation with life and death in the construction and explanation of the social world. Prayer, in this way, is an intrinsic human meaning-making activity that relates the known and the unknown. Prayer grounds humans to earth, yet orients them to a higher spiritual point.

The genre and practice of prayer is richly varied across cultural groups. Prayers can be specially sanctioned by religious institutions, as in the case of The Lord's Prayer in Christian tradition. Such prayers are scripted, following a prescribed pattern in both text and delivery. Prayers can also be situational, arising from moment-to-moment experience. Prayers may be sung or said by an intercessor, co-constructed by a congregation, or recited privately by the individual. And while the act of praying is understood more as an intentional act, at times, it can be involuntary, as in the case of mediums in trance, the exhilarated state of mystics, or of individuals "possessed by the Spirit." Prayers are inherently transcendent in that they are always directed to a superior spiritual being with whom humans seek to align. While prayers can give praise to and acknowledge the bounties of the superior being, prayers can also acknowledge human frailty and, in times of need, petition assistance. In all these situations, worshippers discursively position themselves asymmetrically to a transcendent being, and on occasion, praying may involve an offering or the promise of a vow. Prayer thus discursively extends the domain of the self in anticipation of future life events. People learn particular ideologies about prayer from their early socialization experiences. A 1997 national poll reports that a little over half of American adults pray as part of their daily routine. But the consciousness that leads to prayer is not only limited to believers or practicing individuals. This consciousness can become manifest at any moment in life. Reminiscent of Labovian narratives, everyday stories of conversion describe the non-believer praying while in heightened awareness, most particularly, during near-death experiences.

Prayer has a liminal structural quality, which leads to its description in anthropological work as part of a range of genres that often includes song, dance, divination, and even poetry. Prayers are characteristically parallel in structure. However, metaphorical and syntactic parallelism often extend beyond the confines of text to practice. In fact, in Muslim tradition, repetition is not only inherent to the internal structure of prayer, but also to the act of praying itself. Believers must learn a particular body demeanor and must orient the body to a sacred point in order to pray at regularly prescribed times of the day. Among indigenous groups of the Americas, spatial recognition and the discursive orientation of the praying individual in relation to other beings and spiritual forces is invoked and performed in prayer. It is also not uncommon to find that body demeanor in prayer is accompanied by special diet and other rituals that cleanse the body in preparation for communicating with the transcendent. In this way, prayer consciously unites body and spirit.

A common characteristic of prayer is its narrative quality – its potential as a sense-making discursive act. Prayer can be a powerful means to piece together life experience. Elinor Ochs and Lisa Capps have studied the overlapping nature of prayer and personal narrative, and in their study of family dinnertime grace and of a Los Angeles Sunday School kindergarten class at an Episcopalian church, prayers are the means to retell past and present conflict. In other contexts, prayers can be about absent others and may involve a larger collectivity. In my study of Spanish-taught Catholic religious education classes for Mexicano children at a parish in Los Angeles, classroom prayers extend to include the community. When children pray for the health of an absent teacher, they pray for their families, the sick in hospitals, the incarcerated, and the elderly in nursing homes, in this way linking their present experience to the experiences of other members of the community.

Prayer, however, is no longer situated solely within the domain of religious institutions, particularly in Christian tradition. It is increasingly becoming a commodity and a link to a capitalist economy. Prayers can be requested, exchanged, and even bought. An example of prayers that are commissioned includes those as part of religious ceremonies in remembrance of the dead. Prayers are also being marketed for consumers, as in, for example, the popular dial-a-prayer telephonic services increasingly advertised through mass media. Prayers can also be accessed through on-line prayer links on the Internet. Lanita Jacobs-Huey reports on a group of affluent African-

American Christian cosmetologists who heal both spirit and hair. In their monthly meetings, these Christian cosmetologists talk about their unique spiritual mission, but also about the business of hair care. Prayer has also made its way into popular culture. American singer Madonna's 1989 album *Like a Prayer* catapulted the sexual emancipation begun in the social movement of the 1960s (as well as collected millions of dollars in record sales for the singer). The lyrics of the feature song juxtaposed two irreconcilable domains of the Christian worldview as the song equated prayer with sex.

The preoccupation to understand the mystery of life and death, and the role prayer plays in it, is becoming more ecumenical and pragmatic, no longer limited to philosophers or theologians. Research on the healing power of prayer is currently being conducted by a Georgetown University School of Medicine study, where rheumatoid arthritis patients receive treatment through the practice of laying on of hands. The initial results report on the improved health of the patients. This pragmatic reconceptualization of prayer has the potential to deploy prayer's synergistic power to effect palpable, controllable change. Wherever these efforts might take us in the future, prayer remains a primordial discursive means through which many people interpret and come to terms with the purpose of their lives.

(See also *body, healing, meter, narrative, performativity, poetry, prophecy, theater, truth, voice*)

Bibliography

Baquedano-López, Patricia
  1998 Language Socialization of Mexican Children in a Los Angeles Catholic Parish. Ph.D. dissertation, University of California, Los Angeles.
Bauman, Richard
  1983 Let Your Words Be Few: Symbolism of Speaking and Silence among Seventeenth-century Quakers. Cambridge: Cambridge University Press.
Black Elk, Wallace, and William Lyon
  1990 Black Elk: The Sacred Ways of a Lakota. New York: Harper Collins.
Firth, Raymond
  1996 Religion: A Humanist Interpretation. London: Routledge.
Gossen, Gary
  1974 Chamulas in the World of the Sun. Cambridge, MA: Harvard University Press.
Jacobs-Huey, Lanita
  1998 We Are Just Like Doctors, We Heal Sick Hair: Cultural and Professional Discourses of Hair and Identity in a Black Hair Care Seminar. Paper presented at the Proceedings of the Fifth Symposium on Language and Society. SALSA V. Conference Proceedings. Austin: University of Texas.
Leavitt, John, ed.
  1997 Poetry and Prophecy: The Anthropology of Inspiration. Ann Arbor: University of Michigan Press.

Ochs, Elinor, and Lisa Capps
    2001   Cultivating Prayer. *In* The Language of Turn and Sequence. Cecilia Ford,
        Barbara Fox, and Sandra Thompson, eds. Oxford: Oxford University Press.
Samarin, William
    1976   Language in Religious Practice. Rowley, MA: Newbury House.
Woodward, Kenneth
    1997   Is God Listening? Newsweek, March 31:57–64.

■ *John Leavitt*

Prophecy

I n the modern West, prophecy implies public discourse with a future-oriented social or political message, so that the word can simply mean foretelling the future. The model figure is that of the Old Testament prophet crying God's word and decrying the sins of his people. Prophecy in this sense is found in only a limited number of societies. Yet it is not hard to expand the meaning of the term in a way that respects our own lexical intuitions: if we open up what we mean by divine to include all gods and lesser spirits, then the word *prophecy* comes to designate a much broader phenomenon. In every society, some among the speech forms available to speakers are recognized as closely related to, often as emanating from, what, for lack of better words, we might call a non-ordinary realm. Out of the speaker's mouth comes the voice of a possessing demon, revealing god, or inspiring muse; or the speaker tells, usually in highly marked language, what he or she has experienced in an otherworldly adventure. These kinds of practice are associated with a variety of terms in Western languages – *prophecy, inspiration, possession, mediumship, oracle, mysticism, trance, ecstasy* – all involving language the speaker of which is "outside" him or herself or who is reporting such an "outside" experience. Given the connotations of *prophecy*, it might be advisable to find another word for such language and experience; following Nora Chadwick, here I will use the less loaded term *mantic*, from a Greek word for an inspired soothsayer.

In many societies, mantic speech forms are of evident social and cultural importance. Work toward a better understanding of them can proceed in two ways: first, by continuing the comparative study of theories of language; second, by working toward opening up our own theoretical models.

1. A central concern of the ethnography of speaking has been the documentation and analysis of non-Western and popular theories of language. In the well-documented cases that we have, mantic language is recognized in one or more categories typified by such qualities as degrees of "heat" or power or even, in the Central Himalayas, of "shabbiness." Often these ways of classifying speech forms crosscut what seem to us to be evident divisions.

2. If we accept the legitimacy of other ways of theorizing, what are the implications for our own, one of the characteristics of which is to seek universal status? In the case in question, we can start with the fact that we think we recognize mantic language in many societies; it may thus be considered a form comparable to those we call poetic language, conversation, narrative, and so forth.

The literature on mantic experience has brought out a number of overlapping polarities, each of which directly involves language.

1. One is between situations in which one's consciousness journeys to a non-ordinary realm (a phenomenon sometimes, and controversially, labeled shamanism) and those in which non-ordinary agencies come into the body (spirit possession or oracular experience). Voyages "out" seem to be a central element in North and South American, Siberian, and Central Asian traditions; voyages "in" by spirits, for good or ill, seem more prevalent in Africa, South Asia, and ancient and traditional Europe. Other regions – Oceania, the ancient Middle East, including the Hebrew prophets – seem to combine both or alternate between them. Language plays a central role in both of these forms of spirit movement: to have a social effect, the spirit-journey must be recounted, and visiting spirits usually signal their presence discursively. The differences in these situations will be reflected in narrative vs. declamatory styles and marked by differences in deictics and discourse structure.

2. Who is doing the talking? Possessed language and other forms of ritual language involve a shift in speaking voice so that the prime speaker is no longer, as in less-marked situations, identified with the proximate speaker (to use John Du Bois's terminology). This shift will be linguistically keyed and suggests comparisons with the linguistics of multiple personalities or the classic model of hysteria, in which apparently distinct agencies share a single body and signal their presences largely by linguistic means.

3. Overlapping with the first distinction, between modes of spirit movement, is one between degrees of control. The common definition of the shaman as a healing spirit master, as in Siberia or the higher Himalayas, contrasts with forms of possession and oracular practice in which the practitioner gives up his or her body and voice to the god. Here the language used will index the nature of power relations between practitioner and spirit or god.

4. As the word *prophecy* implies, mantic language usually has a sociopolitical dimension: an oracle speaks from the god and to the society; a case of spirit possession allows the powerless to speak openly precisely because they are not the ones taken to be doing the speaking, something that has been repeatedly documented in South Asia and for traditional African religions.

5. The degree of bodily control involved in mantic experience can range from apparent catatonia, as is sometimes the case in the mystic traditions of the world religions, to the wildest movement. Since language is a bodily function, how one speaks (or squeaks or shrieks) will be an aspect of an overall body technique, a mantic habitus.

6. To what degree can or should a mantic experience be expressed in words?

Here the range is from absolutely ineffable experience, which must be pointed at rather than expressed directly, as in Buddhist, Hindu, Islamic, and to a degree Christian and Jewish mystical traditions, to experiences that call for description or direct expression, as in many traditions, often called shamanic or oracular, that use mantic experience as a direct link to non-ordinary powers for social ends.

7. Mantic ways of speaking range from silence to non-linguistic noises to unintelligible yet phonologically structured glossolalia, as in Christian and other traditions of speaking in tongues, to more or less intelligible language that is sung, versified, riddling (Greek oracles and Greco-Roman sibyls), hortatory, marked by specialized or archaic vocabulary, all the way to conversation that is virtually indistinguishable from any other except that it happens to be a spirit who is speaking, not this body's usual subject, a situation most abundantly documented by Michael Lambek for the island of Mayotte off the East African coast.

8. Roman Jakobson has proposed understanding poetic language as language that calls attention to the message itself, thus implying an additional level of reflexivity. Mantic language, while often poetic, is recognized as such by its quality of either emanating from a state that the proximate subject does not control or telling an imaginal experience in which the subject is wholly absorbed. This suggests parallels between mantic language and, on the one hand, inspired, automatic, or dreamed poetry, on the other, the telling of dreams. What all of these share is the reverse of the heightened reflexivity of poetic language, a kind of collapse of reflexivity.

These polarities may help to orient a more serious study of mantic language. The nature of such language has hardly been addressed by linguistics; anthropology, psychology, and comparative religion have long studied the situations, states, and systems that give rise to it, but seem, with some honorable exceptions, not to have noticed that they are dealing centrally with forms of speech.

(See also *dreams, poetry, prayer, reflexivity, voice*)

Bibliography

Chadwick, Nora Kershaw
   1942   Poetry and Prophecy. Cambridge: Cambridge University Press.
Du Bois, John W.
   1986   Self-evidence and Ritual Speech. *In* Evidentiality: The Linguistic Coding of Epistemology. Wallace Chafe and Johanna Nichols, eds. Pp. 313–336. Norwood, NJ: Ablex.
Gossen, Gary H.
   1989[1974]   To Speak with a Heated Heart: Chamula Canons of Style and Good Performance. *In* Explorations in the Ethnography of Speaking. 2nd ed. Richard Bauman and Joel Sherzer, eds. Pp. 389–413. Cambridge: Cambridge University Press.

Güntert, Hermann
   1921   Von der Sprache der Götter und Geister. Halle: Max Niemeyer.
Lambek, Michael
   1981   Human Spirits: A Cultural Account of Trance in Mayotte. Cambridge: Cambridge University Press.
Leavitt, John, ed.
   1997   Poetry and Prophecy: The Anthropology of Inspiration. Ann Arbor: University of Michigan Press.
Lewis, I. M.
   1989   Ecstatic Religion: A Study of Spirit Possession and Shamanism. 2nd ed. London: Routledge.
Maskarinec, Gregory
   1995   The Rulings of the Night: An Ethnography of Nepalese Shaman Oral Texts. Madison: University of Wisconsin Press.
Rouget, Gilbert
   1985[1980]   Music and Trance: A Theory of the Relations between Music and Possession. B. Biebuyck and G. Rouget, trans. Chicago: University of Chicago Press.
Samarin, William
   1972   Tongues of Men and Angels: The Religious Language of Pentecostalism. New York: Macmillan.

■ *Kwesi Yankah*

Proverb

R egarded as "the wit of one and the wisdom of many," the proverb is a terse and witty philosophical saying that conveys a lesson. It couches conventional wisdom in a poetic capsule, making it esthetically pleasing and memorable. Over time, individuals invent such nuggets of wisdom, using traditionally sanctioned ideas and ways of speaking. The sayings, when repeated and applied by others over time, may win acceptance and gain admission into the community's treasury. The proverb is widespread, but surprisingly missing among a few cultures including Australian Aborigines, American Indians, and Bushmen in Southern Africa.

Grounded upon years of experience and close observation of life and natural phenomena, the proverb, through metaphorical language, may warn, advise, or reprimand by drawing attention to the moral or ethical consequences of human behavior. It may advocate patience, co-operation, and perseverance, and repudiate greed and selfishness. A Turkish proverb says "He who does not listen to proverbs remains screaming for help"; according to Russians, "For the sake of a proverb, a peasant walks to Moscow"; and the Yoruba of Nigeria would say, "The man who knows proverbs reconciles difficulties."

The lessons often embedded in proverbs make them tools for moral education. In actual fact, however, it is only in rare instances that proverbs are ostensibly used to educate, for proverbs are generally not used in isolation. Instances of didactic uses of proverbs as an end in itself may be found among the Chaga and a few other societies in Africa. Among the Chaga, proverbs may be used as a mode of instruction during initiation ceremonies. The Maori of New Zealand offer another example of the proverb as an agent for tuition. To ensure that valuable facts about economic lore in the environment are grasped, various proverbs are repeated to the youth by elders side by side with instruction; and in parts of West Africa, proverb icons staked serially on a string may be held by itinerant griots, who educate the public with their inherent philosophies. Other than that, the element of education in proverb use can be subsumed under the rhetorical function, the proverb as a tool for persuasion in social interaction. The proverb user seeks to alter or reinforce the listener's conviction by referring him to timeless parallels within the proverb universe. By getting the addressee to agree with the moral precept in the proverb, the speaker thereby hopes to win him over. An Akan mother in Africa may thus cite the proverb "The chicken nearer to its mother eats the thigh of the grasshopper" to a truant child who has missed a delicious dinner. And an eloquent litigant among the Anang of Nigeria may seek to persuade a jury about an accused's guilt as a thief with the proverb "If a dog plucks palm fruits from a cluster, he does not fear a porcupine" as a reminder that the defendant has a previous conviction.

Part of the rhetorical power of the proverb derives from its authoritative outlook, or rather its notional ascription to authoritative sources. Among the Punjabi of India proverbs are "the drum of God," and in Turkey proverbs from the prophets are said to have originated from the Koran and Hadith holy traditions. In several African cultures, proverb authorship is ascribed to elders and ancestors. Even though proverbs may also be attributed to specific individuals, and sometimes to non-human entities, the collective category considered responsible for proverbs are elders, to whom the qualities of wisdom, responsibility, and exemplary behavior are attributed. "The elders say . . ." is the prefatory formula that triggers the proverb in several African cultures. The belief in the prophetic power of words spoken by elders is supported by the Ba-Congo saying "Water drawn by old men quenches thirst." In several Western cultures, though, the proverb is prefaced with a formula attributing it to an indefinite source: "They say . . ." Besides the use of a "source" formula to enhance a proverb's rhetorical force, a "factivity" formula may also be used, such as "You know that . . ." or "Remember that . . ." to imply that the impending pithy statement is conventional wisdom or a cultural fact or truth that should not be contested.

Societies where proverbs are intensely used also recognize their high esthetic value, their role as discourse ornaments. The proverb is a "lamp of the word" among the Arabs and an "ornament of speech" in Iran. According to the Somali, proverbs "put spice into speech." The Igbo say that "proverbs are the palm oil with which words are eaten," implying that words are hard to swallow without a proverb lubricant. The proverb's vitality in speech is marked by the observation among the Yoruba that it is "the horse of conversation – when the conversation droops, the proverb picks it up."

In various societies, proverb use is governed by specific social norms; and a good proverb speaker does not only know its logical application and meaning, but also its appropriate social uses: which proverb imagery to select or avoid in what social situations. Sometimes proverbs are used among peer groups or by social superiors speaking to subordinates. If a proverb should be used by one addressing a social superior, the speaker may either use an apologetic formula disclaiming a didactic intent or incorporate his audience in the collective authorship, "It is you elders that said . . ." This mitigates any possibility of patronizing a cultivated audience.

Even though proverbs are mostly spoken, other channels may be used for their expression. These include the talking drum, particularly in societies whose languages are tonal. Akan and Yoruba drum proverbs are well known. These are proverb verses that are uniquely identified with the drum and are uncommon in speech. Also common are visual proverbs on umbrella tops, orators' staffs, and as gold weights and textile design in Africa, as well as proverb drawings and paintings in Japan. The proverb in certain parts of the world may even be danced or dramatized.

Regardless of the proverb's channel of expression, it takes considerable cultural sensitivity to grasp its full semantic nuances in social interaction.

(See also *act, agency, body, genre, healing, humor, music, orality, participation, performativity, poetry, power, style, theater, voice*)

Bibliography

Arewa, E. Ojo, and Alan Dundes
  1964   Proverbs and the Ethnography of Speaking Folklore. *In* The Ethnography of Communication. John J. Gumperz and Dell Hymes, eds. Special Issue of American Anthropologist 66(6) (pt. 2):70–85.
Finnegan, Ruth
  1970   Oral Literature in Africa. Oxford: Clarendon Press.
Firth, Raymond
  1926   Proverbs in the Native Life with Particular Reference to Those of the Maori. Folklore 37:135–153.
Mieder, Wolfgang, and Alan Dundes, eds.
  1981   The Wisdom of Many: Essays on the Proverb. New York: Garland Publishing Inc.
Taylor, A.
  1962   The Proverb. Hartboro, PA: Folklore Associates.
Yankah, Kwesi
  1989   Proverbs: The Aesthetics of Traditional Communication. Research in African Literatures 20(3):326–346.
  1995   The Proverb in the Context of Akan Rhetoric. Berne and New York: Peter Lang.

■ *Victor Golla*

Reconstruction

The fundamental tenet of the comparative method in historical linguistics is that systematic similarities shared by two or more languages that are not attributable to borrowing, universality, or chance must be attributed to a common proto-language. Hypotheses constructed in this framework stand or fall on the evidence that can be adduced for the systematicity and regularity of the similarities. The most convincing evidence is provided by regular phonological correspondences in words with related meanings (e.g., the correspondence of Latin *c* (*k*) to English *h* in *cor: heart, capere: haft, canis: hound*, etc.). Such regular correspondences can only be explained as the result of common origin. They may be presented in various formats, but objectifying them as hypothetical proto-phonemes in specific lexical items in the proto-language (e.g., Proto-Indo-European *k in *kerd- 'heart', *kap- 'seize', and *kwon- 'dog' for the correspondence above) is the one that most convincingly demonstrates the historicity and predictive power of the comparative method.

The earliest extensive use of reconstruction in comparative linguistics is found in the work of August Schleicher (1821–1868). He appears to have been ambivalent about the historical reality of forms he created (and marked with an asterisk – his innovation) to represent the unattested prototypes of words that regularly corresponded in form and meaning in various Indo-European languages. On the one hand, Schleicher usually cited these prototypes as fully inflected words that he did not hesitate to use in phrases and sentences, on one occasion even constructing a short Proto-Indo-European fable. On the other hand, as a pioneer in the rigorous definition of sound laws, he could not have been unaware that many of the details he "reconstructed" were not unambiguously supported by specific phonological correspondences.

The formalism of the following generation of comparative linguists – Brugmann, Osthoff, and others who collectively styled themselves the "Neogrammarians" – was in many ways a reaction to such methodological vagueness. In their view, only the systematic correspondence of phonological elements (the concept of the phoneme had yet to be invented, but was often implicit in their work) could be taken as incontrovertible evidence for the common origin of two or more languages. Thus the only solidly reconstructible elements in a proto-language are proto-phonemes. Although, of course, these are always instantiated in cognate lexicon, the Neogrammarians saw such factors as analogic reformation, borrowing between cognate languages, and the workings of chance, as dooming any attempt to directly compare and reconstruct words, let alone larger syntactic structures. Etymologies can only be the by-products of phonological comparison, and while here and there word-long sequences of reconstructed phonemes can be specified with some assurance, most are problematic in one way or another. Despite the theoretical caveats of the Neogrammarians, most historical linguists then and since have not hesitated to attribute words, paradigms, syntactic structures, and even some discourse phenomena, to the hypothetical parent languages of the families they have studied. Whatever their historical contingencies and inherent uncertainty, the pursuit of etymologies remains the focus of much comparative linguistic work, particularly that undertaken in more general historical and cultural contexts.

To the anthropologist seeking a linguistic perspective on prehistory, comparative reconstruction is of considerable evidentiary value in at least three distinct ways:

1. The rigorous reconstruction of elements of a proto-language is the surest evidence for the common origin of a group of potentially related languages, resting as it must on a detailed understanding of the regular phonological correspondences among these languages, as well as on at least a few highly probable etymologies. A language family for which a proto-language has been reconstructed may be treated as confirmed. Proposed relationships among languages that have not been tested by rigorous comparison in a framework allowing reconstruction must be considered unproved.

2. Lexical (i.e., etymological) reconstructions are an important tool for the investigation of the "proto-cultures" in which the speakers of a proto-language lived, especially in situations where written records are lacking. The reconstruction of the lexicon of Proto-Indo-European (PIE) remains the most extensive and widely discussed instance of such work, but the continuing uncertainty over the location of the PIE homeland and whether PIE speakers were involved with the spread of early agriculture into Europe indicates the tentativeness of the results. Some lexical reconstructions support a PIE homeland in southern Russia and a proto-culture that was primarily nomadic and pastoralist, but other evidence supports (as Tamaz Gamkrelidze and Vyacheslav Ivanov have recently proposed) a PIE homeland in Anatolia and a PIE culture with sophisticated agricultural technology derivative from Mesopotamia. Debate over these ambiguities, however, should not obscure the fact that a considerable amount of detailed information about the social and cultural life of the earliest Indo-Europeans can be recovered from reconstructed terms for various elements of material and symbolic culture. Of particular interest are etymologies that point to the reconstruction of inter-

related sets of terms in such semantic areas as kinship terminology, plant and animal taxonomy, and numeral systems.

Similar results have been achieved in a few other Old World language families, most notably Austronesian. In the New World, a significant body of work, much of it stemming from Edward Sapir and his students, has focused on the reconstruction of proto-languages for many North American Indian language families. Lexical reconstructions in these families have indicated a number of significant prehistoric language–culture correlations, such as that between Proto-Siouan and early farming in the Mississippi Valley, or between Proto-Athabaskan and the diffusion of the bow and arrow in the western part of the continent.

3. Whether or not they are reconstructible from phonological correspondences, elements of the morphosyntactic structure of a proto-language can be inferred from the correspondence of such features in the daughter languages of a family. Such grammatical reconstruction is firmest when the details compared are arbitrary and irregular and the languages are geographically separated. The reconstruction of a few features of discourse, such as poetic formulas and syntactic devices distinctive of highly marked genres, has also been attempted, with varying degrees of success, within Indo-European and a few other well-attested language families. Reconstructions of grammatical and discourse features can provide at best only a partial glimpse of the structure of a proto-language. However, especially where supported by phonological correspondences, they can be of great probative value in establishing a genetic relationship and, more generally, can provide evidence of areal connections, or of structural drift associated with certain typological configurations.

(See also *color, contact, endangered, evolution, genre, grammar, orality, syncretism, variation, writing*)

Bibliography

Blust, Robert
    1976 Austronesian Culture History: Some Linguistic Inferences and Their Relations to the Archaeological Record. World Archaeology 8:19–43.
Bright, William, ed.
    1991 International Encyclopedia of Linguistics. 4 volumes. Oxford: Oxford University Press.
Dyen, Isadore, and David F. Aberle
    1974 Lexical Reconstruction: The Case of the Proto-Athapaskan Kinship System. London and New York: Cambridge University Press.
Friedrich, Paul
    1970 Proto-Indo-European Trees: The Arboreal System of a Prehistoric People. Chicago: University of Chicago Press.
    1991 Semantic Reconstruction. In International Encyclopedia of Linguistics. Vol. 3. William Bright, ed. Pp. 389–394. Oxford: Oxford University Press.

Gamkrelidze, Tamaz V., and Vyacheslav V. Ivanov
  1995[1984] Indo-European and the Indo-Europeans: A Reconstruction and Historical Analysis of a Proto-language and a Proto-culture. Trends in Linguistics, Studies and Monographs 80. Werner Winter, ed. Johanna Nichols, trans. Berlin: Mouton de Gruyter.

Haas, Mary R.
  1969 The Prehistory of Languages. Janua Linguarum. Series minor 57. The Hague: Mouton.

Polomé, Edgar C., and Werner Winter, eds.
  1992 Reconstructing Languages and Cultures. Berlin and New York: Walter de Gruyter.

Sapir, Edward
  1994[1916] Time Perspective in Aboriginal American Culture: A Study in Method. Department of Mines, Geological Survey, Memoir 90, Anthropological Series 13. *In* Collected Works of Edward Sapir. Vol. 4: Ethnology. Pp. 25–120. Berlin and New York: Mouton de Gruyter.

Schleicher, August
  1861–62 Compendium der vergleichenden Grammatik der indogermanischen Sprachen. 2 volumes. Weimar: Böhlau.

Watkins, Calvert
  1991a Culture History and Historical Linguistics. *In* International Encyclopedia of Linguistics. Vol. 1. William Bright, ed. Pp. 318–322. Oxford: Oxford University Press.
  1991b Stylistic Reconstruction. *In* International Encyclopedia of Linguistics. Vol. 4. William Bright, ed. Pp. 86–89. Oxford: Oxford University Press.

■ *John A. Lucy*

Reflexivity

By reflexivity in language we mean the capacity and indeed the tendency of verbal interaction to presuppose, structure, represent, and characterize its own nature and functioning. Reflexivity is one of the defining features of natural languages and the discursive practices implemented through them, and it has, therefore, been of increasing concern in linguistic anthropology and related fields over the last quarter century.

Reflexivity can be *explicit*, as when we make language form and use the subject matter of our speech. This is most transparent when we directly speak about the language code, interpreting, for example, the meaning of a lexical form. Similar interpretations can be made regarding larger idiomatic constructions (e.g., "*He has lost his marbles* is an expression that means 'he has gone crazy'"). Examples of grammatically oriented comments would include classifying words as to formal type, stating grammatical rules, or evaluating grammatical correctness. Similar statements can be made about phonological rules or larger discursive patterns. All these cases focus on relatively stable aspects of the language code structure especially as they contribute to acts of reference.

However, regular patterns of language usage can also be subject to comment. Hence we encounter characterizations of typical or appropriate use (e.g., "the expression *He is losing his marbles* is more likely to be used by an older person and most appropriately in reference to an older person"). In cases of this type, the focus is on pragmatic rules of use – that is, who uses certain forms, in what contexts, and to what effect. The concern is not referential correctness as such but broader discursive appropriateness. Whether these explicitly reflexive utterances concern structure or use, they focus on general patterns rather than particular utterances.

It is also possible to use speech to report or characterize particular utterances. Such utterances may have actually occurred or they may not have, being then only purported or imagined. Here we find the various explicit forms of reported speech, namely, direct report (e.g., "Tom said 'Oh no, I have lost my marbles'"), indirect report (e.g., "Tom said that he had lost his marbles"), and free indirect report (e.g., "Tom said: oh no, he had lost his marbles"). As such reports lose contact with the form of the purported original utterance, they tend to become more like characterizations of persons or events or renderings of essential message rather than mere reports. Some can follow the original fairly closely (e.g., "Tom lamented the loss of his marbles"), while others only very distantly represent or allude to it by reference to its pragmatic effects ("Tom lost them today"). Included here would be all those cases where we explain what someone meant by a particular utterance. All these reflexive forms, whether focused on general patterns or on particular utterances, explicitly signal the presence of two or more functional orders by clear markings whether they involve specialized metalinguistic terms, conventional syntagmatic arrangements, or some combination of the two. Some portion of the utterance functions as metalanguage while another part functions as object language, that is, as the object of metalinguistic presentation, representation, interpretation, or comment.

In all the cases considered thus far, the language spoken and the language spoken about have been the same. Of course, it is also possible to use one language to speak about another language in all the ways just described: giving the meaning of a lexical item in another language, characterizing its rules of grammatical structure and usage, reporting particular utterances, interpreting meaning, and so forth. Translation proper presents a particularly interesting problem from this point of view. Although typically treated as a type of glossing such that a construction in one language is equated with a construction in another, this is only viable at the level of explaining general patterns. As soon as we go to the level of translating a particular utterance, the proper model is that of reporting speech. Indeed, direct translation constitutes a fourth logical type of reporting, sharing with direct report the preservation of deictic center and with indirect report the freedom from the original forms. A reporting or matrix frame is necessarily implicated in every translation, however formally elided it might be in practice, a fact that should alert us to the situated nature of even the most neutral translation. In short, translations are close kin to reflexive constructions within a single language.

Reflexivity also operates *implicitly* in the production of each utterance insofar as it takes account of its own nature and functioning. However, in place of explicit lexical or syntagmatic marks, implicit reflexivity emerges from paradigmatic equivalences across different aspects of the speech event.

First, implicit reflexivity of one sort operates in the very construction of utterances as we use indices of person, tense, status, and so forth that require the listener to take account of the immediate contexts of use for their proper interpretation. Here a paradigmatic calibration must be made between the parameters of the speech event and the elements in the utterance for a proper interpretation. The situation rapidly becomes more complex in those cases where we rely on configurations of markers, so-called contextualization or framing cues, to signal how these very contexts of use, and hence the forms that index them, are to be interpreted.

Looking next within the utterance itself, ensembles of cross-referencing and hence implicitly reflexive structuration elements work together to compose and interrelate higher order units. On the one hand, boundary markers, clausal cohesion, stylistic unity, structural parallelism (of both structure and trope), and organized embedding work together to create the sense of durable, object-like qualities we routinely apprehend in spoken and written discourse. Such poetic or entextualization processes in conjunction with the content of the utterance make possible the various genres, registers, and voices we identify and distinguish by such terms as poetry and prayer, formal and informal speech, dominant and subordinate voice, and so on. On the other hand, the careful intercalation of these larger verbal paradigms, that is, reflexively taking account of the existence of stable structures of this type, makes possible the creative, expressive multifunctionality of everyday speech, the active coordination of multiple voices in a single utterance.

We have spoken here primarily of the reflexive nature of linguistic form. But such forms do not exist in a vacuum; they respond to and create psychological and cultural conditions. During the course of child development, the latent reflexive potential of language is learned and then brought under voluntary control. Whereas implicit reflexivity of the indexical sort is operative at a very early age, its full elaboration and deployment comes later becoming the foundation for the more complex metalinguistic and poetic processes described earlier. These complex reflexive capacities in turn undergird the development of the reflective and narrative activities of our mature years, activities essential to the emergence of the symbolic structures we call self and culture.

(See also *acquisition, indexicality, interview, narrative, participation, poetry, power, prayer, register, socialization, translation, voice*)

Bibliography

Bateson, Gregory
    1972[1955]   A Theory of Play and Fantasy. *In* Steps to an Ecology of Mind. Pp. 177–193. New York: Ballantine.
Goffman, Erving
    1974   Frame Analysis. New York: Harper and Row.
Gumperz, John J.
    1980   Discourse Strategies. Cambridge: Cambridge University Press.
Jakobson, Roman
    1971[1957]   Shifters, Verbal Categories, and the Russian Verb. *In* Selected Writings II: Word and Language. Pp. 130–147. The Hague: Mouton.
    1980   Metalanguage as a Linguistic Problem. *In* The Framework of Language (Michigan Studies in the Humanities). Pp. 81–92. Ann Arbor, MI: Horace H. Rackham School of Graduate Studies.
Lucy, John A., ed.
    1993   Reflexive Language: Reported Speech and Metapragmatics. Cambridge: Cambridge University Press.

Quine, Willard

1960 Word and Object. Cambridge, MA: MIT Press.

Silverstein, Michael

1976 Shifters, Linguistic Categories, and Cultural Description. *In* Meaning in Anthropology. K. Basso and H. Selby, eds. Pp. 11–55. Albuquerque: University of New Mexico Press.

1984 On the Pragmatic "Poetry" of Prose: Parallelism, Repetition, and Cohesive Structure in the Time Course of Dyadic Conversation. *In* Meaning, Form, and Use in Context: Linguistic Applications. D. Schiffrin, ed. Pp. 181–199. Washington, DC: Georgetown University Press.

Vološinov, V. N.

1986[1929] Marxism and the Philosophy of Language. L. Matejka and I. Titunik, trans. Cambridge, MA: Harvard University Press.

■ *Asif Agha*

Register

A register is a linguistic repertoire that is associated, culture internally, with particular social practices and with persons who engage in such practices. The use of a register conveys to a member of the culture that some typifiable social practice is linked indexically to the current occasion of language use, as part of its context. If the current occasion is independently recognizable as an instance of the social practice, the use of the register seems appropriate to that occasion; conversely, switching to the register may itself reconfigure the sense of occasion, indexically entailing that the associated social practice is now under way.

Formally, registers differ in the type of repertoire involved (e.g., lexemes, prosody, sentence collocations), and many registers involve repertoires of more than one kind. From the standpoint of function, distinctive registers are associated with social practices of every kind – such as law, medicine, prayer, science, magic, prophecy, commerce, military strategy, sports commentary, the observance of respect and etiquette, the expression of civility, social status, etc.

Given this range, a repertoire-based view of register remains incomplete in certain essential respects: such a view cannot explain how particular repertoires become differentiable from the rest of the language, or how they come to be associated with social practices at all. It implies also that a register is a closed and bounded set of forms over which all members of a language community have identical competence. Yet registers typically have a socially distributed existence over populations, so that all members of a language community are not equally familiar with all of its registers. These aspects of a register's repertoires – their identifiability, pragmatic value, and social distribution – are best understood by attention to the metalinguistic practices of language users.

All empirical studies of registers rely on the metalinguistic ability of native speakers to discriminate between linguistic forms, to make evaluative judgments about variant forms. In the special case where a linguist studies a register of his or her native language, such evaluations are available in the form of introspectable intuitions. In general, however, linguists rely on native evaluations that are overtly expressed in publicly observable semiotic behavior. Such behavior may consist of language use: e.g., linguistic utterances that explicitly describe a register's forms and associated values; or utterances that implicitly evaluate the indexical properties of co-occurring forms (as responses to them, for example) without describing what they evaluate; such behavior may include non-linguistic semiotic activity as well, such as gestures, or the extended patterning of kinesic and bodily movements characteristic of ritual responses to the use of many registers.

All such behaviors are metalinguistic in nature since they tell us something about the properties of linguistic forms, whether by decontextualizing the forms and describing their properties or by evaluating their effects while the forms are still in play. Such evaluations tell us something, in particular, about the pragmatics of language – i.e., the capacity of linguistic forms to index culturally recognizable activities, categories of actors, etc., as elements of the context of language use – thus constituting the class of metapragmatic evaluations of language. In their most overt form, such evaluations consist of explicit metapragmatic discourse, i.e., discourse that describes the pragmatics of speech forms. Several genres of metapragmatic discourse occur naturally in all language communities – e.g., verbal reports and glosses of language use; names for registers and associated speech genres; stereotypes about users of a repertoire; proscriptions on usage; standards of appropriate usage; positive or negative assessments of the social worth of the register.

Registers have a socially distributed existence over populations of speakers because all speakers of a given language do not acquire competence in all of its registers during the normal course of language socialization. In the case of registers of scientific discourse, competence in the use and interpretation of technical terminologies requires several years of specialized formal study. In the case of registers associated with particular venues of commercial activity (e.g., the stock exchange, the publishing house, the advertising firm), proficiency in specialized terms is typically attained through socialization in the workplace. In the case of registers of respect and etiquette, only individuals born into privileged circumstances tend to acquire competence over the most elaborate locutions. In many societies, certain lexical registers function as "secret languages" (e.g., thieves' argots, the registers of religious ritual, magical incantation, etc.) since their use is restricted to specialized groups by metapragmatic proscriptions against teaching the forms to outsiders.

Thus, two members of a language community may both be acquainted with a lexical register, but not have the same degree of competence in its use. Many speakers can recognize certain registers of their language but cannot fully use or interpret them. The existence of registers therefore results not just in the interlinkage of linguistic repertoires and social practices but in the creation of social boundaries within society, partitioning off language users into distinct groups through differential access to particular registers and to the social practices that they mediate; through the ascription of social worth or stigma to particular registers, their usage, or their users; and through the creation and maintenance of asymmetries of power, privilege, and rank, as effects dependent on the above processes. In such cases, social regularities involving the value of speech motivate socially regular judgments about types of speakers.

The existence of registers is thus associated with social regularities of speech valorization, potentially involving different aspects of language use. Such social regularities are identified when metapragmatic judgments offered by one speaker are found to be socially replicable – that is, shared, by many categories of speakers within a population. Hence, the replicability of metapragmatic discourse serves as a criterion on the social distribution of register values. By this criterion, the social sharedness of registers is always a matter of degree since the replicability of register judgments over an entire language community is only a limiting special case, rarely observed empirically.

The social existence of a register is therefore not a static, all-or-nothing fact even though the social authority of many registers derives precisely from the appearance of their permanence. The cultural en-register-ment of a speech repertoire is itself a social process, varying in degrees of completeness of consensus, in the social domains of language users who subscribe to a given set of enregistered values (vs. those who engage in counter-valorizations), in the social mechanisms by which authoritative values are formulated and disseminated, in the degree of institutionalization of the metadiscourse that typifies the register.

In the case of highly authoritative, firmly institutionalized and widely circulating metadiscourses, the register values promoted by the metadiscourse are socially shared to a high degree (i.e., are comparably recognizable and, in some cases, describable, by many members of society), thus constituting a widespread social regularity of speech valorization. For example, the "standard language" is perhaps the most robustly institutionalized register of any language, one whose existence in modern societies itself depends on the existence and proper functioning of a network of metadiscursive institutions, such as dictionaries, grammars, pedagogic manuals, school curricula, boards of education, national academies, and so on.

(See also *codes, competence, expert, genre, gesture, indexicality, prayer, prophecy, socialization, variation*)

Bibliography

Agha, Asif
  1998 Stereotypes and Registers of Honorific Language. Language in Society 27(2):151–193.
Ferguson, Charles
  1994 Dialect, Register and Genre: Working Assumptions about Conventionalization. *In* Sociolinguistic Perspectives on Register. Douglas Biber and Edward Finegan, eds. Pp. 15–30. New York: Oxford University Press.

Ghadessy, Mohsen
   1988   Registers of Written English: Situational Factors and Linguistic Features. London: Pinter.
Gregory, Michael
   1988   Generic Situation and Register: A Functional View of Communication. *In* Linguistics in a Systemic Perspective. James D. Benson et al., eds. Pp. 301–329. Amsterdam: Benjamins.
Halliday, M. A. K.
   1964   The Users and Uses of Language. *In* The Linguistic Sciences and Language Teaching. M. A. K. Halliday et al., eds. Pp. 75–110. London: Longman.
   1978   Language as Social Semiotic. London: Edward Arnold.
Hervey, Sándor
   1992   Registering Registers. Lingua 86:189–206.
Irvine, Judith
   1990   Registering Affect: Heteroglossia in the Linguistic Expression of Emotion. *In* Language and the Politics of Emotion. Catherine A. Lutz and Lila Abu-Lughod, eds. Pp. 126–161. Cambridge: Cambridge University Press.
Silverstein, Michael
   1996   Indexical Order and the Dialectics of Sociolinguistic Life. Proceedings of the Third Symposium about Language and Society, 266–295. Austin: University of Texas.
Ure, Jean
   1982   Introduction: Approaches to the Study of Register Range. International Journal of the Sociology of Language 35:5–23.

■ *Alessandro Duranti*

Relativity

Linguistic relativity was born out of the observation that languages provide different ways of describing the world. The next step was to posit that each language establishes a system of meanings that is incommensurable with other systems. On that assumption, the hypothesis was made that speakers, depending upon their language, may see the world differently and pay attention to different aspects of reality. Thus, linguistic diversity became a way of predicting and explaining at least some aspects of cognitive and cultural diversity.

Despite the potential implications of these assumptions for the study of language, the issue of linguistic relativity was largely ignored by formal linguists in the second half of the twentieth century mostly due to (1) Noam Chomsky's insistence on the universal properties of grammatical systems and (2) the misunderstanding of the scope and meaning of linguistic relativity. The stereotypical view of linguistic relativity as pertaining to differences in number of words for the "same" concept (e.g., the supposedly high number of words for snow in Eskimo, a myth finally discredited by Laura Martin) for a while undermined its theoretical importance. And yet linguistic relativity speaks to the core of the anthropological enterprise, to the limits of our ability to understand who we are and what we do. It also forces us to think about the power of words and the relative freedom we have to transcend the world as constructed through discursive practices. It forces us to take seriously Martin Heidegger's thesis that we do not speak language, but language speaks us.

Linguistic relativity is historically tied to Romanticism and the view, expressed by the German diplomat and linguist Wilhelm von Humboldt (1767–1835), that a language represents the spirit of a nation and therefore that to speak another language means to accept its implicit worldview. But even for von Humboldt, each (sociohistorically defined) language should be distinguished from language as a universal human capacity. Thus, contrary to popular belief, from the very beginning linguistic relativity has not been incompatible with the belief that there are universals of language.

The names of two North American scholars are usually identified with linguistic relativity: Edward Sapir (1884–1939) and Benjamin Lee Whorf (1897–1941). The frequent use of the "Sapir–Whorf Hypothesis" as a synonym for linguistic relativity is, however, misleading given that the two scholars never worked out a joint statement about linguistic relativity and a close analysis of their writings shows some important differences. For Sapir, linguistic relativity was a way of articulating one of the fundamental paradoxes of human life, namely, the need that each individual has to use a shared and predefined code in expressing what are subjectively different experiences. Sapir also saw the logic of grammar as similar to the logic of artistic codes (e.g., the rule about marking plural or gender in some languages but not in others is similar to a stylistic preference that needs to be honored by the artist working within a certain type of material and within a particular tradition). Whorf was interested in finding ways of characterizing the worldview expressed in American Indian languages as alternative "fashions of speaking," with the same legitimacy of what he called "Standard Average European," an amalgamation of the formal properties shared by languages like English and French. For Whorf, language is a guide to behavior because its logic is transferred, through analogy, to other domains of human cognitive activity (his most famous example was the discovery of the common and dangerous interpretation of the label "empty" on gas drums as equivalent to "devoid of gas" and thus innocuous). He formulated a "linguistic relativity principle" according to which different grammars direct their users toward different types of observations and different evaluations of what could otherwise be seen as similar circumstances.

After a period of criticism of Whorf's work, which culminated with Brent Berlin and Paul Kay's discovery of cross-linguistic universals in the coding of color across a large number of languages (see "Color"), researchers have returned to Whorf's basic insights with renewed interest and new methods. An important contribution in this area has been John Lucy's project comparing the performance of speakers of Yucatec and speakers of English in a series of cognitive tasks. Starting from the observation that English marks plural overtly and obligatorily on a wide range of noun phrases, whereas Yucatec usually does not mark plural and, when it does, it is optional, Lucy hypothesizes that English speakers should habitually attend to the number of various objects more than Yucatec speakers do and for more types of referents. The results of his experiments support his hypothesis. Similar work is being done on the coding and perception of space by other researchers.

Another line of research on the impact of language on human cognition has been pursued by Michael Silverstein, who hypothesizes that native speakers' "metalinguistic awareness," that is, their ability to have intuitions about the meaning and use of linguistic expressions, is conditioned by certain formal properties of those expressions, e.g., whether or not there is a one-to-one correspondence between parts of a word and units of meaning. Even J. L. Austin's speech act theory, Silverstein argues, was based on the ability to name certain (speech) acts through such (referential) expressions as "I promise that," "I declare that," "I order you to," etc. But there are plenty of social acts done through language that cannot be easily named by such referential expressions and therefore may not be as easily accessible to native speakers' consciousness. These phenomena have consequences for social scientists' ability to use members' intuitions in their research.

Recent studies on a variety of communicative activities and genres have expanded the theoretical and methodological boundaries of what used to be thought of as linguistic relativity. No in-depth study of intentionality, agency, indexicality, formality, or code choice, for example, can be possible without assessing the relative power that words have on our ability to understand, act in, and ultimately affect our psychological and social worlds.

(See also *act, category, color, functions, iconicity, ideophone, indexicality, metaphor, poetry, space*)

Bibliography

Gumperz, John J., and Stephen C. Levinson, eds.
    1996   Rethinking Linguistic Relativity. Cambridge: Cambridge University Press.
Heidegger, Martin
    1971   The Way to Language. *In* On the Way to Language. Pp. 111–136. New York: Harper and Row.
Hill, Jane H., and Bruce Mannheim
    1992   Language and World View. Annual Review of Anthropology 21:381–406.
Koerner, E. F. Konrad
    1992   The Sapir-Whorf Hypothesis: A Preliminary History and a Bibliographical Essay. Journal of Linguistic Anthropology 2(2):173–198.
Lucy, John A.
    1992a   Grammatical Categories and Cognition: A Case Study of the Linguistic Relativity Hypothesis. Cambridge: Cambridge University Press.
    1992b   Language Diversity and Cognitive Development: A Reformulation of the Linguistic Relativity Hypothesis. Cambridge: Cambridge University Press.
Mandelbaum, David G., ed.
    1949   Selected Writings of Edward Sapir in Language, Culture, and Personality. Berkeley and Los Angeles: University of California Press.
Martin, Laura
    1986   Eskimo Words for Snow: A Case Study in the Genesis and Decay of an Anthropological Example. American Anthropologist 88:418–423.
Silverstein, Michael
    1977   Cultural Prerequisites to Grammatical Analysis. *In* Linguistics and Anthropology: Georgetown University Round Table on Languages and Linguistics 1977. M. Saville-Troike, ed. Pp. 139–151. Washington, DC: Georgetown University Press.
Whorf, Benjamin Lee
    1956   Language, Thought, and Reality: Selected Writings of Benjamin Lee Whorf. John B. Carroll, ed. Cambridge, MA: MIT Press.

■ *Penelope Brown*

Repetition

Repetition is central to the establishment of semiotic systems. When we have repetition, we have "the same thing" happening again, over time. What, however, makes something "the same" as something else? Judgments of identity and difference are the basis for all classification, and repetition of "the same" units underlies the recognition of pattern. Repetition is therefore fundamental to the definition of all cultural objects: of the phoneme, of particular kinds of act, of chunks of ritual, art, music, and performance, all of which involve meaningful re-enactments in some sense. Repetition is a prerequisite for learning, providing the possibility of assimilating experience, committing it to memory, and thus also the basis for prediction. Repetition is pervasive in social life, oiling the waters of social interaction, from the micro level (the rhythm of conversational interaction punctuated by repeated units of speech, gesture, prosody), to the level of daily routine (the predictability across contexts of politeness routines, social rituals, mealtimes, work schedules), to the annual cycle, and the life cycle. Repetition of events, based on our cultural definitions of what constitutes "the same event" (such that we can recognize another instance of it as a repetition), provides a variety of kinds of meaning to our social and cultural lives. In the realm of language, repetition enters at the basic level of what constitutes a code. Although two exemplars of a linguistic expression cannot ever be identical, on the basis of a code members of a linguistic community treat some features as criterial and thereby some sequences as if they were the same.

Repetition not only underlies semiosis, it also functions as a semiotic device. Even in the construction of the sentence we find repetition (e.g., concord and agreement repeat the coding of a semantic feature on different words; reduplication is used to indicate emphasis, intensity, iteration, or plural in many languages). Beyond the sentence level, repetition is an important stylistic device in narrative and poetic discourse. Indeed, as Roman Jakobson pointed out, "on every level of language the essence of poetic artifice consists of recurrent returns." Repetition and "parallelism" (repetition with patterned variation) characterize high registers, formal styles, oratory, and ritual language in many societies, especially in oral communication ("We shall fight on the beaches, we shall fight in the fields and in the streets, we shall fight in the hills . . ."). In many speech communities around the world, "speaking in pairs" or couplets is the defining feature of elevated registers, prompting the suggestion that parallelism is a cognitive universal.

Less obvious, perhaps, is the fact that repetition is a ubiquitous communicative device in everyday verbal interaction, much of it below the level of awareness. Some is repetition of pure form, for example meter, alliteration, or the rhythms created by repetition/variation of phonemes, overlaid with prosody and gesture, that establish conversational synchrony. Some is purely on the semantic level, as in synonyms and paraphrases. Much repetition, however, combines both form and meaning; words, phrases, and syntactic structures are repeated in discourse. Repeating something calls attention to the prior thing, brings it into the now, claims its relevance; repetition is therefore crucial in establishing discourse coherence. Of course, not all repetitions are alike: we can distinguish self-repetition from repetition of a prior turn at talk, and exact repetition from repetition with expansion (going beyond the initial version) or ellipsis (leaving something out in the repeat). Repetition by self facilitates language production, enabling rapid fluent talk, by setting up a syntactic frame and slotting new information into it ("He did A, and he did B, and he did C . . ."). Self-repetition also occurs predictably in self-repair, and may be used to make a bid to retain the floor or tie a referent to the prior discourse.

People use repetition across turns, in responding to a prior utterance, to do many different sorts of communicative or conversational management acts, including answer a question; query a piece of information; affectively comment on it or play with it; agree with it, ratify it, or confirm an allusion; convey understanding (of what was said, and of its significance); make counter-claims or matching claims (the "me too" phenomenon); initiate repair; and collaborate in producing a conversational contribution. One important thing repeating all or part of a prior utterance can do is transform the repeated item from new into given information, which can then be commented upon or further developed. This is especially important in noisy or informationally critical settings (e.g., service encounters, air traffic control). But in some linguistic communities (for example, many Mayan ones), such cross-speaker repetition has been conventionalized as the default backchannel, the canonical way to respond to any utterance offering new information. This conversational practice makes Mayan conversations strike the outside observer as extraordinarily repetitive, drawing attention to the fact that tolerance for repetition in speech is culturally, as well as contextually, quite variable.

Another arena where repetition is frequent is in speech to and by children. Some scholars consider that it plays an important role in early language acquisition; for example, repetitive routines (patty-cake, etc.) between mother and baby have been claimed as the basis for how the infant learns what a "signal" is with communicative intent. Several kinds of linguistic repetition from adult caregiver to child also may aid language learning. One kind is "expansions," where a child's utterance is picked up and reformulated in order to express the presumed communicative intent in a grammatically correct way (e.g., Child: "dog road." Mother: "Yes, there's a dog in the road"). Another arises in attempts to attract the attention of a young child, when a single communicative intention is recast – rephrased and repeated with lexical substitutions, addition or deletion of specific reference, and reordering – in response to the child's perceived response (or lack thereof). Children learning some languages (for example, Turkish and Tzeltal) routinely hear "the same" utterance repeatedly in different forms, which by their juxtaposition expose the structure of the language for the learner. There are also cultures where explicit prompting routines – telling the child what to say – are a language socialization practice, as in Bambi Schieffelin's well-known example from the Papua New Guinea Kaluli. The other side of the coin, repetition by a child of caregiver speech, is less clearly implicated in language learning per se, since these "imitations" are on the whole not "progressive" – not longer nor syntactically more complex than the child's spontaneous utterances. In fact, as Elinor Ochs has argued, children so often repeat the utterances addressed to them not necessarily with the intention of imitating, but because inexact repetition is the child's goal to satisfy some communicative obligation. A child using these is learning "communicative competence," the different uses of language.

So whether adult or child, layman or linguist, laborer, poet, orator, or priest, no speaker can do without repetition. It is a grammatical, stylistic, poetic, and cognitive resource associated with attention; as such it is a core resource in our mental and social life.

(See also *acquisition, codes, functions, grammar, meter, poetry, socialization, turn*)

Bibliography

Brown, Penelope
    1998 Conversational Structure and Language Acquisition: The Role of Repetition in Tzeltal Adult and Child Speech. Journal of Linguistic Anthropology 8(2):197–222.
Ervin-Tripp, Susan, and Claudia Mitchell-Kernan
    1977 Child Discourse. New York: Academic Press.
Fox, James J., ed.
    1977 To Speak in Pairs. Cambridge: Cambridge University Press.
Haiman, John
    1997 Repetition and Identity. Lingua 100:57–70.
Jakobson, Roman
    1966 Grammatical Parallelism and Its Russian Facet. Language 42:399–429.
Johnstone, Barbara, ed.
    1994 Repetition in Discourse: Interdisciplinary Perspectives. 2 vols. Norwood, NJ: Ablex.

Schegloff, Emanuel A.
   1996   Confirming Allusions: Toward an Empirical Account of Action. Ameri-
      can Journal of Sociology 102(1):161–216.
Schieffelin, Bambi B., and Elinor Ochs, eds.
   1986   Language Socialization across Cultures. Cambridge: Cambridge Univer-
      sity Press.
Silverstein, Michael
   1984   On the Pragmatic "Poetry" of Prose: Parallelism, Repetition, and Cohe-
      sive Structure in the Time Course of Dyadic Conversation. *In* Meaning, Form
      and Use in Context: Linguistic Applications. Georgetown University Round
      Table on Languages and Linguistics. D. Schiffrin, ed. Pp. 181–199. Washing-
      ton, DC: Georgetown University Press.
Tannen, Deborah
   1989   Talking Voices: Repetition, Dialogue, and Imagery in Conversational Dis-
      course. Cambridge: Cambridge University Press.

■ *Leila Monaghan*

Signing

S igning arises whenever a group of people cannot use speech to communicate with each other. In these cases, gestures, particularly hand movements, become the key medium for conveying the symbolic information found in all languages. Sign languages developed, used, and learned by deaf people, particularly deaf children communicating with each other, have a very different grammar from any spoken language. It is a grammar that uses the three dimensions of space as well as stringing together separate components as happens in spoken languages (and written and signed forms developed from spoken languages).

American Sign Language provides clear examples of this. The English sentence "The girl jumps over the rope" can be translated into ASL as "ROPE, GIRL JUMP." The signing of the word ROPE will give information about whether the rope is curved (like a jump rope held by two other children) or straight. The signing of JUMP will give an indication of how vigorously or gently the girl has jumped. In the grammar of ASL adjectives are often replaced by intensifiers (often facial expressions or exaggerations of signs) that are part of a sign, morphemes layered over a basic sign rather than present as a separate word.

Not only do sign languages differ from spoken languages, they also differ from each other – sign languages, like spoken languages, are not universal. Even when signs are iconic, pictorial representations of actual objects, they will be different in different sign languages. The ASL version of "tree" is the forearm held up with all fingers out-stretched, slightly waving, reflecting a tree waving in the wind. The Danish Sign Language version reflects the same bushy top and narrow trunk as the ASL sign but does so by outlining an image of a tree with both hands rather than representing it with one hand.

The study of sign languages using linguistic tools is relatively recent. In 1960 William Stokoe began describing signs in ASL as a collection of parts. He distinguished between the place, handshape, and movement of signs, arguing that these were the equivalent of phonological forms used to describe parts of spoken sounds. Changes in any one of these three variables could create a new sign. If a bent index finger is twisted at the cheek, it is the sign for APPLE, but moved to the side of the eye this sign becomes ONION. RED is done by flicking the index at the chin while CUTE is done with the same motion but using both the index and middle fingers. The verb TO IRON, done by imitating the motion of an iron over a distance of about six inches, becomes the noun IRON when done with a much smaller repetitive movement. Today, orientation of the hands is also recognized as a key parameter when describing any sign.

A viable sign language needs a critical mass of users, but this critical mass can be achieved in a number of different ways. Small communities with high degrees of hereditary deafness (a rate of 1/100 inhabitants being deaf instead of the typical 1/1000 ratio) such as found in Bhan Khor, Thailand, or (historically) Martha's Vineyard are one way to achieve this density. A second way is a network of deaf people in an urban area. In Kano in Northern Nigeria, deaf men (like their hearing Hausa counterparts) meet daily at the marketplace and communicate in the language they have developed over time. This language is known by linguists and anthropologists as Hausa Sign Language. Another circumstance, and probably the most common one, under which deaf children come together and create sign languages is in schools for the deaf, particularly boarding schools. Sign languages can develop sub rosa – when sign languages are banned because authorities expect children to learn to speak and lipread as part of an oral education system – or be part of a formal program.

Sign languages in school settings, particularly those openly taught, use a variety of devices to incorporate spoken or written language concepts into sign language including fingerspelling, mouthing of spoken language words, and air writing. American signers are well known for their fluent and fast one-handed fingerspelling – names, places and unfamiliar terms will be transliterated letter by letter into a signed form. Unlike signing, where each form conveys one or more meanings, fingerspelling is a reflection of written language, and each letter is meaningless in isolation. Just as there is no universal sign language, there is no universal fingerspelling alphabet. Americans inherited their one-handed alphabet from French Sign Language, brought in by Laurent Clerc in 1817, while British and Commonwealth signers use a two-handed fingerspelling alphabet. Although most deaf New Zealanders know the British two-handed alphabet, many do not use it on a regular basis. Instead (reflecting their oral schooling), they will emphatically mouth English forms that they wish to include in their conversation, sometimes pointing at the lips to let others know that an unfamiliar term was appearing. Air writing, tracing letters or characters in the air, is another way of incorporating written language into a signed conversation. It is a particularly efficient way for incorporating Chinese characters into the various versions of sign language found in China – the clear order of strokes taught when teaching characters aids perception.

The complex nature of sign languages was not recognized by the academic establishment until William Stokoe and his colleagues' work on American

Sign Language became well known. This academic acknowledgement of sign language as a language has had many ramifications, including the expansion of rights of deaf people. A major complaint of the student protestors in the "Deaf Prez Now" strike at Gallaudet (a university for the deaf) in 1987 was that newly appointed president Elizabeth Zinsser was hearing, with no knowledge of American Sign Language and therefore was not an appropriate leader. Sign languages around the world have been documented in dictionaries and grammars, leading not only to recognition of local languages but to the recognition that deaf communities have separate cultures as well. These cultures in turn are beginning to be studied in their own right by anthropologists.

(See also *body, codes, community, deaf, gesture, iconicity, identity, socialization, space, writing*)

Bibliography

Klima, Edward S., and Ursula Bellugi
  1979 The Signs of Language. Cambridge: Harvard University Press.
Monaghan, Leila, Karen Nakamura, and Graham Turner, eds.
  In press Many Ways to be Deaf: International Linguistic and Sociocultural Variation. Hamburg: Signum Press.
Sacks, Oliver
  1989 Seeing Voices: A Journey into the World of the Deaf. Berkeley: University of California Press.
Schmaling, Constanze
  In press A for Apple: The Impact of Western Education and ASL on the Deaf Community in Kano State, Northern Nigeria. *In* Many Ways to be Deaf: International Linguistic and Sociocultural Variation. L. Monaghan, K. Nakamura, and G. Turner, eds. Hamburg: Signum Press.
Stokoe, William C., Dorothy C. Casterline, and Carl G. Cronenberg
  1976 Introduction to the Dictionary of American Sign Language. Rev. ed. Silver Spring, MD: Linstok Press.
Sutton-Spence, Rachel
  In press The British Manual Alphabet in the Education of Deaf People since the Seventeenth Century. *In* Many Ways to be Deaf: International Linguistic and Sociocultural Variation. L. Monaghan, K. Nakamura, and G. Turner, eds. Hamburg: Signum Press.
Valli, Clayton, and Ceil Lucas
  1995 Linguistics of American Sign Language: An Introduction. 2nd ed. Washington, DC: Gallaudet University Press.
Van Cleve, John Vickery
  1993 Deaf History Unveiled: Interpretations from the New Scholarship. Washington, DC: Gallaudet University Press.
Van Cleve, John Vickery, and Barry A. Crouch
  1989 A Place of Their Own: Creating the Deaf Community in America. Washington, DC: Gallaudet University Press.

Woodward, James

In press   Sign Languages and Deaf Identities in Thailand and Viet Nam. *In* Many Ways to be Deaf: International Linguistic and Sociocultural Variation. L. Monaghan, K. Nakamura, and G. Turner, eds. Hamburg: Signum Press.

Socialization

L anguage socialization research examines how language practices organize the life span process of becoming an active, competent participant in one or more communities. Communities comprise households, neighborhoods, peer groups, schools, workplaces, professions, religious organizations, recreational gatherings, and other institutions. Unlike language acquisition research, the analytic focus rests neither on less experienced persons as acquirers nor on more experienced persons as input but rather on socially and culturally organized interactions that conjoin less and more experienced persons in the structuring of knowledge, emotion, and social action. This is an important point, for it implicates a methodology in which the gaze and camera lens of the data collecting researcher is primarily directed at the activities undertaken rather than zooming in and tracking the actions of any one participant. Activities (e.g., telling a story, playing a game, preparing and consuming food, attempting to solve a problem, having an argument) are examined for their social and linguistic organization, including the spatial positioning of more or less experienced participants, the expressed stances, ideas, and actions that participants routinely provide or elicit and, importantly, the responses that such expressions receive. With an eye on interaction, we examine the language structures that attempt to socialize (e.g., the use of strong evidentials to claim facts or the use of affect morphology to instantiate moral values) and the interactional effects of such attempts (e.g., Are stances, ideas, or actions acknowledged? Do others display alignment? Nonalignment? Minimally? Elaborately?). From this perspective socialization is a collaborative enterprise, and language socialization researchers are in the business of articulating the architecture of that collaboration.

We tend to think of socializing interactions as repeated and enduring encounters dedicated to the mastery of some community-defined domain. Yet socializing interactions may be fleeting as well – as when one interlocutor momentarily asks another for directions or points out some hitherto unnoticed phenomenon. This property means that ordinary conversation is an informal resource for transforming self and society and that an understanding of how conversation unfolds in specific situations and communities, and the roles of author, animator, hearer, overhearer, and principal or protagonist that less and more experienced participants assume, is central to understanding socialization as a continuous way of life.

While committed to the close examination of ordinary communicative exchanges, language socialization research differs from a conversation analytic or developmental pragmatic approach in its insistence on understanding interactions between neophyte and veteran interlocutors as cultural arrangements. This perspective also has methodological ramifications, for it means that the gaze and wide-angle camera lens of the observer is pulled back to situate what is happening ethnographically in a web of local theories of mind and emotion, local concepts of paths to knowledge, local modes of legal and political decision-making, language ideologies, and the like. Thus a Euro-American parent's praising of a child is tied to local notions of individual accomplishment. A parent's attempt to formulate the meaning of a child's partially intelligible utterance is tied to the idea that it is possible and appropriate to publicly guess at what another person may be thinking and feeling. Simplifying one's speech to an infant is tied to the notion that infants can be conversational partners. And all of the above practices can be tied to a child-centered versus task- or situation-centered orientation of participants in an activity.

Language socialization research is aware that generalizations of this sort have several undesirable effects: for one thing, cultures are essentialized, and variation in communicative practices within communities is underemphasized. We say, for example, that Samoan caregivers communicate one way, Euro-American caregivers another way, Kaluli yet another, and so on. Our accounts also seem like fixed cameos, members and communities enslaved by convention and frozen in time rather than fluid and changing over the course of a generation, a life, and even a single social encounter. Further, in our rush to point out to developmental psychologists that there are diverse cultural paths to communicative competence and not to mistake diversity for deviance, we have tended to overemphasize the unique communicative configurations of particular communities and underspecify over-arching, possibly universal, communicative and socializing practices that may facilitate socialization into multiple communities and transnational life worlds.

I end here with a brief account of how Bambi Schieffelin and I have considered such matters in individual and co-authored work. We look at a community's linguistic repertoire as a set of resources for representing ideas, displaying stances, performing acts, engaging in activities, and building social personae. Many of the linguistic resources and the ways they are socially deployed appear to be widespread and are candidate pragmatic universals. For example, there are common ways of marking the stances of certainty and uncertainty and expressing emotional intensity, and common ways of performing the socializing acts of prompting, giving directions, guessing, questioning, and clarifying. Although universal, the communicative stances and acts themselves are locally organized in terms of who attempts to communicate them, to whom, when, how often, and how elaborately. Thus prompting has been reported widely, but its situational scope varies. In middle-income Euro-American families, for example, prompting is infrequent, endures a few turns, and typically involves only an adult–child dyad. Alternatively, prompting in Kaluli households is pervasive, endures across long stretches of interaction, and involves triadic as well as dyadic participation. Similarly, while clarifying may be universal, it is a highly dispreferred response to children's unintelligible utterances among the Kaluli and Samoan Islanders, while commonplace in Euro-American adult–child encounters.

Depending upon situational rights, access, expectations, and/or personal style, children and other novices come to understand the linguistic repertoire as a palette of subtle, expressive variations and possibilities. They become aware that members draw upon linguistic forms in the palette in different ways. For example, members use language not to portray themselves and others as generic personae such as mother, father, child, teacher, or expert, but rather to paint themselves and others as distinct kinds or blends of mother, father, child, teacher, expert, and so on. Further, rather than sticking to a single portrayal, members transform or rather attempt to transform their own and others' identities continuously over interactional and autobiographical time. While language socialization research concentrates on the role of language in the cultivation of social convention, it also considers invention and attempts to distill conditions that promote or inhibit it, including communicative settings, activities, recognized level of expertise, stage of life, and assigned state of mental and physical health of interlocutors. Socialization is ultimately a two-way street, in that more and less experienced members learn from each other by creatively deploying linguistic resources to navigate and construct the human condition.

(See also *acquisition, community, expert, healing, identity, ideology, turn*)

Bibliography

Goodwin, Marjorie Harness
  1990 He-Said-She-Said: Talk as Social Organization among Black Children. Bloomington: Indiana University Press.
Heath, Shirley Brice
  1983 Ways with Words: Language, Life and Work in Communities and Classrooms. Cambridge: Cambridge University Press.
Kulick, Don
  1992 Language Shift and Cultural Reproduction: Socialization, Self, and Syncretism in a Papua New Guinean Village. Cambridge: Cambridge University Press.
Miller, P. J., R. Potts, H. Fung, L. Hoogstra, and J. Mintz
  1990 Narrative Practices and the Social Construction of Self in Childhood. American Ethnologist 17(2):292–311.

Ochs, Elinor
　1988　Culture and Language Development: Language Acquisition and Language Socialization in a Samoan Village. Cambridge: Cambridge University Press.
Ochs, Elinor, and Bambi B. Schieffelin
　1984　Language Acquisition and Socialization: Three Developmental Stories. *In* Culture Theory: Essays on Mind, Self, and Emotion. R. A. Shweder and R. A. LeVine, eds. Pp. 276–320. Cambridge: Cambridge University Press.
　1995　The Impact of Language Socialization on Grammatical Development. *In* The Handbook of Child Language. P. Fletcher and B. MacWhinney, eds. Pp. 73–94. Oxford: Blackwell.
Rogoff, Barbara
　1990　Apprenticeship in Thinking. New York: Oxford University Press.
Schieffelin, Bambi B.
　1990　The Give and Take of Everyday Life: Language Socialization of Kaluli Children. Cambridge: Cambridge University Press.
Schieffelin, Bambi B., and Elinor Ochs
　1986　Language Socialization across Cultures. Cambridge: Cambridge University Press.

■ *Elizabeth Keating*

Space

S pace is an integral part of social life and language events and is an important resource in the ordering of social experience. The distribution of space can instantiate particular systems of social control, for example, conventionalizing differences between people, and making such delineations material and substantive, as well as anchoring them within historical practice. Space is central in the creation and communication of status and power relations in many cultures; Michel Foucault analyzed the role of space in social disciplining, for example, in restricting the mobility and access of certain members of society. Space and its phenomenological counterpart place are used widely in the construction of gender relations, as feminist geographers and anthropologists have described. Limitations on access and mobility are directly related to the acquisition of particular knowledge domains and often to participation in political process; certain spatial configurations can make linguistic participation by some members impossible.

In investigating the social uses of space, the relationship between place, participation, and particular speech practices is important. Who can speak here? What kinds of communicative interactions are appropriate here? How do individuals organize themselves temporally and spatially in an event? Charles Frake's discussion of the Yakan house in the Philippines is emblematic of some of the culture-specific complexities of spatial arrangements and their relation to linguistic practice. He shows that a house, even a one-roomed Yakan house, is not just a physical space, but a structured sequence of settings where events are understood not only by the position in which they occur but also by the positions the actors move through, the manner in which they make those moves, and the appropriate language practices. Communicative interaction takes place in particular places, and language practices are partly defined by the spatial boundaries within which they occur.

Houses are constitutive of principles of social organization in all societies. Buildings are typically organized as systems of social relations, e.g., into male and female sides or areas, public vs. private, sleeping places according to age or marital status, etc. Some settings index meaning in particular ways, other spaces are settings for a wide variety of events, so that different meanings are mapped onto the same location at different times. In some societies it is common to find different spaces allocated for different speech events – rooms for classes, structures for religious observances, buildings for litigation, entertainment, etc. Looking at the specifics of the built environment or built forms and the specialized activities that surround these forms includes looking at places such as plazas and pathways. Space is not only organized according to locally situated representation practices, but serves as a model for reproducing such forms. However, the notion of space is not necessarily static or self-regulating. One question to be addressed is how the meaning of space is reframed when the same space is used for very different activities.

Spatial relationships and spatial frames of reference are construed not only through the organization of daily life, but through grammatical properties inherent in languages. Linguistic resources for expressing spatial relations are multiple, for example, directional particles, prepositions, nouns, verbs, and possessive constructions. Those studying grammatical encodings of spatial relationships have described some correlations between how language encodes space and other non-linguistic cognitive operations, such as solving spatial puzzles. This research centers on how differences in semantic structure concerning spatial relations relate to properties of conceptual structure, and how cognitive practices come to be shared through encoding in language. Deixis is another area of great interest to linguistic anthropologists looking at the role of space, since context adds crucial specificity for the interpretation of deictic forms.

The significance of a particular location in space emerges through complex relational processes that link it to other locations. Horizontal and vertical relations are particularly salient ways to reflect asymmetrical social relationships between individuals. The cultural valuing of the right side over the left is extremely common, though not universal. This privileging of one side of the body constructs asymmetry out of a mirror-like symmetry. Relationships between lexical expressions such as "above" and "below," "front" and "back," and "east" and "west" are regularly used to link arbitrary differences between members of society to the physical environment. Above is more highly valued than below, front is often more highly valued than back.

Space is, of course, an important resource for sign language. Space is used to contrast event time or to express hypotheticals and counterfactuals. Shifts in head and body orientation index imaginary locations of quoted speakers and also index intended addressees. Spatial concepts are regularly used in both spoken and signed languages as resources in representing ideas about time, music, mathematics, emotions, and social structure including kinship. This has led to the view that spatial conception is central to human thinking.

Space has an important relationship to codified knowledge in some communities. Ingjerd Hoëm describes how in Tokelau (Polynesia), elders take children on tours around the atoll, using particular sites to organize their recitation of historical narratives. Such situated spatial tellings themselves create specific notions of space. Geographical knowledge is also reproduced in songs and speeches. Similarly, for the Pintupi and other aboriginal Australian groups, space is an important component of The Dreaming, through which time, human action, and social processes are understood and interpreted. Particular places are linked to ancestral power and ideas of truth.

Space is a resource with different communicative properties than language. In Pohnpei (Micronesia), where the social structure is regularly displayed through seating position in the community feast houses, space indicates a person's hierarchical relation to others in way that can amplify or resist linguistic constructions of status. In Samoa, space can be a more important marker of status than language. Ideas about authority or privilege can be communicated as well as contested through not only language but through forms of spatial organization.

Some work on the social meaning of space is structuralist in orientation, based on the idea that space communicates polarities that are reified through other cultural expressions, but recently this has been criticized for an interpretation that is often too static and ahistorical. Other work emphasizes the situated meanings that emerge out of a complex relation between sign systems, visual (space and the body) and aural (voice). One of the newest aspects of space of interest to anthropologists is virtual space, and how this space constrains and enables new forms of discourse and interaction.

(See also *gesture, grammar, indexicality, participation, particles, power, relativity, signing, theater, truth, vision*)

Bibliography

Duranti, Alessandro
   1992   Language and Bodies in Social Space: Samoan Ceremonial Greetings. American Anthropologist 94:657–691.
Frake, Charles
   1975   How to Enter a Yakan House. *In* Sociocultural Dimensions of Language Use. Mary Sanches and Ben Blount, eds. Pp. 25–45. New York: Academic Press.
Goffman, Erving
   1963   Behavior in Public Places: Notes on the Social Organization of Gathering. New York: Free Press.
Hoëm, Ingjerd
   1993   Space and Morality in Tokelau. Pragmatics 3(2):137–153.
Keating, Elizabeth
   1998   Power Sharing: Language, Rank, Gender and Social Space in Pohnpei, Micronesia. New York: Oxford University Press.
Kuipers, Joel
   1984   Place, Names, and Authority in Weyewa Ritual Speech. Language in Society 13:455–466.
Lawrence, Denise, and Setha Low
   1990   The Built Environment and Spatial Form. Annual Review of Anthropology 19:453–505.

Levinson, Stephen
    1996   Language and Space. Annual Review of Anthropology 25:353–382.
Myers, Fred R.
    1986   Pintupi Country, Pintupi Self: Sentiment, Place, and Politics among West-
        ern Desert Aborigines. Berkeley: University of California Press.
Women and Geography Study Group
    1997   Feminist Geographies: Explorations in Diversity and Difference. Harlow,
        England: Longman.

■ *Norma Mendoza-Denton*

Style

S tyle, long shunned by postmoderns and identified in critical theoretic circles with an author-centered approach to literature known as stylistics, now enjoys a resurgence driven by an explosion and rearticulation of its definition. Structuralist concepts of style as the deviation of a message from its coded (habitual) norm now lie in tatters, as do the sociolinguistic all-or-nothing dichotomies: formal/casual, read/spontaneous. In the aftermath of the turmoil, linguistic style is defined not as still product but as relentless epiphenomenal process, a context-sensitive interaction between speakers' balance of innovative and conventional elements in their repertoire and hearers' expectations, together with the resultant attributions and interpretations that may or may not be intended by or known to the speaker. Linguistic style is the implementation, at any given time, of a combination of features from the many varieties (such as California Chicano English, or Standardized British English), registers (such as baby talk), and performance genres (e.g., sermon, advice, proverb) at that speaker's disposal. But style does not emerge unmediated from the speaker: it is continuously modulated as it is accomplished, co-produced by audience, addressees, and referees, sensitive to characteristics of these as well as to delicate contextual factors such as presence of an overhearer. Style can be extremely self-conscious, laying claim to identity even in the most "informal" circumstance (as any walk through a high-school cafeteria will make evident); at the same time it can be habitual and routinized, so well worn a groove that it resists attempts at change.

Early sociolinguistic studies found linguistic differences at all levels of the grammar between carefully elicited formal and informal speech in interview settings. These studies viewed style as a metric for attention paid to speech, a meta-awareness of the linguistic correlates of social hierarchy that would motivate a speaker to attempt to use the most prestigious, standard code in the formal section of the interview. An overshoot of this prestigious target became known as hypercorrection. Hypercorrection was taken as a powerful piece of evidence that the entire speech community oriented toward – but not all parts of it had access to – the same standard code. Sociolinguists (usually strangers to the interviewees) attempted to manipulate the level of formality as the interview progressed, trying to make it more informal; the aim was both to simulate the conditions of an ordinary conversation and to reduce the effects of observation. Interviewers tried to elicit the vernacular by identifying particular topics of common experience (such as the danger of death) where interviewees were thought to become more attentive to content and less to the form of their own speech. The result over the course of thirty years has been the establishment of a paradigm: impressive, replicable graphs show linguistic patterns in diverse sites correlating with speakers' elicited style and cross-correlating with other factors similarly predefined by the researcher (such as age group or socioeconomic status). These cross-correlations have ossified into associations between two rigidly polarized definitions of styles, with one end of the continuum associating informal–vernacular–stigmatized–innovative–working-class–young and the other formal–standard–prestigious–conservative–middle-class–old. One of the problems that we have inherited from this line of research is the difficulty of disentangling these sets of opposites and of considering that linguistic features do not have a one-to-one correspondence with either social identity or functional meaning. An inevitable observer's paradox also remains, as interviewers concede that even casual asides by interviewees to their relatives differ tremendously from the most informal speech that a strange interviewer can elicit. From the sociolinguistic springboard of controlled interview data have emerged studies of style that focus on naturally occurring and naturalistic speech settings, where research turned to the question of style-shifting in the course of speech events or as a function of variable factors in the speech situation. Audio recordings of workplace settings, especially broadcast media, have provided researchers with extensive data sets and led to various theories on the correlation between style-shifting and contextual factors such as topic, participants, familiarity, channel, audience, addressee, and attitudes, among others. In many cases speakers' responses to contextual factors were measured by the quantified presence of local dialect features (versus broader, implicitly styleless standard features), and found to mirror characteristics of the listening audience, specific addressees, and persons to whom the speakers referred (referees). Studies under this framework commonly hold that rather than paying attention to their own speech, speakers actively design and target their speech for an audience based on implicit assessments of its characteristics. Without a specific audience, speakers associated topics with an imaginary audience. Work-related topics, for instance, would trigger the use of speech like that of people in a speaker's workplace. Feature co-occurrence and alternation are important for establishing the patterning of features that constitutes a given style. Another strand in style research is that of style as poetics and performance, where features of utterances are organized in such a way that the organization calls attention to itself, and style is put on display for enjoyment, evaluation, and scrutiny by an audience.

The emphasis on performance connects to the question of how different styles emerge. Studies of repetition and ritualization in language suggest that item frequency, markedness, and social evaluation are all important factors in the crystallization of styles. Additional components of style that are currently being brought into focus are extralinguistic, embodied, and material components which contribute to a new understanding of the articulation of linguistic styles with larger frames of symbolic behavior. In my own research with adolescent Latinas in the Bay Area of Northern California, fine distinctions in social networks and gang membership were associated with differences in the use of makeup and clothing, and correlated with the variable use of morphophonologically salient, high-frequency discourse markers. Like any other social actors, these adolescent girls simultaneously draw from the linguistic and extralinguistic realms for bricolage, fashioning styles that are not only linguistically identifiable and socially named, but also embodied, symbolically coherent, and aesthetically unified.

(See also *codes, genre, heteroglossia, inference, participation, performativity, register, switching, variation, voice*)

Bibliography

Bell, Alan
    1984   Language Style as Audience Design. Language in Society 13:145–204.
Biber, Douglas, and Edward Finegan, eds.
    1994   Sociolinguistic Perspectives on Register. New York: Oxford University Press.
Coupland, Nikolas
    1980   Style-shifting in a Cardiff Work Setting. Language in Society 9:1–12.
Eckert, Penelope
    1988   Adolescent Social Structure and the Spread of Linguistic Change. Language in Society 17:183–207.
Ervin-Tripp, Susan M.
    1972   On Sociolinguistic Rules: Alternation and Cooccurrence. *In* Directions in Sociolinguistics: The Ethnography of Communication. John J. Gumperz and Dell Hymes, eds. Pp. 213–250. New York: Holt, Rinehart and Winston.
Labov, William
    1972   Sociolinguistic Patterns. Philadelphia: University of Pennsylvania Press.
Mendoza-Denton, Norma
    1997   Chicana/Mexicana Identity and Linguistic Variation: An Ethnographic and Sociolinguistic Study of Gang Affiliation in an Urban High School. Ph.D. Dissertation, Department of Anthropology, Stanford University.

■ *Benjamin Bailey*

Switching

C ode-switching is the use of two or more languages in one speech exchange by bi- or multilingual speakers. Switches between languages can occur between turns, within turns, and between constituents of single sentences. Code-switching is one of many language contact phenomena, and analysts do not always agree on the precise demarcations between code-switching and other contact phenomena such as lexical transfer. Syntactic analyses of code-switching have repeatedly shown that code-switchers attend to the syntax and morphology of switched languages in making their switches, rebutting the notion that code-switching is a haphazard, ungrammatical jumble of linguistic elements. Even when assumed to be grammatical, however, code-switching tends to be seen by analysts as requiring explanation, in contrast to monolingual speech, which is implicitly treated as the unmarked, or natural state of affairs.

Code-switching is of particular interest for linguistic anthropology because it is both a *language* contact phenomenon and a *social* contact phenomenon. Language is the central semiotic tool for representing social reality and transmitting sociocultural orientations, and in multicultural, multilingual contexts, particular codes are often associated with particular social roles, relationships, institutions, activities, and ideologies. Code-switching is both reflective and constitutive of the social processes that occur in such multilingual situations. Because code-switching involves discrete linguistic forms that can be recorded and transcribed, analysis of code-switching can make visible social negotiation processes that are otherwise veiled.

Defining code-switching in terms of outward form – as the alternation of codes in a speech exchange – backgrounds the diversity of practices and meanings that code-switching encompasses. The occurrence, shape, distribution, and meanings of code-switching vary across and within communities, depending on members' access to cross-boundary social roles and domains and to groups' relative and situational interests in boundary-maintenance versus boundary-leveling. The nature of these social boundaries and the social associations of particular codes are a function of specific histories of social relationships. The children of many international labor migrants, for example, have access to both immigrant and host society languages and sociocultural roles and thus straddle national, linguistic, and ethnic boundaries. Code-switching in this second generation is often frequent, intra-sentential, and unmarked in intra-group peer interactions, an emblem of identity for individuals who live simultaneously in multiple social and linguistic worlds. In situations of more stable bi-/multilingualism, codes and social identities are often more highly compartmentalized, individuals have fewer opportunities to develop multiple roles and relationships across social boundaries, and there are higher sociopolitical costs for crossing boundaries. In such situations, code-switching tends to be less frequent, inter- or intra-turn rather than intra-sentential, and socially and linguistically marked.

Although code-switching is irreducibly polysemous and multifunctional, researchers have highlighted several overarching functions of code-switching by assigning switches to one of several, overlapping, functional types: (1) situational switching, (2) metaphorical switching, and (3) unmarked discourse contextualization switching. As defined by Jan-Peter Blom and John Gumperz, in *situational switching*, distinct codes are employed in particular settings and speech activities, and with different categories of interlocutors, i.e., there is a direct and predictable relationship between code use and observable features of the situation. Codes are switched as observable changes in the context occur, e.g., to accommodate a monolingual speaker who joins the group or as interlocutors move to a different institutional setting associated with a distinct code. *Metaphorical switches* are defined in terms that complement those of situational switches. In contrast to situational switches, metaphorical switches partially *violate* conventionalized associations between codes and context/activity/participants. In such metaphorical switching, changes in language effect changes in context and social roles, without tangible changes in the outward context. Alternative frameworks for interpreting experience and constructing social reality that are associated with a code can thus be invoked by a switch into that code. In *discourse contextualization switching*, individual switches do not co-occur with external changes in the context or significant shifts in sociocultural framework. Individual switches serve instead as contextualization, or framing, cues to mark off quotations, changes in topic, etc. from surrounding speech. In such unmarked discourse contextualization switching, conventionalized associations between particular codes and social worlds are suspended by participants (although not necessarily by non-member bystanders), and the act of code-switching itself, rather than the particular social associations of given codes, is central.

Such categories serve as a heuristic for highlighting particular functions of code-switching and should not be understood as representing entirely discrete or manifest types. Switches that co-occur with shifts from small talk to the beginning of a formal speech, for example, can be simultaneously (and ambiguously) situational, metaphorical, and discourse contextualizing. There can be conventionalized assumptions about separate codes for casual and for formal speeches, making such a switch a situational one that accompanies an observable shift in institutional activities. The switch *itself* can also effectively change the context, from one of informal conversation to more formal speech-making, without other observable shifts in context, thus making it a meta-phorical switch. Finally, such a switch also serves as a local discourse framing device in that it signals contextual information – without necessarily invoking alternative cultural worlds – that might be conveyed in a monolingual setting through prosody or other contextualization conventions.

Code-switching reflects sociohistorical meanings and boundaries, but it can also be used to negotiate and redefine them. Speakers' juxtaposition of codes with divergent social associations within single speech exchanges – simultaneously violating and redefining conventionalized expectations – highlights speakers' creative powers to negotiate linguistic and social boundaries.

(See also *codes, contact, crossing, endangered, heteroglossia, identity, ideology, indexicality, inference, register, variation*)

Bibliography

Auer, J. C. Peter, ed.

  1998   Code-switching in Conversation: Language, Interaction and Identity. London: Routledge.

Auer, J. C. Peter

  1984   Bilingual Conversation. Amsterdam and Philadelphia: John Benjamins Publishing Company.

Blom, Jan-Peter, and John Gumperz

  1972   Social Meaning and Linguistic Structure. Code-switching in Norway. *In* Directions in Sociolinguistics: The Ethnography of Communication. J. Gumperz and D. Hymes, eds. Pp. 407–434. New York: Holt, Rinehart and Winston.

Gumperz, John

  1982   Discourse Strategies. New York: Cambridge University Press.

Heller, Monica, ed.

  1988   Codeswitching: Anthropological and Sociolinguistic Perspectives. New York: Mouton de Gruyter.

Milroy, Lesley, and Pieter Muysken, eds.

  1995   One Speaker, Two Languages: Cross-disciplinary Perspectives on Code-switching. Cambridge: Cambridge University Press.

Myers Scotton, Carol

  1993   Social Motivations for Codeswitching: Evidence from Africa. Oxford: Oxford University Press.

Romaine, Suzanne

  1995   Bilingualism. 2nd ed. Cambridge, MA: Basil Blackwell.

Zentella, Ana Celia

  1997   Growing Up Bilingual: Puerto Rican Children in New York. Malden, MA: Blackwell Publishers.

■ *Jane H. Hill*

Syncretism

Today we recognize that all utterances – not just obvious examples of borrowing and code-switching – are in a certain sense "mixed." They are multivocalic, simultaneously evoking the complex and often highly charged histories of each element of their component pronunciations, words, and expressions. We recognize this when moderates struggle to say "family" without aligning themselves with the political right, or when the use of the syllable *nig-*, especially when stressed in words like *niggardly* and *niggling*, starts a battle between strict-constructionist etymologists (who argue that the words are from Scandinavian roots that have no common source with forms meaning "black" that originated in the Romance languages) and anti-defamationist activists (who argue that to use words that so closely resemble a racist epithet is insensitive and insulting). Why are some of these histories retrievable and contestable by particular interlocutors in particular interactional moments, while others are not? Today we seek answers to this question by examining the active practice of speakers and interlocutors, as they attempt to control what utterances will mean.

One way to think about mixing and multivocality is by using the concept of "syncretism," imported from the history of religion into linguistics by the Indo-Europeanist Jerzy Kuryłowicz, who defined it as "suppression of a relevant opposition under certain determined conditions." This definition admits that interlocutors may wish, variably, either to highlight or to obscure some dimension of the way that they understand the histories of their utterances, in order to construct some new synthesis. Kuryłowicz's definition contains several terms that are useful for a theory of such syncretic practice. By "opposition" we refer to culturally situated systemic relations that are meaningful. While the classic case is that of phonological opposition, the oppositions can be identified at all levels of semiosis. For instance, one might recognize a difference between "Mexicano" and "Castellano," or between "African American" and "White" English. Thus one analytic step in the analysis of syncretic practice is the identification of "relevant oppositions" that are at stake in a moment of utterance, and the way in which particular linguistic elements are associated with those. The second term, "suppression," implies that syncretism is a *practice*, a form of social work through which speakers may render obscure the retrievable histories of particular expressive modalities. Finally, Kuryłowicz speaks of "certain determined conditions" that must be identified as the third step in the ethnography of syncretic practice.

Studying usage among speakers of Mexicano, a Uto-Aztecan language of central Mexico also known as Nahuatl, I recognized syncretic practice at all levels of linguistic production – in syntax, in phonology, in lexical choice, in text construction, and in vernacular etymology and other kinds of metalinguistic talk. Through this work speakers constructed the Mexicano language as a "syncretic project" that drew on a range of semiotic materials. The syncretic project creates a continuum from "more Mexicano" to "more Spanish" utterances. The poles – known as *legítimo mexicano* "real Mexicano" and *castellano* – are unobtainable: speakers will assert that all their talk is marred by mixing (in reference to *legítimo mexicano*) and by error (in reference to *castellano*). Yet while these speakers represented themselves as defeated by structure, it was clear that they were manipulating it at every turn. For instance, the diversity of verb classes within Nahuatl permitted speakers to treat Spanish infinitives as a new type of verb stem, which could be thematized and inflected within a Mexicano system. Thus speakers could code-switch to a Spanish form, like *depende* "it depends," or create quite a different effect by saying *dependerihui* [dependeríwi] in the same meaning. They could exploit the flexibility of the preverbal complex in their verb-initial language to incorporate many Spanish sentence adverbs, such as *entonces* and *cuando*. Their phonological manipulations of Spanish loan words were especially notable. For instance, the Spanish word *cajón* "coffer, chest" could be pronounced in Mexicano as [kaxón], or it could be shifted toward the Mexicano end of the syncretic continuum by shifting the stress to [káxon], reflecting the invariant penultimate stress of indigenous Mexicano words, or, even further, by pronouncing the [x] as [ʃ], reflecting the phonological pattern of the earliest borrowings from Spanish. Thus [káʃon] might be a self-conscious performance of indigenous identity, especially on the part of a young or middle-aged male speaker, while [kaxón] might be an equally self-conscious gesture of political potency and forward-looking urbanity.

Another set of examples can be drawn from the relations between English and Spanish. In the Southwestern United States, from Texas to California, arid conditions required that Anglo-American cattlemen borrow ranching techniques from Mexican herders who had managed stock in these desert environments for two hundred years before the Anglos arrived. A rich Spanish lexicon for this complex of techniques and equipment entered English, but the Spanish source of words like "lasso," "lariat," "chaps," "mustang," and the like is today completely unknown except among specialists. Instead, these words are considered to be peculiarly "American," evoking not Mexican culture, but the rich history of the western cowboy. Much evidence suggests that the current situation owes much to the syncretic practices of the early Anglo settlers, who preferred parodic and hyperanglicized pronunciations of the Spanish words. This linguistic erasure was accompanied by ferocious economic and military suppression of the original Mexican pioneers in the region. Today, however, the Southwestern tourist industry has found that evocation of a Hispanic aura can be lucrative, so Spanish linguistic materials are often unexpectedly foregrounded, as when streets in Southwestern subdivisions are designated as *avenidas* rather than "avenues," or when a popular bicycle race in a hilly Arizona town (notable as the point of origin of a dramatic expulsion of "Mexican" miners from the United States in the 1930s) is called *La Vuelta de Bisbee*. Another case is that of "Mock Spanish," where English speakers make jokes and insults by producing Spanish words, tag lines, and morphological materials as with "Hasta la vista, baby," "no problemo," and "el cheapo." Here, complex pragmatic effects are created by making a "Spanish" history obvious, while parodization and broad English pronunciation simultaneously make it clear that we are in the presence of an English-language voice. Mock Spanish seems to draw on a history of anti-Latino racism while in the same moment reproducing its terms.

In summary, "syncretic" linguistic projects are active and strategic efforts by speakers, who draw on their understandings of the historical associations of linguistic materials to control meaning and to produce new histories by variably suppressing and highlighting these histories through linguistic means.

(See also *contact, crossing, endangered, heteroglossia, style, switching, variation*)

Bibliography

Hill, Jane H.
    1993 Hasta la Vista, Baby: Anglo Spanish in the American Southwest. Critique of Anthropology 13:145–176.
    1998 Language, Race, and White Public Space. American Anthropologist 100:680–689.
Hill, Jane H., and Kenneth C. Hill
    1986 Speaking Mexicano. Tucson: University of Arizona Press.
Rampton, Ben
    1995 Crossing: Language and Ethnicity among Adolescents. London: Longman.
Woolard, Kathryn
    1998 Simultaneity and Bivalency as Strategies in Bilingualism. Journal of Linguistic Anthropology 8:3–29.

■ *Ingjerd Hoëm*

Theater

In the common definition, theater is seen as a particular genre within the broader spectrum of human communication and interaction; a genre that has developed internal aesthetic codes and where action follows rules unique to the theater setting. Understood in this sense, activities on stage may be seen as governed by behavioral norms applied in a different manner than is usually the case off stage, that is, in other areas of life. Traditions of classical drama that employ predefined scripts and fixed roles are illustrations of the kind of norm-boundness that prototypically governs action on stage.

However, other common characteristics of theater or theatrical activities are play, improvisation, and subversive action. Despite the sometimes rigorous orchestration of action on stage, behavioral norms associated with arenas outside of the theater are not necessarily identical with those applied or reinforced on stage. Roles and institutions of everyday life tend to be challenged and shifted around within the defining frame of theater.

In all theatrical activity, there is thus a tension between a fixed and a fluid dimension. The fixed may be manifest as part of the components that constitute theater as an institution, and be seen as present in such resources as a given script, predefined roles, and in the defining frame of the activity itself, that is, the stage or boundary of the theatrical setting. In more experimental or improvisational theater, the fixed dimension may be moved to the institutions or roles represented in a play, that is, the fixity is projected as an aspect of societal activities off stage. The fluidity is achieved as a result of experimenting with the above-mentioned resources. In the study of theater, the tension between structure and anti-structure, fixedness and fluidity, is explored.

Theater is perhaps the one human activity where we can see most clearly the mimetic quality of social interaction. To take an Other's perspective through the act of presenting or representing someone else is an integral part of most forms of theatrical activities. This act allows for a perspective different from the everyday to emerge. In the process, something familiar becomes, at least for a while, something strange. In this way, one or more aspects of the cultural setting of which the play is a part is objectified. Thus, in this sense, play is inherently reflexive.

In a comparative perspective, cross-culturally and diachronically, how theater is defined, and what forms acting and interpretation may take, vary to a great extent. To illustrate, skits depicting socially significant events are part of most Tokelau (an atoll society in the South Pacific) gatherings. These skits function as a running political commentary, as entertainment, and as part of the local management of relationships. There is no strict boundary between the players and the audience: anyone present may be asked to participate, and the topic of a skit always draws on material familiar to those present. The typical way humor and satire are achieved is through role inversion – for example, in the case where the visiting anthropologist was cast in the role of a native. The person directing the skit asked me to "say some words in my own language," demonstrate some "native dances," and so on. And the whole community joined with great pleasure in the exposure of my unusual role in the everyday life of the village. In this and similar cases we may find that the defining characteristics of theatrical activities vary to a considerable extent from the prototypic classical definition referred to above. The distinction between players and audience may not be relevant, there may be no stage as such, improvisation may be the rule rather than the exception, and so on.

Theater and ritual are frequently described as having common roots. However, there are clear indications that theatrical and ritual activities tend to exist simultaneously in most societies, to some extent feeding into each other. The liminal quality and transformative aspect of theatrical and ritual performance has been stressed, and examined particularly in the tradition following Victor Turner. In the cases where theater and ritual exist in opposition, the distinction tends to be achieved through theatrical activities being linked with deception and immorality, and ritual activities being aligned with religious practice and ontological truth.

When studying the role of language in theater, or in examining how linguistic form may be affected by being used for theatrical purposes, both approach and results are highly dependent on what definitions of theater and language are adhered to. If theater is defined broadly as performance or as the performative aspect of human behavior in general (as Erving Goffman's work may serve as an illustration of), it becomes important to examine relations between genre(s) with an eye to the interplay between form and content, with the purpose of establishing what the significant interpretative frames informing this particular language game may be.

The characteristic of theatrical activities, that is, their constant shifting between fixedness and fluidity, makes it a case where the general challenge confronting theories of language is highlighted to a particular degree. To find models that allow us to describe this shifting quality without ending up in the blind alley of empirical particularism, we may have to abandon a conception of language that identifies it with grammatical or cognitive structure.

One way of doing so is through a perspective that focuses on processes of linguistic structuration. We need then to look at linguistic agency, that is, how causal connections come to be established and are represented grammatically. By this means we find keys to the ontology and lifeworld of the language game under study. The focus on linguistic agency crosscuts the further analysis of voice (who is speaking, to whom), content (what is said), and form (how it is said). We thus get a perspective that allows us to depict the interplay between the fixed (codes, norms, grammar) and the fluid existing in the processes of structuration and inscription.

To question who is speaking, to whom, on whose behalf, and with what kind of authority is to ask questions which bring us to the heart of playacting and which may allow us to reveal the hidden ontology that play carries the potential to expose. To pose such questions is to demonstrate the connection between theater and politics. The intimate relationship between any exegetical practice and the score it serves to interpret also holds true for linguistics and anthropology as areas of study. Theatrical activities make us realize that to read and interpret a script means to have the power to define our social world. In this way, theater serves to remind us of the arbitrary quality of all human institutions, including our conceptions of language and performance.

(See also *codes, dreams, gesture, grammar, humor, improvisation, participation, reflexivity, space, voice*)

Bibliography

Duranti, Alessandro, and Charles Goodwin, eds.
    1992 Rethinking Context: Language as an Interactive Phenomenon. Cambridge: Cambridge University Press.
Goffman, Erving
    1959 The Presentation of Self in Everyday Life. Garden City, NY: Doubleday.
    1974 Frame Analysis: An Essay on the Organization of Experience. New York: Harper and Row.
Hoëm, Ingjerd
    1998 Clowns, Dignity and Desire: On the Relationship Between Performance, Identity and Reflexivity. *In* Recasting Ritual. Felicia Hughes-Freeland and Mary M. Crain, eds. Pp. 21–43. London: Routledge.
Kapferer, Bruce
    1986 Performance and the Structuring of Meaning and Experience. *In* The Anthropology of Experience. Victor W. Turner and Edward M. Bruner, eds. Pp. 188–203. Urbana and Chicago: University of Chicago Press.
Schechner, Richard
    1994 Ritual and Performance. Companion Encyclopedia of Anthropology. Humanity, Culture and Social Life. Tim Ingold, ed. Pp. 613–647. London: Routledge.
Sennett, Richard
    1977 The Fall of Public Man. New York: Alfred A. Knopf.

Stallybrass, Peter, and Allon White
  1986   Introduction. The Politics and Poetics of Transgression. London: Methuen.
Taussig, Michael
  1993   Mimesis and Alterity: A Particular History of the Senses. New York and London: Routledge.
Turner, Victor
  1992   From Ritual to Theater. The Human Seriousness of Play. New York: PAJ Publications.

■ *Regna Darnell*

Translation

V irtually all linguistic anthropologists acknowledge translation as crucial to their praxis, even that all ethnographic work of sociocultural
anthropologists may be interpreted at least metaphorically as translation. Considerably less consensus, however, surrounds the methods and
goals by which translations are evaluated and their relations to the larger
anthropological project of cross-cultural research specified. Translations fall
on a continuum from the literal to the poetic, each extreme having passionate
adherents and constituting characteristic linkages between target and source
language. This continuum reflects the hybrid, rhizomatic roots of linguistic
anthropology across the sciences and humanities.

With a commitment to translation as science, Franz Boas, Edward Sapir,
and their colleagues constructed a tradition of textual scholarship as the ideal
database for both linguistics and ethnology. Texts in the words of native speakers of Native American languages were touted as windows into "the native
point of view," the *Weltanschauung* of so-called primitive cultures. This train
of thought led Benjamin Whorf, Sapir's student, to explore the interdepend-
ence of language, thought, and reality. Linguistic relativity, coded in grammatical categories potentially incommensurable with those of familiar
Indo-European languages, rendered true bilingualism rare to impossible and
translation at best a makeshift affair. Perhaps, indeed, the linguistic habits of
first language could never be transcended fully. Yet the Boasians proceeded
as if texts were objective, translatable, capable of yielding up insights into the
myriad ways of being human.

This Americanist text tradition has been lampooned as mere memory culture, isolated from actual behavior, from ongoing social interaction. Among
peoples without writing, however, texts recorded, at least initially, by outsiders have become vehicles of cultural maintenance and revitalization. Ironically, authorship in this collaborative tradition has long been attributed to
the translator, although artistry and intellectual property alike reside with
the original performer.

Recent translations, those of Dennis Tedlock being exemplary, emphasize ongoing performative parameters that remain viable in oral traditions across the aboriginal Americas. Ideally, often also in practice, written texts extend and document dialogic and exegetic processes of interpretation inherent in the adaptive capacities of living oral traditions.

Scientific translation of distant languages has sacrificed elegance for ethnographic verisimilitude, foregrounding word-for-word glosses that allow *metaphras* the linguist/reader to reconstruct the grammatical complexity of the original. Textual poetics remains in the original rather than in the translation, understood as a vehicle back to its source. Such a theory of translation often provides a smoother version but this remains secondary, a sop to the faint of heart.

The long-term collaboration of linguist H. C. Wolfart and Plains Cree elder and linguist Freda Ahenakew exemplifies this textual tradition. Extensive cultural background and detailed linguistic notes substitute for readers' lack of memory and indigenous socialization, making Plains Cree oral literature accessible to a wider audience, both Native and non-Native.

Further adaptations of the Americanist text tradition have emerged from conditions of rapid social change, accelerating over the last two hundred years. Many aboriginal languages are endangered, leaving traditional knowledge to be transmitted necessarily in English, an imposed and alien language. Increasing evidence, however, suggests that textual features ranging from phonological to discourse performative are carried over into English, even transmitted to individuals who do not speak a traditional language. My own work with Lisa Valentine over the past decade has explored performance of First Nations identity in the English discourse of Cree, Ojibwe, and Iroquoian communities.

Translation as poetry partially eschews scientific goals of literalism to celebrate the uniqueness of what can be said under particular conditions by particular individuals recognized in virtually every human culture as poets. Translation is utopian, an unattainable goal, a receding target. No translation can be fully adequate. A. L. Becker, following Ortega y Gasset, calls for a "modern philology" in which the exuberances and deficiencies of particular texts, the reciprocal failures of source and target language to replicate one another's distinctions, remain incommensurable. Even with cultural background and linguistic exegesis, a single sentence may retain irreconcilable indeterminacy resolvable only by imposing a coherence absent in the original.

The impossibility of ever settling for a single translation looms large. Douglas Hofstadter structures an entire edifice around multiple translations, his own and those of collaborators across linguistic and cultural background, to (re)create in English potentialities perhaps inherent in a single small poem written in French five centuries ago by one Clement Marot. Nuanced translation is a miniaturist art, for Hofstadter as for Becker.

The great poets of other Western literary traditions, for example the Hungarian, are translators, writing for audiences expectant that texts in another language will yield to triangulation from multiple translations, each singling out different aspects of the original and creating a unique work in the target language. Despite the number of linguistic anthropologists who are poets in their own right – from Sapir to Dell Hymes, Dennis Tedlock, and Paul Friedrich – our own literary canon tends inadequately to assume that translators should be invisible.

The Boasian text tradition has emphasized the uniqueness of each linguistic and cultural tradition. More recently, Dell Hymes has pioneered in identifying patterns of repetition and formal structure that are serious candidates for universal features of poetic discourse. Treating formal texts in a variety of oral and written traditions as poetry rather than prose allows translation to focus on form. Canadian poet Robert Bringhurst has been particularly effective in recreating in English the encapsulated intentions and creativity of specific Haida narrators.

Translation reaches deep into the core of anthropological thinking, facilitating what Whorf called "multilingual awareness," the capacity to transcend categories of habitual thought by virtue of knowing how knowledge is codified in a range of languages. Multilingualism and its cross linguistic analysis lead to a critique of our own society's monolingualism and ethnocentrism. Translation, understood as effective communication, becomes the very key to survival in a global order constructed on local variabilities of expressive capacity and form.

(See also *orality, plagiarism, poetry, reflexivity, relativity, writing*)

Bibliography

Ahenakew, Freda, and H. C. Wolfart, eds. and trans.
    1992   Kohkominawak Otacimowiniwawa. Our Grandmothers' Lives, as Told in Their Own Words. Saskatoon, Saskatchewan: Fifth House.
Becker, A. L.
    1995   Beyond Translation: Essays toward a Modern Philology. Ann Arbor: University of Michigan Press.
Bringhurst, Robert
    1999   A Story as Sharp as a Knife: The Classical Haida Mythtellers and Their World. Vancouver: Douglas and McIntyre.
Darnell, Regna
    1998   And along Came Boas: Continuity and Revolution in Americanist Anthropology. Amsterdam and Philadelphia: John Benjamins.
Hofstadter, Douglas R.
    1997   Le Ton Beau de Marot: In Praise of the Music of Language. New York: Basic Books.
Hymes, Dell
    1981   "In Vain I Tried to Tell You": Essays in Native American Ethnopoetics. Philadelphia: University of Pennsylvania Press.
Tedlock, Dennis
    1983   The Spoken Word and the Work of Interpretation. Philadelphia: University of Pennsylvania Press.

Tedlock, Dennis, and Bruce Mannheim, eds.

    1995   The Dialogic Emergence of Culture. Carbondale: University of Illinois Press.

Valentine, Lisa, and Regna Darnell, eds.

    1999   Theorizing the Americanist Tradition. Toronto: University of Toronto Press.

Whorf, Benjamin Lee

    1956   Language, Thought, and Reality: Selected Writings of Benjamin Lee Whorf.
       John B. Carroll, ed. Cambridge, MA: MIT Press.

■ *Susan D. Blum*

Truth

Truth has been studied anthropologically and philosophically from three principal perspectives: the correspondence theory, the coherence theory, and the social theory. Several types of non-truth have also been attractive research topics: falsity, non-truth (deception and lying), and truth-irrelevance. Each perspective relies on a view of meaning and pragmatics, and supports its viewpoint either formally or ethnographically.

In the correspondence theory, truth is a matching of words to world. A closely related category, "sincerity," is a matching of words to internal states. Evaluation of the truth of a given utterance depends on understanding of three things: word(s), world, and the relationships between them. These are among the abiding topics of many branches of Western philosophy: ontology, metaphysics, epistemology, logic, and semantics. Thinkers as diverse as Aristotle, Immanuel Kant, Bertrand Russell, Alfred Tarski, and Ludwig Wittgenstein have written about truth. Kant proposed a distinction between synthetic truths, which depend on contingent facts, and analytic truths, which depend only on components and their logical relationships. Truth conditions (analytic truths) are central to formal propositional and predicate calculi in which meaning may be represented by logical operators.

The coherence theory of truth suggests that truth derives from coherent relations within a given social, semantic, and epistemological framework. In this theory, presupposition and rationality are critical for understanding truth. Truth or falsity of religious ideas or metaphysics may be assessed only within a given system. Studies of religion and explanation such as E. E. Evans-Pritchard's work on Azande notions of magic and witchcraft attempt to demonstrate that a positionless model of truth cannot apply to social life. Philosophers of science also often operate within this theory.

The social theory of truth relies on the understanding of relations of power and control over knowledge and claims to possess truth. Plato and Machiavelli proposed the usefulness of social superiors controlling the truth that must be adhered to by inferiors. In this model, truth has been discredited from many directions. Postmodernists, feminists, and Foucaultians criticize claims to objectivity, master narratives, and regimes of truth. If knowledge is power, then claims to have knowledge of the truth – transcendent, objective, universal, panchronic, biological, scientific – obscures others' rights to their own truths. Powerful social sectors often claim to possess the truth; how truth claims serve power, often in religion, economy, politics, and science, is a central question for some anthropologists.

Though it might sometimes seem that truth occupies only theologians and philosophers and lawyers, all societies must ground their interactions in some sort of validation and provide limits to play. Linguistic anthropological research on evidence and responsibility demonstrates widespread concern for knowing the sources of remarks and their origins/transmissions/consequences. People attempt to measure the truth and lies of others, seeing into their souls or minds or hearts through polygraphs, body language, discourse, psychotherapy, and oracles. Quests for truth(s) abound in human life, sometimes through language.

Non-truth takes many forms. Deception is pervasive throughout all life forms, if we extend this term to include camouflage and protective coloring, expansion to appear bigger, mimicry of an enemy's cry, and so forth. Lies and lying have been explored by philosophers, linguists, sociologists, psychologists, primatologists, and linguistic anthropologists. Moral considerations in social life usually involve many matters other than abstract truth. Politeness phenomena may include non-true language uttered for purposes other than those of conveying or seeking information. "What a beautiful dress" may be uttered for pragmatic reasons such as furthering relationships or giving face rather than for literal conveying of true opinion. Sincerity and intentions are in some societies, such as China and Japan, assessed apart from their match between inner states and words. In China moral valuation depends on one's willingness to act appropriately in context; speakers' inner states or desires are irrelevant. Most important are the consequences of utterances, just as of any other act; responsibility is critical, but truth may not be.

Truth-irrelevance in language use is usually traced to Bronislaw Malinowski's notion of phatic communion. He argued that in the Trobriands, language (for example, in greetings) was often used to emphasize contact between speakers, but it conveyed no information. J. L. Austin showed that language performs rather than describes actions. Austin's felicity conditions require sincerity on the part of the speaker. The importance of sincerity and intentions is central to an ideology of language that desires access to a self lying deeply within. In societies where selves are constructed differently, access to them is viewed differently and the role of sincerity is not central. Paul Grice's "Maxims" posit that social actors operate with a tacit shared contract to be informative; violations of maxims are interpreted as conveying other kinds of information. His implicitly universal claim motivated anthropologists to demonstrate how different maxims operate in different field sites. Elinor Ochs, for instance, showed that in Madagascar it was undesirable to be informative; the burden fell on women to provide information in some contexts.

Much of linguistic anthropology's relationship to truth is to show how many things language accomplishes in addition to or instead of expressing the truth and how truth and sincerity occupy variable roles across cultures. Language, produced collaboratively in social interaction, can convey a dazzling variety of truths and non-truths – things displaced in time and space, hypotheticals, counterfactuals – in greatly varying ways. Human beings create characters who have never lived, or animals like unicorns or dragons that live in every generation's imagination. We tell outright lies, either for our own personal benefit or for some greater good or just for fun. We can be mistaken or misunderstood; we can have imperfect transmission or imperfect mastery of a language. We speak of our gods, who are different from other people's gods. We can aspire to the purely referential language of mathematics and logic in which $p = p$. We play with rhyme or rhythm or repetition; we while away the hours spinning yarns or telling legends or playing the dozens. Language does much more than simply describe the conditions of the world.

Linguistic anthropologists contribute to an understanding of the variety of human behavior by recording and analyzing the many things people do with words – which in some times and places includes "telling the truth." By attending to matters beyond truth, we arrive at much of the joy and the passion – and tension – involved in human interaction. Linguistic anthropology's challenge remains to explore the rich diversity of beliefs and practices regarding truth and its manifold variations (performance/stories/deception/lies/gossip) – and to account for similarities, if any. No society can permit complete disregard for responsibility to some physical reality, yet how each society conceives of the consequences and forms of non-truth differs greatly. All these contribute to an understanding of what it is to be human.

(See also *act, inference, intentionality, maxim, plagiarism, prophecy*)

Bibliography

Bailey, F. G.
  1991 The Prevalence of Deceit. Ithaca and London: Cornell University Press.
Barnes, J. A.
  1994 A Pack of Lies: Towards a Sociology of Lying. Cambridge: Cambridge University Press.
Bok, Sissela
  1979 Lying: Moral Choice in Public and Private Life. New York: Pantheon Books.
Coleman, Linda, and Paul Kay
  1981 Prototype Semantics: The English Word "Lie." Language 57:26–44.
Duranti, Alessandro
  1993 Intentionality and Truth: An Ethnographic Critique. Cultural Anthropology 8:214–245.
Hill, Jane H., and Judith T. Irvine, eds.
  1992 Responsibility and Evidence in Oral Discourse. Cambridge: Cambridge University Press.

Keenan, Elinor Ochs
1976   The Universality of Conversational Postulates. Language in Society 5(1):67–80.
Lutz, Catherine A., and Lila Abu-Lughod, eds.
1990   Language and the Politics of Emotion. Cambridge: Cambridge University Press.
Nyberg, David
1991   The Varnished Truth: Truth Telling and Deceiving in Ordinary Life. Chicago: University of Chicago Press.
Rosaldo, Michelle Z.
1982   The Things We Do with Words: Ilongot Speech Acts and Speech Act Theory in Philosophy. Language in Society 11:203–237.
Shapin, Steven
1994   A Social History of Truth: Civility and Science in Seventeenth-Century England. Chicago: University of Chicago Press.
Sweetser, Eve E.
1987   The Definition of "Lie": An Examination of the Folk Models Underlying a Semantic Prototype. *In* Cultural Models in Language and Thought. Dorothy Holland and Naomi Quinn, eds. Pp. 43–66. Cambridge: Cambridge University Press.

■ *Sally Jacoby*

Turn

In any culturally situated communicative activity involving at least two people, participants rely on recurring communicative practices through which they contingently bring about speaker change at appropriately non-random points in everyday, institutional, face-to-face, co-present, and electronically mediated conversational settings. Analysis of such practices indicates that turns at talk are emergent units dynamically designed in real time to be recognizable as now just beginning, now still in progress, and now ending.

There is no universal definition of "turn" for all types of culturally situated communication because different activities are organized by different turn-taking systems. For example, a turn in one form of institutional two-way radio is not considered complete (and thus not implicating an appropriate change in speakership) until the current speaker says "Over." In oratory, a participant may have an extended turn lasting many minutes and comprising many utterances, until some culturally familiar discourse genre is recognizably created. In broadcast news interviews, journalists may preface a question with one or more background assertions, and interviewees will typically refrain from responding until a hearable question has been articulated. In turn, journalists may negatively sanction interviewees for responding to a preparatory assertion instead of waiting for the question. Even in everyday casual conversation, in which speaker change tends to occur frequently, one participant may get an extended turn, comprising many utterances, to tell a funny story or explain something in detail, because recipients, having recognized the speaker's bid to maintain the floor past the next possible turn unit completion point, are willing to refrain from taking a next turn until the story or explanation has hearably come to an end. Recipients may then collaborate in the achievement of the speaker's multi-unit extended turn by producing only minimal verbal and non-verbal recipient responses, such as "unh-hunh," "you're kidding!," and nodding the head.

Scholars who study turn-taking in everyday conversation have provided rich descriptions of many of the practices through which participants design and recognize the most basic unit of a turn: the Turn Constructional Unit (TCU). These scholars' interactional perspective on turn-taking is that speakers' multiple and simultaneous practices for designing turns at talk provide the resources which allow potential next speakers to monitor an emergent TCU so as to locate possibly appropriate (and even inappropriate) points to begin a next turn.

One such resource is the linguistic design of a TCU. The emergent grammatical shape of a TCU in progress makes it possible for a potential next speaker to estimate the first possible point of TCU completion and thus to be ready to start the next turn at talk as soon as that first possible speaker Transition Relevance Place (TRP) is arrived at. Based on English-language corpora, the earliest conversation analytic descriptions of turn-taking identified four grammatical types of TCU:

(1) lexical (a single word)
   ((phone rings))
   → A: Hello?

(2) phrasal (two or more words in a non-clausal arrangement)
   A: The green line indicates the transition.
   → B: The true phase transition.

(3) clausal (a dependent clause)
   A: Is there anything you don't eat?
   → B: That you're bringing?

(4) sentential (an independent clause)
   → A: Do you need cigarettes?
   B: YES.

Researchers have also shown that grammatically "complex" TCUs (e.g., if–then structures, well-known aphorisms) are more vulnerable to speaker change before a next possible completion point is reached. This means that some instances of speaker change do not coincide with the start of a wholly new turn but instead achieve the collaborative completion of one TCU by more than one speaker, as in the following example (a co-constructed sentential TCU):

   → A: Okay, so are you coming up to, ummmm . . .
   → B: Vermont.

The dynamically emergent intonational and paralinguistic contours of a TCU in progress also permit a potential next speaker to predict the next possible completion point. Intonation patterns (rising, falling, etc.), syllable and word stress, and placement of pitch peaks in a tone unit all combine to give a projectable musical shape to a TCU. Current speakers can even manipulate the intonational and paralinguistic design of a TCU in progress so as to discourage speaker change at the first possible point of grammatical completion. Potential next speakers also monitor the emergent grammatical and intonational shape of a TCU in progress to determine where not to start a new turn and where to co-construct a single TCU in progress before it reaches possible completion.

Non-vocal comportment of participants in face-to-face and co-present communication also contributes to the design and recognition of a possibly complete TCU. The dynamic trajectory of a speaker's hand gestures, gaze direction, facial expressions, body positioning, and breath capacity can be routinely monitored by potential next speakers looking for an appropriate (or inappropriate) turn transition relevance place. While their own TCU is in progress, current speakers may also inspect a recipient's non-vocal comportment for signs that she or he is gearing up to take the next turn. Shifts in a recipient's body positioning or a visible taking in of breath may instantaneously influence how a current speaker designs the rest of the TCU in progress, i.e., whether to allow for or discourage imminent speaker change.

The design and positioning of utterances in an ongoing sequence of utterances also contributes to whether a TCU in progress is likely to be vulnerable to speaker transition at the first possible completion point. For example, if a speaker begins a turn saying, "I want to make two points," a recipient may refrain from responding until two hearable points have been made, regardless of how many TCUs it takes for the speaker to make them. Thus the extent to which a TCU in progress can be heard as approaching a point of possible ideational, actional, or pragmatic completion is a further aspect of emergent talk that participants orient to, as speakers and as recipients. In short, if a TCU in progress can be heard as coherently linking to prior talk and accomplishing something in its own right such that a next action is made sequentially relevant, it can be heard as a possibly complete turn at talk and an opportunity for speaker change.

(See also *acquisition, competence, control, gesture, grammar, narrative, participation, poetry, socialization, theater, vision*)

Bibliography

Ford, Cecilia E., Barbara A. Fox, and Sandra A. Thompson
  1996 Practices in the Construction of Turns: The "TCU" Revisited. Pragmatics
      6(3):427–454.
Ford, Cecilia E., and Sandra A. Thompson
  1996 Interactional Units in Conversation: Syntactic, Intonational, and Pragmatic
      Resources for the Management of Turns. *In* Interaction and Grammar. Elinor
      Ochs, Emanuel A. Schegloff, and Sandra A. Thompson, eds. Pp. 134–184. Cambridge: Cambridge University Press.
Jefferson, Gail
  1984 Notes on Some Orderliness of Overlap Onset. *In* Discourse Analysis and

Natural Rhetorics. V. D'Urso and P. Leonardi, eds. Pp. 11–38. Padua, Italy: CLEUP Editore.

Kelly, John, and John Local
  1986 Projection and "Silences": Notes on Phonetic and Conversational Structure. Human Studies 9:185–204.

Lerner, Gene
  1996 On the "Semi-permeable" Character of Grammatical Units in Conversation: Conditional Entry into the Turn Space of Another Participant. *In* Interaction and Grammar. Elinor Ochs, Emanuel A. Schegloff, and Sandra A. Thompson, eds. Pp. 238–276. Cambridge: Cambridge University Press.

Ochs, Elinor, Bambi Schieffelin, and Martha Platt
  1979 Propositions across Utterances and Speakers. *In* Developmental Pragmatics. Elinor Ochs and Bambi Schieffelin, eds. Pp. 251–268. New York: Academic Press.

Sacks, Harvey, Emanuel A. Schegloff, and Gail Jefferson
  1974 A Simplest Systematics for the Organization of Turn-taking for Conversation. Language 50:696–735.

Schegloff, Emanuel A.
  1982 Discourse as an Interactional Achievement: Some Uses of "Uh Huh" and Other Things That Come between Sentences. *In* Georgetown University Round Table on Languages and Linguistics. Deborah Tannen, ed. Pp. 71–93. Washington, DC: Georgetown University Press.
  1996 Turn Organization: One Intersection of Grammar and Interaction. *In* Interaction and Grammar. Elinor Ochs, Emanuel A. Schegloff, and Sandra A. Thompson, eds. Pp. 52–133. Cambridge: Cambridge University Press.

Streeck, Jürgen, and Ulrike Hartge
  1992 Previews: Gestures at the Transition Place. *In* The Contextualization of Language. Peter Auer and A. di Luzo, eds. Pp. 135–157. Amsterdam: Benjamins.

■ *John Baugh*

Variation

E dward Sapir's extraordinary contributions to anthropology and linguistics underlie all of the following observations regarding linguistic
variation. He was ever mindful of the fact that language and linguistic
behavior tie human cognition to the social organizations that maintain the
life of any language. Following in that tradition, ethnographers of communication affirmed incontrovertible linkages between linguistic forms and their
social functions in speech communities throughout the world. William Labov
described linguistic variation as "linguistic differences that don't make a difference." For example, English can freely substitute "kids" for "children"
without any loss in denotational meaning; this type of free linguistic variation is common.

Studies of linguistic variation travel under different guises, depending substantially upon theoretical orientation and the nature of the data under analysis. All studies of linguistic variation are rooted in social contexts, typically
where language is used by ordinary people engaged in day-to-day activities.
Other studies of linguistic variation are highly specialized, perhaps concen-
trating on education, or the use of language in the courts. Analyses of language in the workplace, or during telephone conversations, as well as in
remote villages where literacy is embodied within oral traditions, all exhibit
degrees of linguistic variation.

Linguistic variation also takes place at all levels within the grammar; more
specifically, syntactic variation can be observed (e.g. Tom hit Dave, vs. Dave
was hit by Tom). It also occurs lexically, as mentioned above. Phonetic and
phonological variation are perhaps most commonly observed because we
often tend to associate many characteristics of dialects or accents with their
specific phonetic and/or phonological properties. Quantitative analyses of
phonology and morphophonology lie at the heart of many sociolinguistic
studies, but such quantitative analyses represent one of several approaches
to analyses of linguistic variation.

My own interest in linguistic variation grows directly from personal observations regarding linguistic discrimination against African Americans.

Although I now have considerable command of standard English, this was not always the case. I grew up in inner-city neighborhoods in Philadelphia and Los Angeles. I also attended public schools where the vast majority of my teachers – regardless of their racial background–were openly critical, if not hostile, to African American English.

Indeed, my earliest awareness of linguistic variation occurred during early childhood when I observed striking differences between the language of my teachers, my playmates, and people throughout the community. Like most people, their life experiences and educational backgrounds strongly influenced their speech. Such is the case with the linguistic variation illustrated in Figure 1.

Four African American males are displayed, along with evidence of their usage of non-standard English negation. The adolescent data were collected in 1975, and the young adult data were collected in 1985. As teens the young men almost always used non-standard negation. That is, whenever possible, they would say, "I ain't got none," or "He ain't seen it," in contrast to standard English, "I don't have any," or "He hasn't seen it."

Coco and Juan are brothers by blood, as is the case for Russell and Leon. However, Coco and Juan lived in poverty with a single mother who was drug dependent and on welfare. Russell and Leon were middle class; their father was an attorney and their mother an elementary school teacher. Again, as teens they rarely – if ever – used standard English. However, their circumstances changed as adults, and so did their relative usage of standard English.

Coco enlisted in the army as a private and had risen to the rank of sergeant by 1985; he is presently a colonel with plans to retire from active military duty. His brother Juan had been convicted of murder during a robbery, and he continues to serve a life sentence in prison; he could not be tried as an adult for his crime, otherwise he may have received a death penalty. Russell owns three small stores "in the old neighborhood"; in 1985 he owned a single

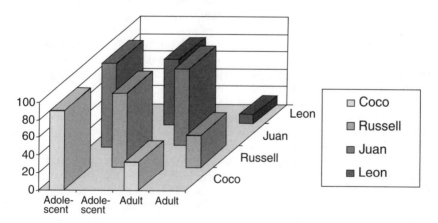

Figure 1
% of non-standard negation for four African American males as teens and adults

hardware store. His brother Leon received an MBA, and after leaving IBM in 1992 he formed a software corporation with some of his former colleagues. He has prospered as an entrepreneur and philanthropist.

The linguistic variation that they demonstrate is both typical of many communities and somewhat unique as part of the African American experience. First of all, many Americans vary usage between standard and non-standard English, and I frequently hear many well-educated people use "ain't" or other non-standard forms, often for emphasis. The point at hand seeks to affirm that linguistic forms are frequently influenced by their function. In the case of my African American consultants, their life experiences resulted in different exposure to standard English, as well as different circumstances that either embrace or reject standard English. Leon observed that he would have been outcast at IBM had he tried to speak "Black English," but Juan noted that standard English was devalued in prison, and those convicts who embraced it did so at considerable personal risk.

Linguistic variation within a single language differs considerably from linguistic variation across languages. Letticia Galindo's study of Chicanas who were former gang members is highly illustrative of the latter case, where linguistic variation includes bilingual code-switching between Spanish and English, as well as Caló, the slang and jargon that was common in prison and within their gang culture. Far from the stereotype of impoverished linguistic abilities, these women demonstrate how knowledge of more than one language or culture can enhance communication, allowing interlocutors to draw on their complete reservoir of knowledge; that is, as long as others share comparable communicative competence. Galindo's studies take on added relevance because of politicized efforts to dismantle affirmative action and the passage of laws intended to eliminate bilingual education. The informants whom she interviewed were not only socially disenfranchised, they were linguistically disenfranchised, and educationally disadvantaged.

Her account of the use, or lack thereof, of cursing among Chicanas who had served time in prison offers insights into cultural and linguistic norms that could only be obtained by an outstanding fieldworker. I stress this point because Galindo's exceptional skill as a fieldworker is understated in her research; she does not boast about her ability to draw out conversation that is intimate or salacious, nor does she imply that others can not do what she has done. However, those of you who read her work will no doubt agree with the observation that she has managed to record extremely casual speech, which, at times, was potentially incriminating of the speakers (all of whom she has protected with pseudonyms).

Upon concluding her linguistic survey she returns to the functional realm of Pachuca discourse in context, and she builds upon the observations of Gumperz and Hernandez-Chavez who also observed that substantial Mexican-American code-switching only occurs among those with adequate linguistic skill. The newly arrived immigrant from a Spanish-speaking country can not utilize these same linguistic resources; that is, without substantial English proficiency.

Matters of linguistic variation go far beyond minority communities in the United States. Evidence of linguistic variation can be found among individual speakers throughout the world, as well as within the speech communities they occupy. Within the U.S. context, however, matters of linguistic variation take on considerable significance in the life of minority group members who lack fluency in mainstream U.S. English. It is partially for this reason, and my own desire to enlist anthropology and linguistics in the quest for greater social equality, that the chosen examples of linguistic variation are relevant to social concerns beyond that of language usage.

(See also *codes, genre, individual, register, style, switching, voice*)

Bibliography

Baugh, John
　　1983　Black Street Speech: Its History, Structure, and Survival. Austin: University of Texas Press.
Blom, Jan-P., and John Gumperz
　　1972　Social Meaning and Linguistic Structure: Code-switching in Norway. *In* Directions in Sociolinguistics. John Gumperz and Dell Hymes, eds. Pp. 407–434. New York: Holt, Rinehart and Winston.
Cedergren, Henrietta, and David Sankoff
　　1974　Variable Rules: Performance as a Statistical Reflection of Competence. Language 50:333–355.
Galindo, Letticia
　　1993　The Language of Gangs, Drugs, and Prison Life among Chicanas. Latino Studies Journal 6:23–42.
Gumperz, John, and E. Hernandez-Chavez
　　1971　Bilinguals, Bidialectalism, and Classroom Interaction. *In* (1997) English with an Accent. R. C. Lippi-Green, ed. London: Routledge.
Guy, Gregory
　　1996　Form and Function in Linguistic Variation. *In* Towards a Social Science of Language. Volume 1: Variation and Change in Language in Society. Gregory Guy, Crawford Feagin, Deborah Schiffrin, and John Baugh, eds. Pp. 221–252. Philadelphia: John Benjamins Press.
Hymes, Dell
　　1972　Towards Communicative Competence. Philadelphia: University of Pennsylvania Press.
Labov, William
　　1972　Sociolinguistic Patterns. Philadelphia: University of Pennsylvania Press.
　　1994　Principles of Linguistic Change. Vol. 1: Internal Factors. Oxford: Blackwell.
Sapir, Edward
　　1949　Language. *In* Selected Writings of Edward Sapir in Language, Culture and Personality. David Mandelbaum, ed. Pp. 7–32. Berkeley: University of California Press.

■ *Charles Goodwin*

Vision

A primordial environment for the emergence of language in the lived social world consists of a situation in which multiple participants are using talk to pursue courses of action in concert with each other, frequently while attending to, and construing as relevant to their ongoing projects, phenomena in their surround. Practices in which vision and language mutually elaborate each other can enter into this process in a number of different ways.

First, analysts of language have long recognized that talk is not something done by speakers alone, but instead an activity constituted through the mutual orientation of a speaker and a hearer (e.g., Ferdinand de Saussure's famous diagram of the speaking circuit). However, actual analysis of human language has focused almost exclusively on the speaker and treated the hearer as simply an entity that decodes structure in the stream of speech. One primary modality through which mutual orientation between speaker and hearer is organized as public discursive practice is through gaze. Speakers can treat all or a subset of available participants as focal addressees by gazing at them, and moreover by moving gaze from one type of addressee to another with structurally different properties (e.g., in the midst of a story moving from an unknowing recipient – one who hasn't heard the events being recounted – to someone who shared experience of those events with the speaker), and can display relevant changes in the local participation framework, a process that frequently requires changes in the structure of the emerging talk. Non-speaking participants can use gaze toward the speaker to display whether or not they are in fact assuming the social position of hearer. Such socially organized practices for the deployment of gaze are normative and have consequences in detail for the organization of emerging talk. Speakers who find that they lack the gaze of hearers typically interrupt or abandon their utterances. These restarts and pause beginnings have the effect of soliciting the gaze of non-gazing hearers. A transcript that covered only the stream of speech would show sentence fragments (Noam Chomsky's famous "performance errors"). But, in fact, the way in which speakers abandon sentence beginnings that were not being attended to and begin utterances afresh once they have visibly secured a hearer, shows participants' systematic orientation to the production of complete coherent sentences not into the air, but within a framework of mutual orientation between speaker and hearer as visibly displayed through gaze and other embodied practices. An important ethnographic issue for future research consists of the specification of how hearership is displayed in settings and societies where gaze toward the hearer is dispreferred.

Second, rather than being lodged exclusively within the mental life of the speaker, talk as action is constituted through the visible differentiated displays of the bodies of separate participants organized through multi-party interactive fields. The basic mutual orientation of speaker and hearer provides one example. However, this process can become considerably more complicated in more elaborated speech genres. In mundane conversations the characters being animated in stories are frequently present at the telling. In addition to speaker, addressed recipient(s), and non-addressed recipient(s), the participation framework for such a story also includes its principal character. As what he or she did (e.g., a husband who committed a social gaffe in a story being told by his wife) emerges within the story it can become relevant for other participants to gaze not at the speaker but at the principal character, and for that party to arrange their body for the story relevant gaze that can be focused on it. The talk in progress structures not only where gaze should go, but also how someone should be seen within a multi-party participation framework. Rather than existing solely, or even primarily, within the stream of speech, stories are interactive fields in which the participants are engaged in a local, situated analysis not only of the talk in progress, but also of their participation in it. The multiple products of such analysis, as displayed through both talk and the visible body, provide for the differentiated but co-ordinated actions that are constitutive of the story as a social activity.

Third, vision plays a crucial role in the practices through which entities in the participants' environment are made relevant to local talk, and the phenomenal world being constituted through it. At least two interrelated types of organization are relevant here. First, especially when used in conjunction with deictic gestures such as points, talk can not only help to locate and pick out relevant features of the surround, but, of equal importance, construe what is being looked at in a particular fashion. Second, visual structure in the surround can itself contribute to the organization and comprehensibility of talk and action. Visible semiotic structures such as maps, hop-scotch grids, playing fields, and ritual spaces, provide simple examples of resources used to build action that could not be constituted through the stream of speech alone. Such practices shed new light on some traditional concerns within linguistic anthropology. For example, when color classification is analyzed in terms of the historically shaped practices of groups who must classify color as part of their work, it is found that participants use not only a mental color lexicon, but also semiotically shaped material structures such as Munsell color charts.

Graphic representations of many different types play crucial roles in the language practices used to build scientific, legal, and political discourse. This interplay between talk, a domain of scrutiny, and representational practices constitutes the key arena through which work groups organize their professional vision as public discursive practice. In a court case that was followed worldwide, lawyers for the four white policemen who beat an African American motorist, Rodney King, used language to structure the jury's perception of events on the tape from the perspective of the police, and convinced the jury that Rodney King, not the policemen, was the aggressor. While the language used by the lawyers shaped how the tape was to be seen, the visible events being pointed at simultaneously contributed to the organization of the categories proposed in the talk by filling in the sense of those categories (e.g., "aggression") with apparent visual proof.

Fourth, gesture constitutes one crucial modality linking talk and vision. Like alternative approaches to the study of language itself, gesture has been variously analyzed as an external, visual manifestation of the mental processes in the speaker, as visible, socially organized interactive practice, and most recently as a manifestation of the thinking/working body's cognitive engagement with the world. Similarly, both posture and facial displays that might fall outside the scope of gesture provide crucial resources for stance-marking.

In contemporary social theory two master metaphors have emerged: Vision (e.g., Michel Foucault's panopticon) and Voice (cf. Mikhail Bakhtin). By isolating a particular sensory domain, each of these frameworks becomes blind to the way in which talk and vision are embedded within a larger ecology of sign systems that permit each to function by elaborating, and being elaborated by, each other. Neither is a self-contained island. By investigating not just the actions of the speaker, but the visible behavior of all relevant participants, and the structure of phenomena in the surround, it becomes possible to overcome perspectives that lodge the dialogic organization of talk within the stream of speech alone and most frequently within the talk of a single speaker (albeit one who might be quoting the talk of another), and to investigate both human interaction and embodiment as crucial components of language practice.

(See also *color, expert, gesture, indexicality, media, participation, power, turn, voice*)

Bibliography

Goodwin, Charles
    1981 Conversational Organization: Interaction between Speakers and Hearers. New York: Academic Press.
    1984 Notes on Story Structure and the Organization of Participation. *In* Structures of Social Action. Max Atkinson and John Heritage, eds. Pp. 225–246. Cambridge: Cambridge University Press.

1994   Professional Vision. American Anthropologist 96(3):606–633.

1995   Seeing in Depth. Social Studies of Science 25:237–274.

1996   Transparent Vision. *In* Interaction and Grammar. Elinor Ochs, Emanuel A. Schegloff, and Sandra Thompson, eds. Pp. 370–404. Cambridge: Cambridge University Press.

Goodwin, Marjorie Harness

1980   Processes of Mutual Monitoring Implicated in the Production of Description Sequences. Sociological Inquiry 50:303–317.

Heath, Christian

1986   Body Movement and Speech in Medical Interaction. Cambridge: Cambridge University Press.

Kendon, Adam

1990   Conducting Interaction: Patterns of Behavior in Focused Encounters. Cambridge: Cambridge University Press.

LeBaron, Curtis D., and Jürgen Streeck

2000   Gestures, Knowledge, and the World. *In* Gestures in Action, Language, and Culture. David McNeill, ed. Pp. 118–138. Cambridge: Cambridge University Press.

Ochs, Elinor, Patrick Gonzales, and Sally Jacoby

1996   "When I Come Down, I'm in a Domain State": Grammar and Graphic Representation in the Interpretive Activity of Physicists. *In* Interaction and Grammar. Elinor Ochs, Emanuel A. Schegloff, and Sandra Thompson, eds. Pp. 328–369. Cambridge: Cambridge University Press.

■ *Webb Keane*

Voice

The concept of voice, meaning the linguistic construction of social personae, addresses the question "Who is speaking?" in any stretch of discourse. Linguistic anthropologists studying the complex and fluctuating relations among people, their ways of using language, and projected selves take as fundamental several observations. One is the ubiquity of stylistic variation in the speech habits of both communities and individuals. Another is the existence in communities of linguistic ideologies that link stylistic variations to differences in social identities, statuses, value systems, and so forth. A third is the complexity and manipulability of participation roles, by which persons can take on a wide range of possible alignments toward the words being used in any given context, e.g., claiming authorship versus merely reporting another's words.

Research on voice directs attention to the diverse processes though which social identities are represented, performed, transformed, evaluated, and contested. This has bearing on two common ways in which "voice" is invoked by other disciplines. One centers on political representation and authority, that is, "having a voice." The second raises epistemological questions about relations among identity, experience, and point of view, as in "claiming one's own voice." Politics and epistemology often converge, in asking, for example, "Can the subaltern speak?" Faced with such questions, linguistic anthropology takes the details of linguistic form to be crucial for any effort to trace how speakers shift among positions, identities, and alignments toward the words they speak. Political roles, for instance, may demand particular linguistic features, as when the apparently timeless or disinterested voice of preacher or pedagogue facilitates a legitimate capacity to take the floor, speak on behalf of larger groups, or talk about others. But research also demonstrates the artfulness and subtlety at work not just in highly self-conscious forms of expression, such as literary or oratorical texts, but in everyday uses of language. It gives empirical substantiation to the theoretical proposition that speakers are not unified entities, and their words are not transparent expressions of subjective experience.

Voices not only construct identities but also play them off against one another. The influence of Mikhail Bakhtin and V. N. Vološinov has heightened analytic attention to the agonistic and fluid character of the correlations between linguistic and sociological variables. Bakhtin's notion of heteroglossia entails a world of stylistic and social differences in which voices are juxtaposed against one another or jostle for dominance even within the discourse of a single speaker. Every speaker has available numerous ways of speaking that are associated by virtue of linguistic ideologies with different character types, professions, genders, social statuses, kinship roles, moral stances, ideological systems, age groups, ethnicities, and so forth. In a given stretch of discourse these may be expressed by virtually any linguistic contrast, including lexical or language choice, intonation and (physical) voice quality, variations in fluency, phonology, or syntax, shifts in pronouns, deictics, or evidentials. These permit speakers to claim, comment on, or disavow different identities and evaluative stances at different moments. A commonplace example of evaluation is parody, in which a speaker pits one voice, the parodist, against another, the kind of person characterized by the words being parodied; other noticeable examples are clichés, irony, mock accents, allusions, and proverbs.

Relations among voices are also worked out at the level of interaction, especially in the ways in which responsibility for words is distributed among participants in a speech event or text. Participation roles are the parts one may play in what Goffman called the "production format." Different roles can be overtly expressed even within a single turn of talk, as in the embedding of one person's words (the author) in the discourse of another (the animator) by means of reported speech; the imputed author, of course, may be a construction of the animator. Further distinctions are common: a press secretary may animate words whose author is a speech writer but whose principal, the person responsible for the message, is the President (who may, in turn, be claiming to speak in the name of the nation). Roles may leak, as when the animator's emotions affect reported speech, potentially shifting the attribution of voices: the press secretary may be fired. By attending to the production format as a whole, we can observe the construction not only of speakers' identities, but also the social positioning of interlocutors as particular kinds of addressees, overhearers, and "targets" (the President, for instance, addressing one as citizen, not spouse). Notice that whereas heteroglossia refers to multiple voices within a single speaker, participation roles entail aspects of a single voice distributed across several speakers. In either case, voice is not a personal attribute, but involves shared assumptions about recognizable types of character and their attributes.

Much of the current interest in voices concerns questions of identity and agency. By tracking different voices in ordinary conversations we can show the articulation of macro and micro scales of power. The play of voices depends on listeners' capacity to distinguish between a voice and its animator, but the exact identity of a given voice may be contested, ambiguous, or rendered purposely indeterminate, with important social consequences such as the occlusion or diffusion of responsibility. To speak in a singular or monologic voice appears to be the highly marked outcome of political effort rather than a natural or neutral condition. Genres of religious speech such as glossolalia, shamanistic performance, divination, scriptural quotation, preaching, mantras, or prayer, commonly stage or index voices of otherworldly, dead, invisible, or otherwise absent participants in a wide variety of ways. Individuals do not always control the attribution of the voices they animate: in possession, for example, it may be up to the audience to determine if a spirit speaks. Nor do individual speakers necessarily seek to claim for themselves a voice that seems authentically their own, but rather may disavow responsibility for their words in favor of more authoritative, divine, or collective agents. Research on voice reveals how the internal complexity of the language-using subject is inseparable from its articulation with a social world of other subjects, both present and absent in any given context.

(See also *agency, healing, heteroglossia, identity, indexicality, participation, plagiarism, prayer, prophecy, register, style*)

Bibliography

Bakhtin, Mikhail M.
>   1981   The Dialogic Imagination: Four Essays. Caryl Emerson and Michael Holquist, trans. Austin: University of Texas Press.

Goffman, Erving
>   1981   Forms of Talk. Philadelphia: University of Pennsylvania Press.

Hanks, William F.
>   1996   Language and Communicative Practices. Boulder, CO: Westview Press.

Hill, Jane H.
>   1995   The Voices of Don Gabriel: Responsibility and Self in a Modern Mexicano Narrative. *In* The Dialogic Emergence of Culture. Dennis Tedlock and Bruce Mannheim, eds. Pp. 97–147. Urbana and Chicago: University of Illinois Press.

Hill, Jane H., and Judith T. Irvine, eds.
>   1992   Responsibility and Evidence in Oral Discourse. Cambridge: Cambridge University Press.

Hymes, Dell
>   1981   "In Vain I Tried to Tell You": Essays in Native American Ethnopoetics. Philadelphia: University of Pennsylvania Press.

Keane, Webb
>   1997   Religious Language. Annual Review of Anthropology 26:47–71.

Silverstein, Michael, and Greg Urban, eds.
>   1996   Natural Histories of Discourse. Chicago and London: University of Chicago Press.

Urban, Greg
>   1989   The "I" of Discourse. *In* Semiotics, Self, and Society. B. Lee and Greg Urban, eds. Pp. 27–51. Berlin: Mouton de Gruyter.

Vološinov, V. N.

 1986[1930] Marxism and the Philosophy of Language. L. Matejka and I. R. Titunik, eds. Cambridge, MA: Harvard University Press.

■ *Antonio Perri*

Writing

In an anthropological sense, writing includes all social practices that use systems of graphic (sometimes also material) signs, which are recurrent, combinable and conventionally linked to a linguistic content. From this perspective, one could say that writing has been with *homo sapiens* from the beginning. On the other hand, linguistic and philological approaches have expressed more limiting views of writing. In particular, three perspectives have emerged: the evolutionary one (e.g., Ignace Gelb's famous statement about the pictographic origins: "at the basis of all writing stands picture"); the linguistic one (i.e., the idea that writing must, or should, merely represent speech); and the vague (seemingly opposite) relativistic stance according to which "if all writing is information storage, then all writing is of equal value" (Albertine Gaur). These approaches share a view of the written sign as a static entity, informed by the logic of the alphabet (or rather by a partial, Western theory about it, as pointed out by Roy Harris).

More recently, anthropologists have rethought the relationship between orality and literacy, rethinking, with Jack Goody's three-vertexes model, the "unilinear" Saussurean model of the language–writing ratio. One of the goals of the anthropological research on literacy has been to investigate psycho-cultural changes caused by the acquisition of (mostly alphabetical) writing skills in societies previously without writing. Such an approach shows several limitations, among which are a schematic binarism regarding the passage from orality to literacy; the assumption that equates literacy with alphabetical literacy, thus acritically accepting traditional linguistic typologies; and an emphasis on psychological effects (mainly in scholars such as Walter J. Ong). In these studies writing is frequently considered as a non-social activity (even if socially transmitted) that aims at improving individual skills and mental processes. The social side is highlighted mainly in the context of linguistic/orthographic policies implementing a standard written language in a given country.

The myth of a "primary orality" is also highly questionable given that a circulation of graphic messages (i.e., texts produced according to a notation, related primarily to linguistic-conceptual contents and only conditional to reflexive aesthetics) does in fact exist in all cultures. Even what is considered by many the "land of orality," Africa, is a forest of symbols that materialize cultural and linguistic contents that cannot be understood outside of their social context. This is the case for the Akan graphic symbols, the Nigerian *nsibidi*, and the Dogon cosmogonic signs. Rather than "pseudo-non-writing/partial/limited" or forerunners of "true/complete/unlimited writing" (according to John DeFrancis' terminology), they are evidence of the intrinsically social attitude toward all media of communication in many non-Western cultures. In Africa, as well as in Native American cultures, "to write" never meant to produce a static, fixed, and a-pragmatic text reflecting an "ideal" and totally explicit utterance, in a one-to-one ratio with the (phonic) elements resulting from an abstract analysis of a sentence.

The new anthropological approach mentioned at the beginning moves from a flexible taxonomy, grounded on semiotic principles. If languages are equipollent *in abstracto* because they all share the features of omniformativity and omnitranslatability, then *de facto* those features can be implemented only by the concrete speech acts in which many other non-segmental factors (gestures, settings, audience, proxemic, etc.) play a significant role, since meaning is always constructed pragmatically and inferentially. Writing systems are neither omniformative nor equipollent, even though they give rise to new codes emphasizing other dimensions of a communicative act. Thus their degree of pragmatic and contextual sensitiveness will be inversely related to their expressive power. Writings that tend to be exhaustively superimposed on explicit and de-contextualized acts of speech (e.g., the alphabetical, standard written languages) will tend to express more linguistic contents, resorting less to co-textual and performance contexts, or to a shared graphic competence as completely independent from oral communication. On the contrary, writings that tend to re-structure language (Chinese is a good example) will need a degree of pragmatic, graphic, and inferential competence that goes as far as allowing each written element to reshape the linguistic system, rather than simply corresponding to a single spoken element. All writing systems, thus, could be arranged along a continuum whose two (purely theoretical) extremes, according to Louis Hjelmslev's terminology, will be named signal-writing and metasemiotic-writing. As a consequence of this definition, scriptorial sign is considered a dynamic unit, a sign function implementing texts whose meanings are interactively constructed. There follows a basic need for the researcher: one has to investigate (through fieldwork or historical reconstruction) practices, contexts, and uses of writing systems to fully understand their products (i.e., texts).

Specific sociolinguistic situations vary considerably, challenging the binary opposition between orality and literacy. In Aztec Mexico of the colonial period, it is essential to postulate a triadic model of cultural circulation interweaving Latin alphabet, local pictographic writing, and orality, as argued by Serge Gruzinski.

Finally, on the basis of Dell Hymes' SPEAKING model, we can adopt a model for the description of scriptorial events whose components correspond by acronym to the mnemonic word WRITING, the seven different factors being W = Writers (e.g., Who are the writers? Do they have specific status? Are writing skills subjected to institutionally recognized patterns?); R = Readers (e.g., Who are the readers? Is the role of the reader independent from that of the writer? Are there different reading skills, according to sociocultural or status levels?); I = Instrumentalities (e.g., What kind of instruments are used to write a message, and how are they related to keys through which scriptorial events must – or should – be interpreted?); T = Textualization (e.g., Which are the rules governing the passage from cultural – and linguistic – content into written texts? Is there any distinctive pattern of "translation" between linguistic and scriptorial domains?); I = Interpretive context (e.g., What is the role played by the environmental context in which the written text is placed, in the interpretation of that same text?); N = Norms (e.g., Are there graphic and social norms related to the writing and reading of different kinds of texts?); G = Genres (e.g., Is there a "canon," either implicit or explicit, through which texts are classified and hence interpreted?).

(See also *evolution, genre, inference, literacy, media, orality*)

Bibliography

Basso, Keith
> 1974　The Ethnography of Writing. *In* Explorations in the Ethnography of Speaking. R. Bauman and J. Sherzer, eds. Pp. 425–432. Cambridge: Cambridge University Press.

Cardona, Giorgio Raimondo
> 1981　Antropologia della scrittura. Turin, Italy: Loescher.
> 1986　Storia universale della scrittura. Milan: Mondadori.

Gaur, Albertine
> 1984　A History of Writing. London: The British Library.

Gelb, Ignace J.
> 1963　A Study of Writing. Chicago: University of Chicago Press.

Goody, Jack
> 1977　The Domestication of the Savage Mind. Cambridge: Cambridge University Press.

Harris, Roy
> 1986　The Origin of Writing. London: Duckworth.
> 1996　Signs of Writing. London and New York: Routledge.

Hymes, Dell
> 1972　Models of Interaction of Language and Social Life. *In* Directions in Sociolinguistics: The Ethnography of Communication. John J. Gumperz and Dell Hymes, eds. Pp. 35–71. New York: Holt, Rinehart and Winston.

Ong, Walter J.
> 1982　Orality and Literacy. London: Methuen.

INDEX

Note: cross-references are provided at the end of each essay to orient readers to related topics.